A Genre Approach to First Ye...

KINGDOM

Understand and Explore

1

Aly Allsopp, Seanagh McCarthy and Ciara Morris

educate.ie

Introduction

Welcome to *Kingdom 1* – Junior Cycle English for First Year.

This book and its accompanying title for Second and Third Year English, *Kingdom 2*, complete the *Kingdom* series.

Kingdom 1 features genre-based units which act as the foundation of learning for Junior Cycle English. Through such genre-based study, students will develop a strong understanding of the various forms of texts they will encounter *and* create throughout the three years of Junior Cycle, as well as the important features of these texts. The genre-based units are:

1. Writing With Purpose
2. Poetry and Song
3. Fiction
4. Stage and Screen
5. Media and Advertising

A broad variety of material allows mixing and matching of old favourites with fresh, new and exciting texts to suit the skills and interests of the class and reflect their experience of the world. Students will write, research, construct and deliver speeches, work together, debate, create storyboards, listen to documentaries and advertisements and read and perform a variety of poems and extracts as they journey through their First Year course.

The 3 ups answering technique offers students a simple and effective method for answering questions.

Formative and summative assessments have been carefully designed to develop skills linked explicitly to the subset of 22 First Year Learning Outcomes and reflect how the course is assessed. Many of the extracts throughout the textbook are springboards for grammar and language-based learning, while other tasks encourage students to reflect on, discuss or write about their own studied texts. The *Kingdom 1* Portfolio provides a well-scaffolded approach to some of the tasks where students are asked to be creative. Such question and answer templates are in line with the style and demands of the final examination. Students are also given opportunities to draft and redraft with success criteria provided as a guide for improvement.

Kingdom 1 ends with a suggested 'mini theme' focusing on relationships that offers students an opportunity to connect their learning through the study of a broad, unifying theme in preparation for thematic study in *Kingdom 2*.

Kingdom 2 follows a thematic approach. Nine fully developed, exam-style themes are explored using texts from the five genres with which students have become familiar throughout *Kingdom 1*.

A consistent style and approach across both books ensures a seamless transition for your students, with:

- questions and tasks organised consistently under five headings:
    - Discuss
    - Understand
    - Explore
    - Investigate
    - Create

◖ assessment at the end of every unit covering written and oral assessment, classroom-based assessment (CBA) and exam preparation and grammar

◖ dedicated 'Language skills' and 'How to' pages to build vital skills and knowledge.

The *Kingdom* package includes:

◖ a double-sided Portfolio and Grammar Primer for *Kingdom 1* with:

– dedicated space for completion of creative tasks and checklists for redrafting

– practice exercises to develop key language and punctuation skills

◖ a Portfolio for *Kingdom 2* containing draft and redraft tasks, reflective tasks and sample exam-style questions with templates for answering

◖ teachers' CDs containing podcasts, radio advertisements, documentaries and a variety of recorded Shakespeare extracts, poems and short stories

◖ an invaluable Teacher's Resource Book with planning materials for all three years, Christmas and summer tests, extra worksheets and much more.

The complete series offers a realistic approach to the exciting challenge of guiding students through the Junior Cycle English course. As practising teachers who have guided their students through this new course and exam, the authors of *Kingdom* have developed a series that responds to the requirements of the specification, the exam, you the teacher and the variety of students that you teach; with relevant, lively texts and tasks to assist your students in reaching their full potential in their study of English and becoming masters of their own kingdom.

Aly Allsopp, Seanagh McCarthy and Ciara Morris
March 2018

Tasks

 Discuss questions are designed to promote discussion, encourage students to think about the texts and prepare them to answer further questions.

 Understand questions are comprehension-style questions that check the student's understanding.

 Explore questions are higher-order questions that require the student to think more deeply about the text.

 Investigate questions ask the student to conduct their own research.

 Create tasks require the student to produce their own oral and written work.

Icons

 The work together icon indicates that a task should be performed in pairs or in groups.

 The 3 ups icon reminds students to use the 3 ups answering technique to structure their answer.

 The portfolio icon is used to indicate where the task is to be completed in the Portfolio. This work can be helpful for revision and can provide a base for their collection of texts for their classroom-based assessment.

 The grammar primer icon shows that there are further activities in the Grammar Primer.

 The redraft icon is used whenever a task asks students to improve something they have created already.

 The oral language icon is used to show where a task has an oral component.

 The CD icon appears where recorded material is available on the teacher's CD.

Contents

Unit 1
Writing With Purpose 2

Unit 2

Poetry and Song
64

Unit 3

Fiction
124

Unit 4

Stage and Screen
174

Unit 5

Media and Advertising
216

Unit 6
Relationships: A Thematic Approach
252

Thematic Contents

Unit 1

Writing With Purpose

Why study this area?

All writing has a purpose, whether it is to express your thoughts, share your opinions or communicate ideas. Some types of writing follow a certain format and require a structured approach and style.

Learning intentions

- Discover different types of writing.
- Write for a variety of purposes.
- Learn how to answer questions.
- Develop your presentation skills.
- Learn how to draft and redraft your work.
- Understand how to use punctuation.

 **Discuss**

1. What do all of the images above have in common?
2. Why would you comment on someone's social media page?
3. What is a hashtag (#)?
4. When is a hashtag used?
5. How is a diary different to a blog?
6. Why might someone choose to keep a diary?
7. What reasons might someone have for writing a letter?
8. What are the main differences between a tweet and a letter?

 Create

Create a short story using the titles of books that you know.

Place the titles in order so that they create a story.

If you would like to see more examples
search #titletales on Instagram.

Personal profiles

 Create

1. **(a)** Write six sentences describing your day yesterday. Begin with the opening line: 'Yesterday after my alarm went off I ...'

 This is personal writing, as you are writing from your own point of view. Personal writing is a genre (style or category) of writing that gives details about your own experiences of and feelings about an event or a memory.

 (b) Swap your personal piece about your day yesterday with the person next to you and ask them to summarise your day in the style of a tweet.

 Twitter is an online news and social networking service where users can interact and post messages to one another. These messages are called 'tweets' and can be up to 280 characters long.

On social media networks, messages on a particular topic are identified with a #.

 Sue
@sue903   ☼   Follow

School starts back tomorrow. English first class.

#school #english #classwork

When you write about your likes, dislikes, hobbies and family, this is called a personal profile. It is information about you, written by you. Below is an example of a personal profile.

 Hi, my name is Ben. I'm 12 years old and I live in Carlow with my mum, dad and sister, Jenny. I go to Carlow Community College and my favourite subject is History. I play football for the local team and we have a match every Saturday. I train as many evenings as I can because I want to improve and make the senior team when I am older. My favourite film is *Batman V Superman*. Last summer I went to Spain for two weeks. We had to leave our dog, Bruno, in a kennel while we were gone. I missed Bruno and I felt guilty about not taking him abroad, but Dad said that we couldn't have a dog running up and down the plane! I am currently reading *The Demigod Diaries*. I have a habit of listening to music while I relax. Every night I go to bed with Ed Sheeran blaring in my ears.

 Create

 1. **(a)** Create your personal profile on page 3 of your Portfolio.

 (b) Swap your personal profile with another student in your class. Write a short message to them in the space provided on page 3 of their Portfolio about anything that you have in common. Swap your profiles back and discuss your similarities.

Diary entries

A diary is a place where you write your deepest thoughts, feelings, hopes and plans. As this is a personal and informal piece of writing, there are many styles in which a diary entry can be written, but most diaries include the features listed below.

Features	Language
◖ Date	◖ Informal
◖ 'Dear Diary' greeting	◖ Conversational
◖ Reference to time and place	◖ Intimate
◖ Written in the first person	
◖ Detailed account of events	
◖ Description of thoughts, feelings and intentions	
◖ Sign off	

Informal and conversational language is a natural way of talking. For example, the way you speak to your friends.

Oh my gosh, I'm wrecked today. I stayed up so late watching films.

Here is an example of a diary entry.

11 April 2018   *Date*

Dear Diary,   *Greeting*

Today was a wonderful day. I went to Herbert Park to feed the ducks.   *Reference to time*
We brought a bag of birdseed with us. Mum sat on the bench while I   *and place*
divided out the birdseed among the ducks. I had to fling a few handfuls *First person*
of it really far to reach the shy ducks that didn't paddle up to me. I was
nervous of the swans, as Mum said that they can nip you with their   *Description of events that*
beaks if they feel threatened.   *happened that day*

I think that tomorrow I will call in to Aunt Mary in the nursing home, as I
haven't seen her in a few weeks. Mum took a few photos of me feeding the *Intentions for tomorrow*
ducks on her phone. I'd like to show Aunt Mary, as she loves Herbert Park.

Lately I feel as though the time is flying by and I won't get all of my
school projects finished in time for Easter. If I set aside two hours every
evening I think that should be enough to complete most of the work.   *Expresses thoughts*
                                                                         and feelings

I have to stop writing now, but I will let you know how it all goes
tomorrow.

Jill

                                                                        Sign off

Below is an extract from *The Secret Diary of Adrian Mole Aged 13 ¾* by Sue Townsend.

The Secret Diary of Adrian Mole Aged 13 ¾

Saturday January 3rd

I shall go mad through lack of sleep! My father has banned the dog from the house so it barked outside my window all night. Just my luck! My father shouted a swear-word at it. If he's not careful he will get done by the police for obscene language.

I think the spot is a boil. Just my luck to have it where everybody can see it. I pointed out to my mother that I hadn't had any vitamin C today. She said, 'Go and buy an orange then.' This is typical.

She still hasn't worn the lurex apron.

I will be glad to get back to school.

obscene:
offensive

lurex:
a fabric with a metallic appearance

....

Sunday January 4th

Second after Christmas

My father has got the flu. I'm not surprised with the diet we get. My mother went out in the rain to get him a vitamin C drink, but as I told her, 'It's too late now.' It's a miracle we don't get scurvy. My mother says she can't see anything on my chin, but this is guilt because of the diet.

The dog has run off because my mother didn't close the gate. I have broken the arm on the stereo. Nobody knows yet, and with a bit of luck my father will be ill for a long time. He is the only one who uses it apart from me. No sign of the apron.

....

Monday January 5th

The dog hasn't come back yet. It is peaceful without it. My mother rang the police and gave a description of the dog. She made it sound worse than it actually is: straggly hair over its eyes and all that. I really think the police have got better things to do than look for dogs, such as catching murderers. I told my mother this but she still rang them. Serve her right if she was murdered because of the dog.

My father is still lazing about in bed. He is supposed to be ill, but I noticed he is still smoking!

Nigel came round today. He has got a tan from his Christmas holiday. I think Nigel will be ill soon from the shock of the cold in England. I think Nigel's parents were wrong to take him abroad.

He hasn't got a single spot yet.

Discuss

1. What impression of Adrian Mole's parents do you get from his description in the diary?
2. Why do you think Adrian Mole does not sign off his diary entries?

Understand

1. Find two features of a typical diary entry in this extract.
2. What did Adrian's mother tell him to do when he pointed out that he had not had any Vitamin C that day?
3. Why does Adrian hope that his father will be ill for a long time?
4. How did Adrian's mother describe the dog to the police?
5. Why does Adrian think that Nigel's parents were wrong to take him abroad?

Explore

1. Choose two words that you would use to describe Adrian Mole, based on the extracts from his diary. Explain your choice.
2. Would you like to read more of *The Secret Diary of Adrian Mole Aged 13 ¾*, based on the extract you have read? Why/why not?

Create

Create an illustration (picture) to accompany one of the diary entries above. Draw a picture or select an image from the internet that you think best suits the day you have chosen. Give two reasons why you have chosen this image.

Below are two extracts from *Zlata's Diary: A Child's Life in Sarajevo*. Sarajevo is the capital of Bosnia and Herzegovina. Zlata Filipović kept a diary, that she named Mimmy, during the siege of Sarajevo, which lasted from 1992 until 1996.

siege: military blockade

Zlata's Diary: A Child's Life in Sarajevo

Monday, 29 June 1992

Dear Mimmy,

BOREDOM!!! SHOOTING!!! SHELLING!!! PEOPLE BEING KILLED!!! DESPAIR!!! HUNGER!!! MISERY!!! FEAR!!!

That's my life! The life of an innocent eleven-year-old schoolgirl!! A schoolgirl without a school, without the fun and excitement of school. A child without games, without friends, without the sun, without birds, without nature, without fruit, without chocolate or sweets, with just a little powdered milk. In short, a child without a childhood. A wartime child. I now realize that I am really living through a war, I am witnessing an ugly, disgusting war. I and thousands of other children in this town that is being destroyed, that is crying, weeping, seeking help, but getting none. God, will this ever stop, will I ever be a schoolgirl again, will I ever enjoy my childhood again? I once heard that childhood is the most wonderful time of your life. And it is. I loved it, and now an ugly war is taking it all away from me. Why? I feel sad. I feel like crying. I am crying.

Your Zlata

Friday, 7 August 1992

Dear Mimmy,

It thundered here today. I don't know how many shells fell near by. It was quiet when Daddy went with Samra to get the aid package. But then the shelling suddenly started. An explosion. It thundered. Emina was at our place. There was a terrible boom. Glass shattered, bricks fell, there were clouds of dust. We didn't know where to run. We were convinced that the shell had fallen on our roof. We were on our way to the cellar when we heard Nedo frantically calling out to us, running towards us through the dust, bricks and broken glass. We ran over to Bobars' cellar. They were all down there. We were shaking. Mummy most of all. In tears, she asked about Daddy, whether he had come back. When we calmed down a bit they told us that a shell had fallen on the roof of Emina's house, above her flat. We were lucky, because that's only about ten metres away from the roof over our flat. Everything turned out OK. Daddy and Samra soon came running in. They had been worried about us too. When we got back to the flat it was full of dust, pieces of brick, and we found a piece of shrapnel in the bathroom. We rolled up our sleeves and started cleaning the place up. I was scared it would start again. Luckily, it didn't. Another horrible day.

Your Zlata

 ## Understand

1. What does Zlata wonder if she will ever enjoy again?
2. Where did they begin to run to after they heard the boom?
3. Why did Zlata feel she was lucky?
4. Describe the condition of Zlata's flat when she returned.

 ## Explore

1. You have read extracts from two diaries, *The Secret Diary of Adrian Mole Aged 13 ¾* and *Zlata's Diary*. One of these is fiction and one is non-fiction. Which do you think is fiction and which is non-fiction? Give reasons for your answer.
2. Identify three typical features of a diary entry found in the extracts from *Zlata's Diary*.

 ## Investigate

 What can you find out about the war in Sarajevo? Discuss your findings with the class.

 ## Create

1. **(a)** Write five questions that you would like to ask Zlata.

    (b) With a partner, take turns to imagine you are Zlata. Answer one another's questions as though you are her.

2. Imagine that you are a soldier at war. Write a diary entry about your experiences.

Capital letters and full stops

Capital letters are used for:

◖ **beginning a sentence**

She went to the shop yesterday to purchase a litre of milk.

We need to make sure that we take down all of the homework into our diaries.

◖ **the personal pronoun 'I'**

When I was six I broke my leg after I fell from the treehouse.

They looked in my direction and I decided to go over and try to make some new friends.

◖ **days of the week, months of the year and holidays**

We go away on the first Monday in January.

I think I will go to my aunt's house for Christmas.

◖ **countries, languages, nationalities and religions**

The language spoken in France is French.

In China, 18.2% of the population are Buddhists.

◖ **people's names and titles**

Professor Dave   *King Henry VIII*

◖ **names of companies and organisations**

Pepsi   *United Nations*

◖ **places and monuments**

Eiffel Tower, Paris   *Grafton Street*

◖ **titles of books, poems and songs**

The Lion King   *Thinking Out Loud*

 Grammar Primer: pages 2–5

◖ **abbreviations**

BBC   *TV*

Full stops are used to end your sentences.

The car's brakes screeched and it came to a sudden stop.

After dinner Polly sat down to do her homework.

 Understand

Write out the following sentences, inserting the correct capital letters and full stops.

1. valerie visited the national history museum and then she toured around dublin
2. enda bought new shoes in jack jones, a wallet in house of fraser and a jacket in dunnes stores
3. ciara bought her new toyota corolla in sligo and drove it home to cork
4. dr murphy always goes on holiday to italy
5. amy and ella queued to get tickets to see despicable me 3 in the cinema in limerick

Blogs

Blog posts are similar to diary entries in that they contain personal thoughts and opinions. However, blog posts are posted online. Diaries and blogs are a series of entries or posts collected together.

Features

- Title
- Date
- Blogger's name
- Opinions
- Written in the first person
- Details of events
- Information

Language

- Language appropriate to the topic/audience (e.g. a blog discussing make-up may use casual language, whereas a blog discussing a serious topic, such as animal cruelty, may use more formal language)

The main difference between diaries and blogs are as follows:

Diaries

- Private – intended only for the writer to read
- Dated at the top
- Can be called a name
- Can be written or typed
- Usually do not contain images

Blogs

- Public – posted online for others to read and comment on
- Dated with a time stamp
- Have a title
- Typed on a webpage
- Often contain photos and images

 Discuss

1. Do you follow any blogs?
2. What type of blogs might interest you?

Below is an example of a blog entry by Irish lifestyle blogger Nathalie Marquez Courtney.

🔒http://nathalie.ie/blog/2016/08/30/learning-lettering/ *Domain (website address)*

Nathalie Marquez Courtney

Title

Photos and finds for the creative and curious. A personal journey of photography, design, food, travel and adventures in Dublin, Ireland.

Information about the blogger and the blog

Learning Lettering

Entry heading

August 30, 2016

Date and time stamp

Do you know what's great? Being bad at something. Being a total beginner and slowly and steadily seeing yourself improve. It's massively rewarding.

If you have come across any of my Insta stories, you'll know that I've been playing around with a couple of new creative outlets, mainly watercolour and calligraphy. I got lots of messages asking about what I was using, so thought I would share some of the great buys and online resources that might help other beginners looking to get started.

Content about whatever interests the blogger

The basics: Calligraphy and hand lettering are kind of like cousins – certain techniques overlap in certain ways, but they're quite different. Calligraphy is the traditional dip-pen approach, using ink and a metal nib to create beautiful sentences. Hand lettering, though it contains words, is often about creating an overall composition; more drawing than writing. It can be done using any number of materials, from ballpoint pens to watercolour brushes.

Images to make the post more visual

The book: I decided to begin with traditional calligraphy to get a solid grasp of fundamentals before playing around with hand lettering. I ordered *Nib & Ink* by Chiara Perano, founder of Lamplighter London, a cool calligraphy, decorative lettering and illustration studio. It's a great introduction to the basics and comes with letter by letter exercises.

The tools: You don't need much to get going – ink, a nib and a holder (and something to clean up inevitable ink smudges). I picked up Lamplighter's really gorgeous starter kit, pictured above, which contained a wooden pen holder, a Zebra G nib, and a glass pot of Higgins Eternal black ink as well as some Rhodia dot pads for extra practise. If you're looking to pick up tools in Dublin, I found that Kennedy Art had the best supply of nibs and ink.

As you can see from my wonky efforts above, it's very early days for me. But I'm enjoying embracing the suck and learning something new. Let me know if you decide to give it a try!

COMMENTS (1)

Sign in now to post a comment

LUCY September 1, 2016 at 12:24 p.m.

Your efforts are so not wonky, they are beautiful! Perfect timing on this post, I am going to my very first intro to calligraphy workshop at the Print Museum on Sunday. Tried a couple times to teach myself online and hoping a couple of hours with a teacher will get me started right.

Reply 👍 👎

A blog is interactive, which means there can be a conversation. Blogs offer the readers the option of leaving a comment. Always be careful and considerate about what you post online.

 Investigate

Look up the Irish Blog Awards to see if there are any blogs you would be interested in reading.

 Create

 1. (a) Write a blog entry on a topic of your choice in the space provided on pages 4–5 of your Portfolio. Remember to include a domain, a blog title, an entry heading, a date and a time stamp.

 (b) There is a space at the end of your blog for comments. Pass your blog entry to the person sitting next to you and ask them to write a comment on your blog post.

Commas

Punctuation can save a life! Both of the sentences below are the same, apart from the use of a comma.

Let's eat Grandma.   *Let's eat, Grandma.*

 Grammar Primer: pages 6–8

Discuss

1. How does the use of a comma change the meaning of these signs?

2. Can you think of any other circumstances where a missing or incorrectly placed comma could cause confusion?

 SLOW, ANIMAL CROSSING

 SLOW ANIMAL CROSSING

Commas are used to:

❨ **separate adjectives,** until you reach the last adjective before the noun: *She has long, curly, wavy, blonde hair.*

❨ **separate a list,** until you come to the last item on the list which is indicated by an 'and': *We had coffee, tea, cakes and biscuits.*

❨ **indicate a pause:** *Darragh did not just leave the room, he ran out of the room.*

Understand

1. Write the following sentences in your copy, inserting commas where appropriate.

   (a) They brought tents sleeping bags food and books on their camping trip.

   (b) I am not just hungry I am starving.

   (c) Ben felt tired hungry and cold after football training.

   (d) My favourite subjects are History Science Art and Irish.

2. Write the following blog entry in your copy and insert commas, full stops and capital letters where appropriate.

ALEXKNOWITALL7

16 SEP **The Thoughts and Musings of Alex, Age 11**

on our second morning in new york city we went to an amazing diner called ellen's stardust diner where the staff sing famous songs from musicals while you order your food the portions were massive a kid's meal had nine chicken nuggets that's the same as a large mcdonald's adults meal in the uk crazy right?! anyway my little brother who sleeps everywhere slept through the whole thing!

Later we walked the highline it is a converted old railway track a beautiful escape from the urban world beneath in the evening we went to watch the new york mets vs the cincinnati reds it was a fantastic match ending with the mets winning 5 home runs to 1 it was really fun as it was t-shirt night and we all got a free mets shirt

Once you have finished, read over your work to ensure that you did not miss anything. Check alexknowitall7.com/2017/09/16/the-capitol-washington-dc/ to see if you are right!

Vlogs

Vlogs are blogs that are created through video – video blogs.

Vloggers upload their videos to the internet on media platforms, such as YouTube, Snapchat and Instagram, for viewers to watch. You can follow particular vlogs and receive a notification each time a new video is posted. Vloggers can upload videos for entertainment or even educational purposes.

Similar to blogs, vlogs are interactive and allow viewers to comment.

Watch the following video explaining how to vlog:

https://s3-eu-west-1.amazonaws.com/ videos.educateplus.ie/vlog.mp4

 Discuss

Do you follow any vlogs that you could recommend to the class?

Atua Mo'e is a teenage vlogger who documents his adventures. Watch the following post from his vlog: https://youtu.be/QX067TS5isU

 Understand

1. What music can you hear in the background of Atua's vlog?
2. Name two things that Atua finds during his exploration.
3. What advice does Atua give about eating what you find on these explorations?
4. How high do the boys estimate the waterfall is?
5. What does Atua compare the blue tree to?
6. What two words would you use to describe the view that the drone captures?

 Create

 Record a three-minute vlog on one of the topics below.

◄ How to write a diary entry.
◄ The best mode of transport to get to school.
◄ How to avoid distractions while you study.

Autobiographies

An autobiography is a longer version of a personal profile. It is written by a person about their own life. Famous people often write autobiographies so that you can read all about their lives.

Features

- Personal details
- Facts and information
- Written in the first person
- Narrative style (storytelling)
- Events are often told in sequence (explained in order)
- Revelation of secrets and private events

Language

- Honest
- Descriptive
- Can be informal and conversational or formal, depending on the preference of the writer

Below are two covers of autobiographies.

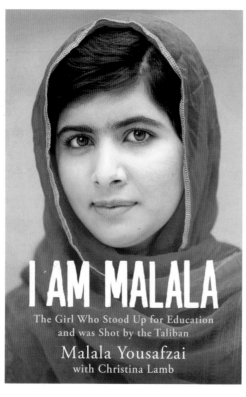

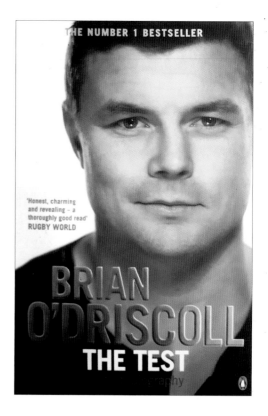

 **Discuss**

1. Based on the covers of these autobiographies which would you prefer to read and why?

2. How do you imagine these autobiographies would be similar or different to one another?

3. What do the photographs on the cover of each of these books tell us about the authors?

Below is an extract from the autobiography of Jessica Ennis, an Olympic track and field athlete.

Unbelievable – From My Childhood Dreams to Winning Olympic Gold

I am crying. I am a Sheffield schoolgirl writing in her diary about the bullies awaiting me tomorrow. They stand menacingly by the gates and lurk unseen in my head, mocking my size and status. They make a small girl shrink, and I feel insecure and frightened. I pour the feelings out into words on the page, as if exposing them in some way will help, but nobody sees my diary. It is kept in my room as a hidden tale of hurt.

Fast forward two decades and I am crying again. I am standing in a cavernous arena in London. Suddenly, the pain and suffering and frustration give way to a flood of overwhelming emotion. In the middle of this enormous arena I feel smaller than ever, but I puff out my chest, look to the flag and stand tall. It has been a long and winding road from the streets of Sheffield to the tunnel that feeds into the Olympic Stadium like an artery.

cavernous: large space

I am Jessica Ennis. I have been called many things, from tadpole to poster girl, but I have had to fight to make that progression. I smile and am polite and so people think it comes easily, but it doesn't. I am not one of those athletes who slap their thighs and snarl before a competition, but there is a competitive animal inside, waiting to get out and fight for survival and recognition. Cover shoots and billboards are nice, but they are nothing without the work and I have left blood, sweat and tears on tracks all over the world. It is an age where young people are fed ideas of quick-fix fame and instant celebrity, but the tears mean more if the journey is hard. So I don't cry crocodile tears; I cry the real stuff.

young people think fame comes easy but there's actually a lot of work put in to it

Understand

In the case of each of the following, write the letter corresponding to the correct answer in your copy.

1. What is Jessica Ennis writing about in her diary?
   (a) She is writing about the bullies who are waiting for her.
   (b) She is writing about her homework.
   (c) She is writing about training.

2. Where does Jessica Ennis keep her diary?
   (a) In her school locker.
   (b) In her bedroom.
   (c) In her school bag.

3. Which of the following does Jessica Ennis say she has been called?
   (a) Super girl.
   (b) Poster girl.
   (c) Sporty girl.

4. Based on your understanding of the word 'cavernous', which of the following images would you say best captures what a cavernous space looks like? Give two reasons for your choice.

 5. What features of an autobiography do you notice in the above extract? Work in pairs to list the features with examples from the text for each.

 Investigate

 Find out more about Jessica Ennis. Work in pairs or groups to come up with a written list of her accomplishments.

Answer questions

An answering technique is a useful tool to help guide your answers. You should use this technique for your written answers. It ensures that you stick to the point and answer the question fully, without including too many details, so that you have enough time to answer all of the questions.

There are three simple steps you can follow to ensure that your answers always include enough detail, while sticking to the point. These steps are known as the **3 ups**.

Start up your answer by referring to the question and answer it in your own words.

Back up your answer with evidence from the text.

Sum up your answer by explaining how your evidence answers the question.

Example

According to Jessica Ennis, why do people think that competing comes easily to her?

Start up Refer to the question and answer it in your own words.

According to Jessica Ennis, people think that competing comes easily to her because she is friendly and mannerly.

Back up Provide evidence from the text. Remember to use quotation marks when quoting directly from the text.

Jessica tells us 'I smile and am polite so people think it comes easily, but it doesn't.'

Sum up Explain how your evidence answers the question.

This tells us that people think she finds competing easy because she conceals her competitive streak from them.

According to Jessica Ennis, people think that competing comes easily to her because she is friendly and mannerly. Jessica tells us 'I smile and am polite so people think it comes easily, but it doesn't.' This tells us that people think she finds competing easy because she conceals her competitive streak from them.

 Understand

Answer the following questions using the **3 ups**.

 1. What does Jessica Ennis tell us about her childhood bullies?

 2. How does Jessica Ennis feel when she is in the middle of the arena?

 3. Why does Jessica Ennis say that she does not cry crocodile tears?

Check that you used capital letters and full stops correctly in your answers.

 From now on when you see this icon you should remember to use the **3 ups**.

Nelson Mandela was a civil rights leader in South Africa. He fought against a system of inequality in his country. People of colour did not have equal rights and were segregated. Mandela served time in prison for his fight against this injustice. He later went on to become the first black president of South Africa. Below is an extract from his autobiography.

Long Walk to Freedom

At midnight, I was awake and staring at the ceiling – images from the trial were still rattling around in my head – when I heard steps coming down the corridor. I was locked in my own cell, away from the others. There was a knock at my door and I could see Colonel Aucamp's face at the bars. 'Mandela,' he said in a husky whisper, 'are you awake?'

I told him I was. 'You are a lucky man,' he said. 'We are taking you to a place where you will have your freedom. You will be able to move around; you'll see the ocean and the sky, not just gray walls.'

He intended no sarcasm, but I well knew that the place he was referring to would not afford me the freedom I longed for. He then remarked rather cryptically, 'As long as you don't make trouble, you'll get everything you want.'

Aucamp then woke the others, all of whom were in a single cell, ordering them to pack their things. Fifteen minutes later we were making our way through the iron labyrinth of Pretoria Local, with its endless series of clanging metal doors echoing in our ears.

cryptically:
mysteriously

labyrinth:
paths and passages that can make it difficult to find your way out

Understand

In the case of each of the following, write the letter corresponding to the correct answer in your copy.

1. At what time was Nelson Mandela awake and staring at the ceiling?
   (a) Midnight
   (b) Midday
   (c) Afternoon

2. Who did Nelson Mandela tell us that he sees through the bars?
   (a) His mother's face.
   (b) Colonel Aucamp's face.
   (c) The door to freedom.

3. What does Colonel Aucamp tell Nelson Mandela he will be able to see in the new place he is taking him to?
   (a) His friends and family.
   (b) The ocean and the sky.
   (c) Mountains and rivers.

4. Which image best represents your understanding of a labyrinth? Give two reasons for your answer.

 Explore

1. What impression of Nelson Mandela do you get from this extract?
2. Why does Colonel Aucamp tell Mandela that he is 'a lucky man'?

 Investigate

 Research Nelson Mandela and find the answers to each of the following questions.

◀ When was Nelson Mandela born?
◀ Where did Nelson Mandela grow up?
◀ What was Nelson Mandela imprisoned for?
◀ How long was Nelson Mandela imprisoned for and when was he released?
◀ When did Nelson Mandela become president of South Africa?
◀ When is Mandela Day and what are people asked to do on this day?

Give a presentation

In your oral presentations, you should aim to communicate effectively and clearly in front of an audience. This is scary at first, but you will find it is a lot easier the more you prepare and practise.

Try not to rely too heavily on notes. Make eye contact with your audience to keep their attention. Practise at home before delivering your presentation to the class. A visual aid can help keep your presentation interesting and engaging for the audience, while acting as a guide for you to know what points you wanted to make.

Presentation checklist

- ✓ Research your topic well.
- ✓ Decide what you want your audience to know about the topic.
- ✓ Introduce your topic at the beginning of your presentation.
- ✓ Speak clearly and slowly – do not rush through your presentation.
- ✓ Engage with your audience – maintain eye contact, use humour and questions.
- ✓ Thank your audience for their attention at the end of your presentation.

Your teacher will examine your presentations and award you for the following:

- ◖ excellent communication skills
- ◖ well-chosen material
- ◖ good knowledge of your topic
- ◖ clear engagement with the audience.

 Create

 Create a short presentation about Nelson Mandela and deliver it to the class.

Paragraphs

A paragraph is a group of sentences on one point or topic.

Each paragraph should make one point that is fully developed to help the reader understand your written work. Start a new paragraph to show a change of topic.

Show your reader that you are beginning a new paragraph by either indenting (leaving a space) or skipping a line.

 Grammar Primer: pages 9–10

Indenting:

> End of paragraph one.
>   Start of paragraph two.

Skipping a line:

> End of paragraph one.
>
> Start of paragraph two.

Read the following description.

> My granny's house is situated on a quiet, residential road. Her house is on the corner, nestled behind a large ash tree. The front garden is full of shrubs and flowers growing neatly in a row. The last time I visited, my granny was making an apple pie. She always uses fresh apples that she picks from her garden.

The writer moves from describing the grandmother's home to talking about her apple pie. When the writer starts a new point they should begin a new paragraph.

> My granny's house is situated on a quiet, residential road. Her house is on the corner, nestled behind a large ash tree. The front garden is full of shrubs and flowers growing neatly in a row.
>
> The last time I visited, my granny was making an apple pie. She always uses fresh apples that she picks from her garden.

Write out the following extract, dividing it into three paragraphs.

Damien carried the large casserole dish into the living room, where his parents' guests were sitting. The whole way in he was careful not to let the dish slip. It was piping hot and he was worried that he could burn the tips of his fingers if he held it for much longer. Damien hated when his parents had guests to dinner. It always meant that he was banished out of sight for a few hours to entertain himself. He decided he would cycle down to Gordon and they could play basketball in his front garden to kill some time. When he arrived at Gordon's house he noticed the front door was open. Damien carefully approached the front of the house and peered into the hall.

 Create

Imagine you have just landed in the landscape below. Write three paragraphs in the space provided on page 6 of your Portfolio. Use your first paragraph to describe your surroundings, your second paragraph to explain how you feel, and your third paragraph to express your hopes and fears for the future.

Biographies

A biography is an account of someone's life that is written by someone else.

Features	Language
◖ Personal details	◖ Honest
◖ Facts and information	◖ Appropriate to the topic (e.g. the biography of a celebrity may be informal and conversational, whereas the biography of a political figure may be more formal)
◖ Written in the third person	
◖ Narrative style (storytelling)	
◖ Often recounts events in sequence (in order)	
◖ Often reveals secrets and private events	

 Discuss

1. What are the main differences between a biography and an autobiography?
2. Can you think of any famous biographies?

 3. Would you prefer to write an autobiography or have a biography written about you? Work in pairs to come up with three reasons to share with the rest of the class.

 Investigate

Use the internet to find an example of each of the following types of biographies:
◖ a biography of a sportsperson
◖ a biography of a singer
◖ a biography of a historical figure.

 Create

 1. **(a)** Work in pairs to share some personal experiences on one of the topics below. Listen to your partner and take notes on their experiences.
   ◖ My first day of school
   ◖ My greatest childhood memory
   ◖ My favourite summer holiday

 (b) Write a paragraph about your partner's experience of this event on page 7 of your Portfolio. You are now writing a biography of an event in their life.

Below is an extract from the biography of author Roald Dahl, written by Michael Rosen.

Fantastic Mr Dahl

To understand how Roald Dahl became such a fantastic writer, I think it's important to find out what he was like as a boy. Let's picture him, aged about nine years old when he first went to boarding school.

It was called St Peter's, and it was a long way from home, near the seaside town of Weston-super-Mare in Somerset, England. There were about seventy boys there, aged between eight and thirteen. No girls. St Peter's didn't really look like a school. It was more like the kind of spooky house you find in ghost stories, with dark, pointed windows and ivy creeping all over the outside walls.

The boys were grouped into 'houses', which meant that they lived together in different parts of the school.

 Understand

1. What does the biographer think is important in understanding how Roald Dahl became such a fantastic writer?
2. What age was Roald Dahl when he first went to boarding school?
3. According to the writer, why didn't St Peter's resemble a school?

Biographies can also be created through video. Watch the following video biography of David Beckham:
www.biography.com/people/david-beckham-9204321

 Create

 Create a video biography of a person who has achieved great success in his or her life. Remember to include background details, images and facts.

Nouns and adjectives

A noun is a person, animal, place or thing.
There are different types of nouns.

◖ **Common nouns:** ordinary, everyday nouns
  tree, pen, dog

◖ **Collective nouns:** a collection of things
  a group of girls, an army of ants, a flock of sheep

◖ **Proper nouns:** people's names, place names, brand names, days of the week and months of the year
  February, Friday, Michael D. Higgins

◖ **Abstract nouns:** feelings and qualities
  love, beauty, anger

Adjectives are words that are used to describe nouns.
white *walls,* ***brown*** *dog,* ***red*** *pen*

 Write a noun on a piece of paper then fold the paper and place it into a container. One by one select a piece of paper from the container at random. In pairs, time your partner and give them one minute to talk about this object without pausing or saying 'eh', 'um' or 'em'. Using adjectives will help you with this task!

 ## Understand

1. Count **(a)** how many nouns and **(b)** how many adjectives you can find in the extract from *Fantastic Mr Dahl* on page 26.

2. Write the following sentences in your copy and underline the nouns.
   (a) Dave painted the walls then washed the brushes.
   (b) Nicola finished reading her book and turned off the lamp.
   (c) Elaine switched off her phone and fell asleep.

3. Write the following sentences in your copy and underline the adjectives.
   (a) The lazy, tired dog slept in his comfortable bed.
   (b) The old, cranky woman shouted angrily at the children making noise.
   (c) Sweet sugar tastes delicious on fresh strawberries.

 Grammar Primer: pages 11–15

Personal essays

A personal essay is a piece of writing that reveals your thoughts, feelings and ideas. Your personality comes through in a personal essay.

Features	Language
◖ Written in the first person	◖ Honest
◖ Deal with memories or events	◖ Descriptive
◖ Describe thoughts, feelings and emotions	◖ Personal
◖ Narrative style of writing	
◖ Events told in sequence	

Read the following example of a personal essay. Notice how each paragraph is linked to the one before, but deals with a separate event within the main story.

A Day I Will Always Remember

Heading

It was a sunny Friday morning in June and Dad came home early from work. He had several planks of wood and his toolbox in hand. I met him at the door and he had the biggest smile on his face. I asked him what he was so happy about and he motioned me to follow him to the end of the garden.

Arresting opening that grabs the attention of the readers

There is an old oak tree at the bottom of our garden. It has been there since before we moved into this house. It was always my go-to place during hide and seek, as the trunk of the tree was so wide that nobody could spot me behind it. I loved running my fingers over its rough bark and smelling the freshly cut grass as I crouched behind it, listening for my friends.

Descriptive setting that appeals to the senses

Dad told me that we were going to build a tree house in the oak tree. Looking back at that moment I was so excited and I knew there and then that this would be a day I would never forget.

Reflective language used as the writer looks back on the event

Dad took care of all the dangerous tasks, such as sawing, drilling and hammering nails. I sanded down and painted the wood. My task made me feel important and grown up.

Reveals thoughts and feelings

At six o'clock Mum called us in for dinner. I raced to eat as fast as I could, as I was dying to get back out and continue working. Dad told me to calm down and not rush my meal, but I was eager to get the most out of the day before it grew dark.

Develops the scene further

Eventually, Dad finished his dinner and we got back to work. The tree house was really taking form. There was a window and a door at the front and the floor was secured by two of the large branches that jutted out from the tree. We worked tirelessly into the evening and as the sun started to go down our tree house was complete.

Dad and I took a step back to admire the small wooden house nestled in the tree. It was as though the tree house had always been there. I was really proud of our handiwork. I could not wait until Saturday so I could have all of my friends over to explore our new base camp.

Reflects on the memory

Dad went into his shed and reappeared with a long piece of rope. He made a ladder that reached the top of the tree house and secured it tightly to the tree. I felt as though this day could not get any better until Mum came out with ice cream as a reward for our hard work. Dad suggested that we eat our ice cream in the new tree house. We both climbed up the ladder, balancing our bowls of ice cream, until we got inside.

As we sat there with our legs crossed, eating our ice cream and admiring our handiwork, I remember thinking how this was a really special day that I would never forget.

Ends with a link to the title

 Discuss

1. Why do you think this was a memorable experience for the writer?
2. Is there any particular day in your own life that you will always remember?
3. Why was this day so memorable?

When writing a personal essay, you should remember the points below.

- You will be expressing your own thoughts and emotions throughout. Remember: the one subject that you know best is you.
- Think carefully about the title and plan your essay – have ideas for each paragraph to guide you through.
- Make your opening engaging. Ask yourself 'Would I want to read on from this opening?'
- Create a strong setting that captures sound, smell, taste, touch and sight.
- End on a reflective piece of writing (an idea for the reader to think about).
- Give vivid details of any other people included.
- Vary the length of your sentences and paragraphs to keep the reader interested.
- Avoid any unnecessary or irrelevant details that veer off topic or that a reader may find boring.

Below are some sample openings of personal essays.

> I was seven when my brother tiptoed into my bedroom and told me he had murdered the tooth fairy.

> I glared at her from across the playground. I was biding my time until the teacher turned his back, then I would seek my revenge.

> My Mom always warned me about checking the pockets of my trousers before I put my clothes in the wash. At that moment I really regretted that I had not listened.

 Discuss

1. Do these openings make you want to read on?
2. Which one of these personal essays would you most want to read and why?
3. Can you think of any openings that you have read that caught your attention?

 Create

 Pick one of the following titles and write the opening paragraph of a personal essay on page 8 of your Portfolio.

- The greatest holiday I ever had
- A time when I was really angry
- The best decision I ever made
- My biggest regret
- If I could do anything for a day, I would …

Remember to write some ideas in the rough work box first to help you organise your thoughts.

Draft and redraft

It is always a good idea to spend time looking over your work to see if there are areas that you can improve on and to ensure that you have included all of the features of your chosen genre. Perhaps you forgot to write the date in a diary entry, maybe you signed off the wrong way in a letter or did not include a subject line in an email.

Reviewing your work gives you an opportunity to correct any mistakes that you may have made, such as spelling or punctuation errors. It can also give you the chance to improve your work, such as adding in more description, moving information around or changing details of your plot or characters.

What is a draft?

A draft is a version of a written piece of work. You can write many drafts before you write your final version.

Why do we draft?

Practise helps us to improve at sports, drawing, playing musical instruments and singing. Writing is no different. We write drafts so that we can improve on them.

What is proofreading?

Proofreading is when you read over your work and correct any mistakes. After you have written your first draft, you should read back over it. You may notice spelling mistakes or errors in grammar. You can correct these so that when you write your next draft you will know to include these changes.

What is the difference between proofreading and editing?

Proofreading focuses on mistakes in your writing, such as errors in your grammar, spelling or punctuation. Editing focuses on correcting these errors, while also making bigger changes, such as adding descriptions or making changes to your plot or characters.

What are the benefits of drafting and redrafting your work?

Editing your work gives you the opportunity to spot any mistakes you have made, and gives you the chance to improve and make sure that your final piece of writing is your best work.

Tips for redrafting your work

Here are a few tips to help you redraft your work once you have completed a first draft.

- **Read your draft aloud.** This will help you to ensure that each sentence is clear and that the reader will not have any difficulty comprehending your work.

- **Ask a peer to read your work and give you feedback on potential areas that you could improve.** Make these changes if you feel they will improve your work.

- **Leave your work aside and come back to it another day with fresh eyes.** Ensure that there are no spelling or grammar mistakes and that you are happy with all elements of your work. You can then rewrite your essay.

 Redraft your opening paragraph of a personal essay in the space provided on page 76 of your Portfolio. Follow the steps below.

1. Proofread your paragraph to ensure that you have made no spelling, grammar or punctuation errors. Use a different-coloured pen to make any changes needed.

2. Reread your paragraph and make a note of any changes you would like to make. For example, could you add more description to draw your readers in?

3. Ask a peer to read over your work.

4. Listen to their feedback on your work and change any areas that you feel you could improve.

5. Read over your piece one last time to ensure there are no spelling or grammar mistakes and that you are happy with all of the changes.

6. Write out your paragraph neatly in the space provided on page 76 of your Portfolio. This is your final draft.

7. Proofread your final draft one last time to guarantee that you have not missed any spelling or grammar mistakes.

 Create

 1. **(a)** Choose one of the titles below and write the first draft of a personal essay in the space provided on pages 9–10 of your Portfolio. There are six paragraphs to fill in, so decide what each paragraph will deal with before you write your first draft.

- The Nicest Thing I Have Done For Someone Else
- The Most Important Things In My Life
- My Greatest Accomplishment
- How I Feel About Growing Up

 (b) When you have completed your first draft, redraft your personal essay in the space provided on pages 77–78 of your Portfolio.

Personal letters

A personal letter, also known as an informal letter, is written to someone you know. When you write a personal letter, you can use casual language.

Features		Language
◖ Sender's address	◖ Introductory paragraph	◖ Casual
◖ Date	◖ Details/information	◖ Personal
◖ Greeting	◖ Closing statement	◖ Language that is appropriate for the recipient (e.g. a letter to your friend may be more casual than a letter to your aunt)
◖ Written in the first person	◖ Sign-off	

Layout of a personal letter

35 Sandy Lane Pebble Avenue	*Sender's address*
3 June 2018	*Date*
Dear Scott,	*Greeting*
It feels as though it has been ages since we last spoke. I know that we only met for a coffee two weeks ago, but it really feels longer.	*Opening paragraph*
So far the holiday has been amazing. The weather is incredible, so I have been spending most of my days on the beach. My swimming is definitely improving. I might re-challenge you to that race I lost last summer. I have made a few friends over here and in the evening we play volleyball on the beach. I'm not very good, but at least it is improving my fitness level.	*Body of letter (3–4 paragraphs)*

My dad logged on to the school database and it turns out the exams went really well. I was surprised that I got a B in French. All those late nights studying verbs really paid off. How did you do?

I have decided that when I get home I am going to start a travel blog. If I keep a diary over here it will help me remember all the hotspots and highs of the holidays to include in my blog. See if you can think of a cool name for it!

I hope your holidays are going well. There are only 10 days left of my holiday. I can't wait to fill you in on everything.

Looking forward to seeing you,

Closing statement

Dave

P.S. My mum and dad say hi.

Postscript for additional thoughts or information

 Discuss

Would you use a different style of language when writing to an older relative than you would when writing to a friend?

 Create

1. Write a letter to a friend in which you tell them how excited you are about the annual school disco.
2. Write a letter to your aunt and uncle thanking them for your birthday present.

Remember to use the features of a personal letter and to include organised paragraphs with a separate point in each.

Formal letters

Formal letters are usually written to someone you do not know personally.

Features

- Sender's address
- Recipient's address
- Date
- Greeting
- Written in the first person
- Introductory paragraph
- Details/information
- Closing statement
- Sign-off

Language

- Professional
- Formal
- Informative
- Direct

Hello. I am interested in applying for a job with your company. I was wondering if it would be possible to leave my C.V. with you?

Formal language is used in more serious situations or when speaking to people that we do not know well.

The main differences between personal and formal letters are as follows.

Personal letters

- Informal language
- Recipient is someone you know well
- Sender's address appears on the right-hand side
- Recipient's address is not included
- Casual greetings and closing statements
- Can include a postscript (P.S.) with additional information

Formal letters

- Formal language
- Recipient is not usually someone you know well
- Sender's name and address appear on the right-hand side
- Recipient's title, name and address appear on the left-hand side, across from the date
- Formal greeting and closing statement
- Usually do not have a postscript

You should begin your letter with the greeting 'Dear' and address the recipient by their proper title (Mr, Ms, Dr, etc.). If you do not know the name of your recipient, you may begin your letter with 'Dear Sir/Madam'.

If you know the name of the person you are writing to, close your letter with 'Yours sincerely'.

If you do not know the name of the person you are writing to, close the letter with 'Yours faithfully'.

Layout of a formal letter

29 Dame Street
West Junction
Co. Wexford

Sender's address and the date in the same position as in a personal letter

19 October 2018

Ms E. Carty
Human Resources Manager
Sports For All
Riverdale
Dublin 6

Recipient's address

Dear Ms Carty,

Formal greeting

I am writing to you in relation to the job advertisement that you posted online last Friday 17 October for a sales assistant in your sports store.

First paragraph states reason for writing

I feel that I would be very well suited for this job, as I am a keen sportsperson who is involved in numerous sports within my community. I play soccer for my school team and we had great success this year, having reached the Leinster finals. I also volunteer with the local swimming club and coach tennis to under sixteens in West Row tennis club.

Body of letter includes further details and information

I also have retail experience. I worked in my local bookshop for the summer months last year and can supply you with a reference from my previous employer.

I look forward to hearing from you, as I would appreciate an opportunity to meet with you in person to discuss the role further. Please do not hesitate to contact me at the above address.

Contact information for a response mentioned

Yours sincerely,

Sign-off and signature

Deirdre Killoran

 Discuss

1. What are the main differences between the letter above and the letter on page 33?
2. Which style of letter, personal or formal, would you write to each of the following recipients?

   (a) A letter to your aunt telling her about your time in Irish college.
   (b) A letter to a local restaurant complaining about the service.
   (c) A letter to your friend inviting them to your birthday party.
   (d) A letter to your local supermarket requesting an application form for a job.
   (e) A letter to your cousin telling them about your summer holidays.
   (f) A letter to your grandparents to wish them a happy Christmas.
   (g) A letter to your school principal requesting a non-uniform day.

Read the following two letters.

Letter 1

19 Meadows Lane
Ballygrange
Co. Kerry

7 April 2020

Oran,

How are you keeping, man? I'm trying to study for my exams and I thought I would take the time to write to you while I am on a break.

I saw your photos from New York on Instagram. It looks amazing. What did you think of my comment?

I was out in town yesterday looking for your birthday gift. When I came across the new Ireland jersey I thought it was definitely something you would like to have for your strolls through Central Park. Everyone will know you're Irish!

I'm looking to book flights over to you once I finish my exams. I'll Facetime you later, but I thought this letter would be a nice treat with your gift.

Anyway, I'd better get back to the books. Chat to you soon.

Your friend,

Rory

P.S. My golf swing is seriously improving. You'll be very impressed next time we play a round!

Letter 2

23 Grange Road
Co. Laois

7 July 2019

Manager
Tasty Treats Restaurant
Main Street
Portarlington
Co. Laois

Dear Sir/Madam,

I am writing to you to complain about my visit to your establishment last Thursday.

I had booked a table for six, as my family and I were celebrating my brother's birthday. When we arrived we were told that there was no record of this booking and we had to wait 40 minutes until a table became available.

Once we were seated it took a further 40 minutes for the waiter to take our order. When the food was delivered to the table it was cold and the order was incorrect.

I complained to the waiter who told me that the restaurant was understaffed and recommended that I forward my complaint to the manager.

I was highly unsatisfied with the service on the night of my reservation and I expect compensation for the cold meal and the delay in seating my party.

You can contact me at the above address. I await your reply.

Yours faithfully,

Enda Whelan

 Discuss

Which of the examples is a formal letter and which is a personal letter? Give reasons for your answer.

 Understand

List the features of a formal letter and the features of an informal letter that you notice in each example.

 Create

Write a letter to a sports club asking if it would be possible to host a football match to raise money for charity. Remember to include the features of a formal letter.

Emails

'Email' is short for 'electronic mail'. Email is used for sending messages instantly from one computer to another. Similar to letters, emails can also be personal or formal in language and tone.

The main differences between letters and emails are as follows.

Letters	Emails
◀ Must be dated	◀ Dated automatically with a time stamp
◀ Sent to an address	◀ Sent to an email address
◀ Can be handwritten or typed	◀ Typed
◀ Must be delivered or posted	◀ Received instantly
◀ Hard copy only	◀ Soft copy stored in your mailbox
◀ Sent directly to one recipient	◀ Can be sent to multiple addresses at once

The top of your email will include the following:

◀ **To:** the email address to which you are sending your email.

◀ **From:** this will be automatically updated with the address of the email account from which you are sending your email.

To:	sean@communitycollege.ie
From:	jenny@gmail.com
Subject:	School Project

◀ **Subject:** a summary of what the email is about.

The top of your email may also include the following:

◀ **Cc (carbon copy):** the email addresses of any others who you want to see the email. These email addresses can be seen by the recipient.

◀ **Bcc (blind carbon copy):** the email addresses of any others who you want to see the email. These email addresses will not be seen by the recipient.

To:	sean@communitycollege.ie
From:	jenny@gmail.com
Cc:	ciara@communitycollege.ie
Bcc:	principal@communitycollege.ie
Subject:	School Project

 Discuss

1. Do you have an email address?
2. Have you ever sent an email?
3. What was the main reason for sending this email?
4. What are the advantages of sending an email rather than a letter?

 Investigate

1. How quickly does an email travel from one computer to another?
2. Who invented email?

Here is an example of an email of enquiry.

To:	booking@bowledover.com	*Recipient's email address*
From:	ianpilkington@email.ie	*Sender's email address*
Subject:	Birthday Bowling 22 February	*A summary of the reason for writing the email*

B *I* U T тT ☺ ▲ ≡ ☰

Dear Manager,

Greeting

I am writing to you to enquire about booking your venue for my birthday on 22 February. There are 10 guests attending and we were hoping to have two bowling lanes for the duration of an hour.

Opening paragraph detailing reason for writing

Could you please inform me as to what refreshments or snacks are available on your premises and forward me on a cost per person for the use of the bowling lane for an hour?

What you hope to find out from your email of enquiry

You can reply to me at the above email address. Alternatively, my mobile number is 087 123 4567.

Contact information for the recipient to get in touch

I look forward to hearing from you.

Yours faithfully,

Sign off

Ian Pilkington

Understand

1. Who wrote the email above?
2. What was their reason for writing this email?
3. List two pieces of information that the manager needs to address in his reply.
4. What two methods of contact does the writer of this email offer the manager?
5. If the writer of this email knew the manager's name would the sign off be different? If so, what would it be?

Create

1. **(a)** Write a draft of the email you think the manager of Bowled Over would send in reply in the space provided on page 11 of your Portfolio.

(b) Rewrite your email in the space provided on page 79 of your Portfolio

Persuasive writing

 Create

 Pretend that you and your partner are a parent and child. Act out a short scene in which the child is trying to convince the parent to let them get a dog.

Persuasive language tries to convince people to support a particular point of view, by using logic and reason and by appealing to their emotions.

Can I get a dog for my birthday this year? I want a golden retriever.

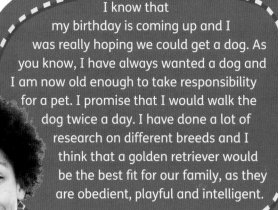 I know that my birthday is coming up and I was really hoping we could get a dog. As you know, I have always wanted a dog and I am now old enough to take responsibility for a pet. I promise that I would walk the dog twice a day. I have done a lot of research on different breeds and I think that a golden retriever would be the best fit for our family, as they are obedient, playful and intelligent.

 **Discuss**

Which teenager do you think is more likely to get a dog and why?

 Create

1. In pairs, write three convincing points to deliver to your classmates as to why wild animals should not be caged.
2. Write a persuasive paragraph to be delivered to the board of management at your school, encouraging teachers to allow students to use their mobile phones at school.

Speeches

A speech is a communication delivered directly to an audience. Speeches use persuasive language to inspire and motivate listeners. Most speeches include the following features.

Features

◀ Personal anecdotes
◀ Facts and statistics
◀ Inspiring content
◀ Engaging topics
◀ Rhetorical questions

Language

◀ Inclusive
◀ Motivational
◀ Direct
◀ Can be conversational or formal, depending on the occasion and the audience

anecdotes:
short, amusing or interesting stories about real events

rhetorical questions:
questions that do not require an answer, as the answer is obvious (e.g. do birds fly?)

The following extracts demonstrate some of the key features in speech writing.

Personal anecdotes make speeches more engaging and interesting.

I was convinced that the only thing I wanted to do, ever, was write novels. However, my parents, both of whom came from impoverished backgrounds and neither of whom had been to college, took the view that my overactive imagination was an amusing personal quirk that would never pay a mortgage, or secure a pension. I know the irony strikes with the force of a cartoon anvil, now.

– J. K. Rowling, Harvard Commencement Speech, 2008

Personal reflection allows the listeners to relate to the speaker.

Really, when I look back on it, I wouldn't change a thing. I mean, it was so important for me to lose everything because I found out what the most important thing is … to be true to yourself. Ultimately, that's what's gotten me to this place. I don't live in fear. I'm free. I have no secrets and I know I'll always be OK, because no matter what, I know who I am.

– Ellen DeGeneres, Tulane Commencement Speech, 2009

Motivational language inspires listeners.

You cannot let a fear of failure or a fear of comparison or a fear of judgment stop you from doing what's going to make you great. You cannot succeed without this risk of failure. You cannot have a voice without the risk of criticism. And you cannot love without the risk of loss. You must go out and you must take these risks.

– Charlie Day, Merrimack College Commencement Speech, 2014

Directly addressing your listeners engages the audience.

Have you ever gone into your favourite neighbourhood café with the paper that you buy every day, and you open it up and inside is a 500-word opinion written by a nice middle-class woman, the kind of woman who probably gives to charity, the kind of woman who you would be totally happy to leave your children with. And she is arguing over 500 words so reasonably about whether or not you should be treated less than everybody else, arguing that you should be given fewer rights than everybody else. And then the woman at the next table gets up and excuses herself to squeeze by you and smiles at you and you smile back and you nod and say no problem, and inside you wonder to yourself 'Does she think that about me too?'

– Panti Bliss, Noble Call speech at the Abbey Theatre, 2014

Statistics and facts help to strengthen a speech.

Fall forward. This is what I mean: Reggie Jackson struck out twenty-six-hundred times in his career – the most in the history of baseball. But you don't hear about the strikeouts. People remember the home runs. Fall forward. Thomas Edison conducted 1,000 failed experiments. Did you know that? I didn't know that – because 1,001st was the light bulb. Fall forward. Every failed experiment is one step closer to success.

– Denzel Washington, Penn Commencement Speech, 2011

Rhetorical questions encourage the audience to reflect.

We are struggling for a uniting word but the good news is that we have a uniting movement. It is called HeForShe. I am inviting you to step forward, to be seen, and to ask yourself if not me, who? If not now, when?

– Emma Watson, HeForShe speech at the United Nations, 2014

 Investigate

Research some famous speeches online and see if you can find any other examples of rhetorical questions. Share the quotes you find with the class.

Hint: try the following speeches:
- Martin Luther King, 'I Have a Dream'
- King George VI, 'Radio address, 1939'
- John F. Kennedy, 'The Decision to go to the Moon'
- Ken Robinson 'Do Schools Kill Creativity?'

Read the following example of a speech welcoming incoming students on their first day of secondary school.

Welcome speech

How many of you are exhausted? If you are anything like I was, then you didn't sleep a wink last night. In fact, you were probably scrolling through social media at all hours of the night dreading today. It's a big day, isn't it? The first day of secondary school.

Questions and inclusive language engage the audience

I'm Scott Fallon and I can remember being in your shoes, those brand-new, shiny shoes, sitting precisely where you are now. I was exhausted and terrified. Looking back on it now, the things I feared the most turned out to be some of my greatest experiences. I knew nobody and I had no friends. Now, six years on, here I am with some of the most talented, supportive and loyal people I have ever met as my friends.

Introduction and personal anecdote maintain the interest of the audience

I was asked to talk to you today about my advice for starting school. This school is 150 years old. You do not get to be that old without gaining some wisdom and experience along the way. This school has the secret – in the corridors, the classrooms, the teachers, the building. It knows better than I do how to shape, encourage and inspire you. This school will motivate you and challenge you. At the end of your secondary education you will realise that you are who you are because of your time spent here.

Facts support and emphasise points

Looking back, I thought Mr Benson was the most terrifying man I'd ever met. Six feet tall with broad shoulders and a stern look. Now, at 18, I am taller than he is, but I haven't nailed that look just yet! On my first day he was a giant and he terrified me. I never spoke up in his Science classes, I barely made eye contact with him and I would neglect football practice, social media and computer

Personal reflection helps the audience to relate

games to ensure I had his homework done. I wish I had not been so scared of Mr Benson and many other members of the teaching staff in my first term, as it turns out the staff in this school are remarkably supportive and friendly. They will go out of their way to guide and assist you in any way they can, so do not let fear hold you back. Embrace your classes, your teachers and your peers.

The best advice that I can give you here today, as you sit in front of me, a batch of fresh new talent brimming with ideas and aspirations, is to get involved. Try everything from sport to music, from art to science, from dance to debate. The school will provide you with countless opportunities to wear out your sparkling new school shoes, and I say to you wear out those shoes and become another legacy of this school.

Motivational and inspirational message that ties back to the opening paragraph

Thank you for listening and welcome to our school.

 Understand

1. Who delivered this speech?
2. Who is this speech addressed to?
3. What advice does the speaker give to the audience? Find two examples and use quotes to support your answer.
4. Why did the speaker think Mr Benson was the most terrifying man he'd ever met?

 Create

1. **(a)** You have been asked to write a speech to deliver to your sports team to motivate them before the final match of the season. Write an opening paragraph for your speech. Include at least one of the following features.

   ◖ Personal anecdote
   ◖ Inclusive language
   ◖ Facts, figures, statistics

    (b) Rewrite your opening paragraph and include one of the features below.

   ◖ Rhetorical question
   ◖ Personal reflection
   ◖ Inspirational message

ch Malala Yousafzai's speech to the United
ions and answer the questions that follow.

https://youtu.be/3rNhZu3ttIU

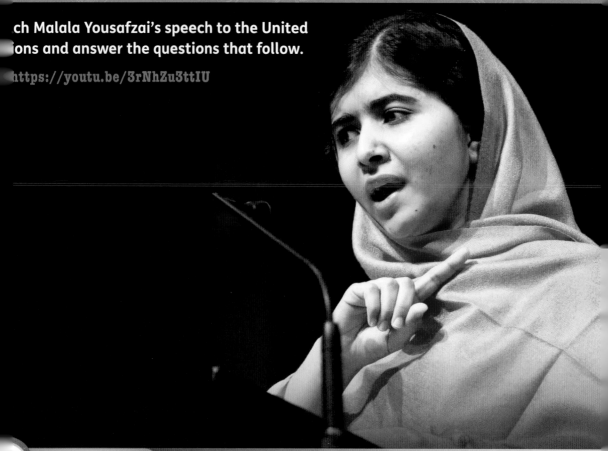

Discuss

What aspects of Malala's speech did you enjoy?

Understand

1. Who does Malala say she is speaking for?
2. What does Malala tell us happened in October 2012?
3. What does Malala say can change the world?

Explore

1. What is Malala's attitude towards the Talib who shot her?
2. What does Malala mean by 'The pen is mightier than the sword'?
3. What is Malala's wish for every child all over the world?

Create

1. **(a)** Write a speech encouraging your classmates to take up an after-school activity in the space provided on pages 12–13 of your Portfolio.
   (b) Deliver your speech to your classmates, then fill out the checklist on page 13 of your Portfolio.

Debates

A debate is a formal discussion between two people or groups on a particular subject in front of an audience. Debate speeches are different to other types of speeches because a debate speech can only explore one side of a topic.

Features

- Welcome the audience
- Introduce the motion
- Put forward an argument for the motion
- Structured approach
- Statistics and figures
- Sources and facts
- Rhetorical questions
- Closing argument

Language

- Formal
- Convincing
- Inclusive
- Engaging

The topic being debated is called a **motion**.

This discussion is divided into two sides. The **proposition** argues in favour of the motion. They are the first side to speak. The **opposition** argues against the motion. They are the second side to speak. The argument goes back and forth between the sides.

A **chairperson** conducts the debate, introduces the speakers, the motion and the guidelines of the debate.

A **timekeeper** keeps the time and lets the speakers know when their time is up.

Adjudicators decide the winners of the debate by judging which side put forward the best argument.

Spectators watch the debate.

Watch the following video to gain a greater insight into debates.

 https://youtu.be/lwXZisYEQZs

 Discuss

1. Select one of the motions below and, as a class, raise your hands to show which side you are on: proposition or opposition. Give a reason as to why you agree or disagree with the motion.

   - *This house believes that football is better than rugby.*
   - *This house believes that Snapchat is better than Instagram.*
   - *This house believes that books are better than films.*

2. Are there any other topics that you think would be interesting to debate as a class?

Debate speeches follow a formal structure.

The opening of a debate should welcome the audience, introduce the motion and state clearly whether you are opposing or proposing it.

> *Chairperson, adjudicators, ladies and gentlemen, my name is ... and I am here today to propose/oppose the motion that ...*
>
> *Good afternoon, my name is ... and I strongly disagree with the motion that ...*

List three main points that you will argue in your debate.

> *I believe that ... for the following reasons ... (point 1, point 2, point 3).*
>
> *It is clear/obvious/evident that ... because ... (point 1, point 2, point 3).*

The main argument of your debate speech should develop your three points in detail.

Firstly ...

In our society/school/ education system today ...

Young people these days ...

It is a sad state of affairs when ...

We must ask ourselves why ...

Let's consider ...

Secondly ...

We must also consider/look at/ discuss ...

Furthermore ...

This is a widespread problem in our society ...

It is the responsibility of the government to ...

Finally ...

It is necessary to look at ...

Further evidence shows that ...

I strongly/firmly believe ...

The end of your debate should summarise your three main points, thank the audience for their attention and urge them to agree with your side.

> *To conclude ...*
> *In summary ...*
> *Once again, I believe that ...*
> *Thank you for your attention ...*

Read the following example of a debate.

This house believes that cats make better pets than dogs

Speaker 1 (proposition)

Chairperson, timekeeper, adjudicators, ladies and gentlemen, my name is Amy and I am here today to propose the motion that cats make better pets than dogs.

Formal introduction, states the motion and side

I believe that cats are better pets than dogs for three reasons. Firstly, cats are more independent. Secondly, cats are cleaner. And finally, cats require less training than dogs.

Outlines main arguments

Cats are more independent than dogs. Dogs require supervision and training. Dogs need to be let in and out, dogs cannot walk themselves and dogs are not as street-smart as cats. Cats can roam the neighbourhood freely without worry, a simple cat flap can save you the hassle of having to open and close doors and cats can fend for themselves.

Addresses the first point in more detail, using a comparison to highlight argument

My second point to demonstrate why cats make better pets than dogs is that they require less maintenance. Dogs love to roll in muck, jump in puddles and lie in dirt. Dogs are not fazed by dirt or smells. Owners must either wash, dry and brush their dogs, which, let's face it, is an inconvenience, or pay as much as €90 to have their dog groomed. Cats, on the other hand, are far cleaner animals. Cats are disgusted by dirt and spend an inordinate amount of their day cleaning themselves. I believe this is one of the strongest reasons why you would have to agree that cats do in fact make better pets than dogs.

Moves on to the second point and uses examples to support argument

This brings me to my last point. Cats do not require the same level of training as dogs. A puppy needs to be trained not to chew on furniture and shoes, drink from the toilet bowl, bark at guests and whine during dinner. Cats do not do these things.

Develops the final point

Cats are more independent, cleaner and easier to manage than dogs. It is for these three reasons that I believe cats make far better pets. Thank you for listening and I urge you to agree with me.

Sums up main points, thanks listeners and asks them to agree

Speaker 2 (opposition)

Good afternoon chairperson, timekeeper, adjudicators, ladies and gentlemen. My name is Sean and I oppose the motion that cats make better pets than dogs.

Formal introduction

I strongly disagree with the proposition's argument. Cats may be more independent than dogs, but this does not make them better pets. Dogs are loving and loyal, whereas cats are cold and dismissive. A dog will always be at the door ready to greet you with the utmost love and affection. A cat would not care if you never came home. Cats may be independent, but this makes them cold and unloving. Are these qualities that you want in a pet?

Engages with and argues against the proposition's points while making a counter argument

Asks a rhetorical question

Secondly, cats may be able to clean themselves, but they also use a litter tray that remains indoors. Your cat may be clean, but this litter tray could cause your house to smell. On the other hand, a dog will ask to be let outside to do his business. I, for one, believe that washing your pet is a moment of bonding. I love nothing more than grooming my dog. This makes for a stronger bond between us.

Personal anecdote to support the point being made

While speaker one is correct in saying that cats can be let out alone, the fact that a dog cannot only encourages the owner to get exercise by walking them. Walking has been proven to reduce the risk of heart disease and stroke by up to 27% and it also has great mental health benefits. It is clear then, that having a dog as a pet can help keep you healthy as well.

Facts and statistics to back up argument

I think you will agree that dogs are loyal, loving companions, and that these traits make them far better pets than cats. I therefore encourage you to agree with me in opposing the motion that cats make better pets than dogs.

Sums up main points and asks listeners to agree

 Understand

1. Outline the three main reasons speaker one puts forward in support of the motion.
2. Speaker one argues that cats make better pets because they are more independent. Why does speaker two disagree with this point?
3. What does speaker two say is an important bonding activity between a dog and its owner?
4. How does speaker two turn the necessity of having to walk a dog into a positive?

 Discuss

1. Which speaker do you believe put forward a better argument? Give two reasons for your answer.
2. Can you think of any other arguments for or against this motion?

Read the following debate speech and answer the questions that follow.

This house believes that written homework should be banned

Good afternoon chairperson, adjudicators, members of the opposition, teammates and audience. I am here to propose the motion that written homework should be banned.

Let me begin by outlining my three main reasons for this argument. Firstly, written homework is an unnecessary stress that all students must endure after a long day at school, which takes from our time to unwind in the afternoon and relax. Secondly, there are no proven statistics to say that written homework is of benefit to a student's development, and, finally, this time would be better spent revising, as most exams are memory and information related.

Let me start by introducing myself. I am Lucy Garvey and I am a third year student at St Martin's Community College. I strongly believe that using our time in the evening to watch television, listen to music, play sport or socialise with friends is far more beneficial to the development of our social skills and protection of our mental health. I conducted an in-school survey and 87% of students agreed that they would feel more prepared for a day at school if they had time in the evenings to relax instead of completing written assignments.

This brings me to my next point. I am not saying that there should be no homework whatsoever. Instead, I am suggesting that teachers designate practical homework, rather than long and tiresome written assignments. As pointed out by the *The Good School's Guide*, unless homework is well thought-out and beneficial to the learning outcomes of the lesson that day, it is pointless. Who here in this room agrees that they have spent countless hours completing written tasks that they feel will be redundant in 10 years' time?

Finally, I would like to address the nature of the exams in Ireland. The State Examinations require us to retain information, learn vital knowledge and process this into our own opinions. I know you will agree that revision of texts and supplementary reading material would be a far more beneficial after-school task for us students.

In conclusion, I believe that this house should ban written homework. It does not improve our grades, it takes away from our recreational time and it does not complement the exams on which we are graded. Ladies and gentlemen, I implore you to agree. Thank you for listening.

Understand

1. Who does the speaker welcome to the debate in the opening paragraph?
2. Is the speaker proposing or opposing the motion?
3. List the three main points the speaker says she will address.
4. What statistical evidence does the speaker put forward?
5. Identify the rhetorical question the speaker asks in this speech.

Explore

1. Do you believe the rhetorical question in this speech was effective? Give two reasons for your answer.

 2. What features of a debate can you identify in this speech? Work with a partner to list all of the features you can find. Include an example of each feature you identify.

Investigate

Can you find any facts or statistics that would oppose Lucy's argument?

Create

  1. Work in groups to write the opposing speech for the motion: *This house believes that written homework should be banned.* Choose a member of your group to deliver it to your class.

 2. (a) Write a speech proposing or opposing the following motion in the space provided on pages 14–15 of your Portfolio: *This house believes that social media should be banned.* Remember to research some facts and figures to help strengthen your argument.

 (b) Time yourself reading your speech aloud. Your speech should be two minutes long. Edit or add to your speech in order to meet the two-minute requirement.

 (c) Deliver your speech to your class.

 3. Split the class in half. The left side is the proposition and the right side is the opposition. Write a debate speech for the following motion: *This house believes that secondary school classes should continue during the summer months.* When you have written your speeches, carry out a class debate on this motion.

Reviews

A review is an opinion on a book, a film, a holiday or any other experience. Reviews can be written or spoken (for example, on radio, television or YouTube). Reviews can be either positive or negative. Reading, listening to or watching reviews can be helpful in determining whether or not you will like or dislike something.

Features	Language
◖ Introduction ◖ Description ◖ Judgement ◖ Recommendation ◖ Details ◖ First person ◖ Information ◖ Facts ◖ Opinions	◖ Language appropriate to topic/audience ◖ Engaging ◖ Persuasive

A review should begin with an **introduction** that names the item or event being reviewed and then gives some brief details. The introduction should be followed with a more detailed **description** of what is being reviewed. A **judgement** should then be made on the pros and cons. The review should end with a **recommendation** as to whether to purchase/go to the thing being reviewed, or who specifically would enjoy the thing being reviewed.

Below is a review of an electronic device. Notice how the advantages and disadvantages of the device are included in the review, with an overall judgement weighing up the positives and negatives.

Review of the Easy Reader

Introduction

The new, highly anticipated Easy Reader e-reader launched in stores today. With a greater memory capacity for storing your chosen books and a built-in dictionary to make looking up new words more accessible, this is sure to be a hit with consumers.

Product named and briefly described

Description

At €79 the new lightweight Easy Reader is a bargain. The sensitive touchscreen makes turning pages a doddle and the inbuilt torch means you never need to be stuck in the dark without your favourite book again. The Easy Reader is available in a variety of colours to suit all tastes. It will also store your favourite books and make recommendations of books you should try based on your reading habits.

Features of the product described in greater detail

Judgement

What sets this e-reader apart from its competitors is the radio functionality, which allows you to listen to music as you read. Alternatively you can select the 'read aloud' mode and have the book read to you.

The one drawback of the Easy Reader is the short battery life. I found that after several hours of charge I only got between five to six hours of reading life. The long charge is worth the wait though, as the functionalities have a lot to offer all readers.

Details the positive and negative aspects of the product

Recommendation

I would highly recommend this e-reader to keen readers of all ages and anyone like me who was skeptical of going from physical books to e-books. The Easy Reader allows you to read more books than ever with its advanced storage. Do not hesitate to avail of a free demo in shops nationwide today. You won't regret it!

States who would best enjoy this product

Makes a recommendation based on their opinion of the product

 Discuss

1. Could you use emojis to give a review?
2. Can comments on social media be a form of review?

 Understand

1. How much is the Easy Reader selling for?
2. What are the features of the Easy Reader?
3. What does the reviewer tell us about this product that sets it apart from other e-readers?
4. What is the one negative comment the reviewer makes about this product?
5. Who does the reviewer recommend this product to?

 Investigate

Look up a review of your favourite book, film or television show. Do you agree with what the reviewer has said?

 Create

Review the last book you read using just a hashtag statement and an emoji. For example: *Harry Potter and the Philosopher's Stone* #Icouldntputitdown ⚡

Read the following review. Notice how the reviewer summarises what the book is about but does not give away any details about the ending.

The Fault in Our Stars by John Green – review

The Fault in Our Stars is a novel by American author, John Green. The title is a reference to a line in Shakespeare's *Julius Caesar*: 'The fault, dear Brutus, is not in our stars/But in ourselves'.

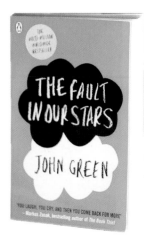

It is about a girl called Hazel, who has Stage 4 Thyroid cancer with metastasis on her lungs, and her boyfriend Augustus, who lost his leg to osteosarcoma. The book deals with the tragedy of their health problems, but not in a mawkish way, and ends up being totally uplifting. It is set in present-day Indianapolis, America.

The book tells the story of how they meet and fall in love, although it isn't some lovey-dovey story.

Whilst it isn't laugh-out-loud funny, it is witty and thoughtful; the characters are honest and likeable. The author makes you connect with Hazel and Augustus, and the book really opens your eyes to the struggle of living with disease. Hazel's relationship with her parents is heartbreaking but extremely touching. It is a sad book and it may make some tearful (I admit I did cry) but it is also a book of joy and appreciation of life. You will not regret picking up this book – I have yet to hear a bad review of it!

 Understand

1. According to the reviewer, what does the title reference?
2. According to the reviewer, what is this book about?
3. Does the reviewer consider this novel to be funny?
4. Does the reviewer recommend this book?

 Explore

 1. What does the reviewer suggest is different about this novel?
2. Would this review make you want to read *The Fault in Our Stars*?

 Create

 1. Create a vlog reviewing a recent school event.

 2. **(a)** Write a review of a book you have read recently in the space provided on pages 16–17 of your Portfolio.

 (b) Swap your review with the person next to you and use the checklist on page 17 of your Portfolio to ensure that they have completed all elements of the task.

Interviews

An interview is a list of questions tailored to and directed at a particular person, in order to find out more information about them.

Interviews can be carried out to discover more about someone's life. They can also be helpful in finding out the suitability of a candidate for a job.

Features

◖ Transcript
◖ Dialogue
◖ Clear purpose
◖ Questions that probe for detailed answers
◖ Word-for-word answers from the interviewee

Language

◖ Personal and honest
◖ Direct answers
◖ Language appropriate to the audience

A **transcript** is a written text of a conversation. An interview can be written as a transcript. This will include the interviewer's questions and the interviewee's answers, word for word.

Ivy: Did you always know you wanted to be a businessman?

Tom: Yes, from a young age I was always interested in business and economics.

Ivy: How did you get into your line of work?

Tom: It was simple really. I studied Business in school and spent my summer holidays shadowing my dad, who worked in advertising, to get an insight into the industry.

 Discuss

Who do you think the interviewer is? Ivy or Tom? Give a reason for your answer.

Reported speech is used in an interview when you are summarising the conversation but also want to quote parts of what the interviewee said in their own words.

Read the following extract from an interview with actor Millie Bobby Brown. This interview is written using reported speech rather than a transcript.

When Vogue Met Millie Bobby Brown

… I ask her what she would wear, given the choice, she tells me that she went to dinner in a Pikachu onesie last night.

The pressing question, of course, is whether Brown will return for the second series of *Stranger Things*. When I ask her about the next step in her career she says that she's 'open-minded' but solemnly reminds me that she's 'focusing on *Stranger Things* and Netflix right now'. Most revealingly of all, when I ask her about whether she's planning to grow her hair out now, she says: 'I don't know if I'm growing it out just yet … To be honest I think if I do come back and I had to cut my hair again I'd be fine with it.'

 Understand

Rewrite the interview with Millie Bobby Brown in transcript form.

 Create

 Work in pairs to come up with a list of potential interview questions that you could ask the following people:

- a sporting hero
- a student running for class captain
- a librarian applying for a job in the school library
- a television personality
- the President of Ireland
- an astronaut.

Quotation marks

Quotation marks should be used if you are writing down what someone has said or written.

When writing what someone has said (direct speech), punctuation, such as question marks and exclamation marks, should be included within the quotation marks.

> *'How are you?' asked Jim.*
> *'I'm fine,' Annie responded, 'and how are you?'*

Quotation marks are used when writing up interviews, as the interviewer will be quoting directly from the interviewee.

> *She feels that her fame is better put to use to spread a message: 'I made a vow that I would stand for something and not just enjoy the materialism of fame.'*

Quotation marks should also be used if you are quoting directly from a piece of writing.

◖ When you are quoting a piece of writing, all punctuation marks that are included in that quote should be kept within the quotation marks.

> *Heaney tells us that there was 'a foot for every year.'*

◖ If a quote begins with a capital letter, you should place the full stop within the quotation marks.

> *Heaney tells us that his brother was in 'A four foot box.'*

◖ If the quote does not begin with a capital letter or end with a punctuation mark, then punctuation marks that signify the end of your sentence should be placed outside of the quotation marks.

> *Heaney's brother was in a 'four foot box'.*

 Grammar Primer: pages 16–18

 Understand

Write out the following sentences, adding quotation marks where necessary.

1. Have you done the homework? asked the teacher.
2. Can I have some chocolate? begged the child.
   No, said his mother, it would spoil your dinner.
3. What do you want to do today? asked Paul.
   I don't know, sighed Zack, how about we go for a cycle?

 Investigate

 Work in pairs and take turns asking one another what you would use your fame for if you became famous. Write down what your partner says.

 Create

Write a short piece summarising your partner's answer to the Investigate task above. Include at least two direct quotations in your answer.

Read the following interview between journalist Rosanna Greenstreet and *X Factor* judge Louis Walsh.

Louis Walsh: 'Which book changed my life? My chequebook'

When were you happiest?

I'm always happy. Ask Simon Cowell: he says if I had a tail, I'd wag it.

What is your greatest fear?

Getting old, getting sick, getting cancer, getting Alzheimer's disease.

What is your earliest memory?

I grew up in a small village in the west of Ireland. My father played things like *My Fair Lady*, *The King And I*, and *The Mikado* on his record player, and I remember looking at the records.

What is the trait you most deplore in yourself?

I say things I shouldn't and I can't stop myself. It's called no filter.

What is the trait you most deplore in others?

Snobbery and bad manners.

deplore:
strongly dislike

What was your most embarrassing moment?

I have one every day: I don't care about making a fool of myself at all.

Who would play you in the film of your life?

Colin Farrell. He auditioned for me for Boyzone and I said no. He couldn't sing.

Which book changed your life?

My chequebook.

What is your most unappealing habit?

I bite my nails – in fact, I'm doing it at the moment.

Aside from a property, what's the most expensive thing you've bought?

I have a Maserati. I love pop art and I collect Warhol, Hirst and Hockney.

 Understand

1. What trait does Louis dislike most in others?
2. What is Louis's worst habit?
3. What type of art does Louis collect?

 Explore

 1. What impression do you form of Louis Walsh based on this interview?

2. Which question from the interview do you think reveals the most interesting information about Louis Walsh? Explain your choice.

3. If you had the opportunity to ask Louis Walsh a question, what would it be and why?

Investigate

1. (a) Research a famous person you admire, either from the sporting world, entertainment or science, using the following headings:

- date and place of birth
- family
- education
- how they started in their career
- the highlight of their career so far
- an interesting fact about them.

 (b) Share your findings with the class.

 Create

1. Come up with eight interview questions that you could ask the person you researched.

  2. In pairs, select one of the images below. One of you must come up with five interview questions. The other will answer these questions as a member of this profession.

Question marks

A question mark is used at the end of a sentence to show that it is a question rather than a statement.

Both of the sentences below are the same, apart from the question mark.

We have no homework.

We have no homework?

Discuss

1. How does the inclusion of the question mark change the meaning of the sentence above?
2. Does the tone of your voice change in your delivery of these two sentences?
3. Can you think of any statements that can become a question by adding a question mark?

In dialogue, the question mark will go inside the inverted commas.

'When will you be home?' asked Jake.

'What do we have to do for homework?'

'How long is the match?' Tommy asked.

Understand

Write out the following sentences, placing a question mark in the correct place.

1. 'Why are you going downstairs' asked Mum.
2. 'What time does the film start' she enquired.
3. 'How long is left until the bell rings' the teacher wondered.
4. 'How many people will the room hold' the lady queried.
5. 'Does a question always end with a question mark' asked the student.

 Grammar Primer: pages 19–21

Revising writing with purpose

Reflect and review

1. Look back at the images at the top of page 3.
   (a) Which image best represents the unit, in your opinion?
   (b) Which image least represents the unit, in your opinion?
   (c) Think of some alternative images that could be used to represent this unit.

2. Fill in the unit review on page 18 of your Portfolio.

3. What did you learn about drafting and redrafting in this unit? Write a paragraph in your copy about why you think this process is important.

Language skills

1. Write out the following sentences including capital letters, commas and full stops where appropriate.
   (a) jenny burst into the room she could not wait to tell sarah and jason the news
   (b) i set my alarm for 7 o'clock this morning as i needed enough time to pack my runners lunch shorts and sunglasses for our school trip to the national gallery
   (c) dermot was so excited about his holiday he was going to paris to visit the eiffel tower and taste the local cuisine

2. Write out the following sentences including quotation marks and question marks where necessary.
   (a) Mum, where are the shoes I bought Sarah roared down the stairs.
   (b) Are there any sweets left in the press Chris asked Alex.
   (c) We've only got two rehearsals left before opening night, the teacher informed the students.

Oral assessment

Work in groups of four to carry out a debate. Select one of the motions below.
   ◀ *This house believes that the driving age in Ireland should be lowered.*
   ◀ *This house believes that there should be a fine for those who do not recycle their waste.*
   ◀ *This house believes that bicycles should be banned from the road.*

Divide into proposition and opposition (two speakers on each side). Decide on a first speaker and a second speaker for both opposition and proposition. Each speaker must research the motion, write and present a two-minute speech outlining their position on the motion.

Written assessment

1. **(a)** Write the diary entry that a character from your studied novel would write after a significant event in the novel in the space provided on page 19 of your Portfolio.

   (b) Redraft your diary entry in the space provided on page 80 of your Portfolio.

2. **(a)** Write a letter to your school principal requesting a specific school tour that you would like to go on with your class in the space provided on page 20 of your Portfolio.

   (b) Redraft your letter in the space provided on page 81 of your Portfolio.

3. **(a)** Write the opening paragraph of a personal essay inspired by the image below in the space provided on page 21 of your Portfolio.

   (b) Redraft your opening in the space provided on page 82 of your Portfolio.

Unit 2

Poetry and Song

Why study this area?

Poems and songs are a way of exploring experiences and expressing emotions. Poems have the power to make us see things differently. The writer Jeanette Winterson said that 'A tough life needs a tough language – and that is what poetry is.' When we read a poem or listen to a song we know that we are not alone, however tough life might be.

Learning intentions

◁ Read and understand a wide variety of poems and songs.

◁ Discover techniques and devices associated with poetry.

◁ Discuss and interpret many poems.

◁ Investigate poets and present the information you discover.

◁ Create your own poetry and writing inspired by poetry.

◁ Compare two poems.

◁ Make links between poetry and song.

◁ Discover how to conduct research.

◁ Learn about apostrophes and pronouns.

 Discuss

1. What words or phrases do you associate with poetry?
2. Which of the images above best represents poetry, in your opinion?
3. The poet E. E. Cummings said 'write poetry, for God's sake, it's the only thing that matters'. Why might he have felt this way?
4. What do song lyrics and poems have in common?
5. We often turn to poetry in times of celebration or sorrow, such as weddings or funerals. Why do you think people read poems at times like these?

 Create

 Write your own definition of poetry in the space provided on page 29 of your Portfolio, by completing the sentence 'Poetry is ...'. You will return to this definition later on.

Introducing poetry and song

Poetry is a form of writing that often evokes an emotional response. Poets use carefully chosen words and arrange them in a certain way to create a particular meaning, sound or rhythm. Poems are often described as 'paintings in words'. They are usually arranged in groups of lines known as stanzas or verses.

In First Year you will learn at least 10 poems. Although some will share a similar theme, each poem is unique. Remember, a poem can have many possible meanings and you should interpret the poem in a personal way. Ask yourself, 'what does this poem mean to me?'

Throughout this unit you will learn several new poems in various styles. You will become familiar with many of the techniques and devices that poets use to get their message across. You will also encounter a selection of songs in this unit. Poems and songs share many similarities. Both poets and songwriters use poetic devices and create memorable sound effects. Look out for the **Focus on ...** boxes, which are used every time you are introduced to a new poetic technique or device. When you see these boxes, be sure to add the definition to the glossary on pages 1–2 of your Portfolio.

Discuss

1. Think of a poem that you have learned in the past.
   (a) What is the poem called?
   (b) What did you like about it?
2. Share some of your favourite lyrics of all time. Compare your choices – are you familiar with the lyrics chosen by your classmates?

Song

It has been said that songs are poems put to music. It is true that music and poetry have a lot in common. After all, poets and songwriters are artists who enjoy the freedom of expression through words and rhythm.

Read the lyrics of the song 'You Can't Judge a Book by the Cover' by songwriter Willie Dixon. What stands out about the sounds of the words at the end of each line?

You Can't Judge a Book by the Cover

You can't judge an apple by looking at a tree, a
You can't judge honey by looking at the bee, a
You can't judge a daughter by looking at the mother, b
You can't judge a book by looking at the cover. b

Oh, can't you see, a
Oh, you misjudged me. a
I look like a farmer but I'm a lover, b
You can't judge a book by looking at the cover. b

Oh, come on in closer baby,
Hear what else I gotta say!
You got your radio turned down too low,
Turn it up!

You can't judge sugar by looking at the cane,
You can't judge a woman by looking at her man,
You can't judge a sister by looking at her brother, b
You can't judge a book by looking at the cover. b

Oh, can't you see, a
Oh, you misjudged me. a
I look like a farmer but I'm a lover, b
You can't judge a book by looking at the cover. b

You can't judge a fish by looking in the pond,
You can't judge right from looking at the wrong,
You can't judge one by looking at the other, b
You can't judge a book by looking at the cover. b

Oh, can't you see? a
Oh, you misjudged me. a
I look like a farmer but I'm a lover, b
You can't judge a book by looking at the cover. b

Focus on ... **rhyme**

Rhyme is similar sounding words in poetry or song.

Rhyme creates a musical quality. Many poets and songwriters make use of a rhyming scheme, where similar sounding words are placed at the end of lines. This is known as end rhyme. Internal rhyme is when some words or phrases within the same line rhyme.

Work with a partner to find words that rhyme with the following:

- lace
- proud
- frame
- middle.

The rhyme in 'You Can't Judge a Book by the Cover' is regular, which means it has a pattern. The rhyming scheme in this song is *aabb*. This means that the last words in the first two and last two lines rhyme. Take a look:

You can't judge an apple by looking at a tree,	*a*
You can't judge honey by looking at the bee,	*a*
You can't judge a daughter by looking at the mother,	*b*
You can't judge a book by looking at the cover,	*b*

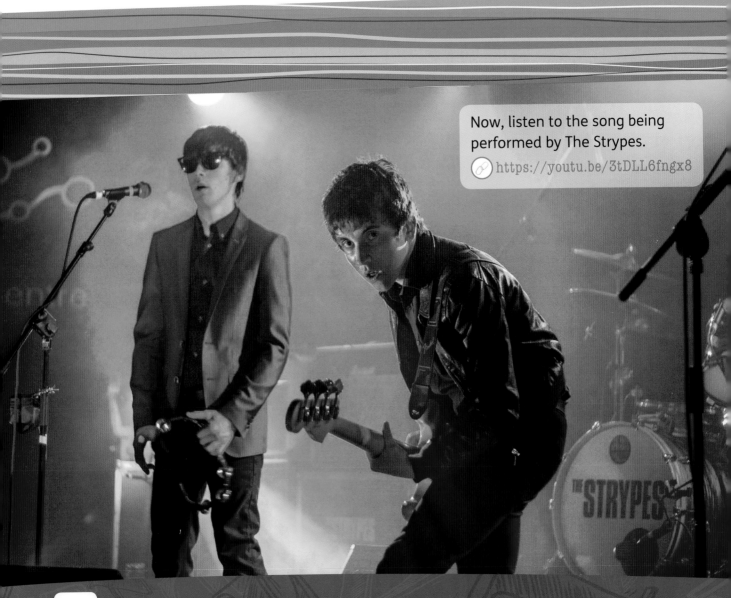

Now, listen to the song being performed by The Strypes.

https://youtu.be/3tDLL6fngx8

Discuss

1. Did you enjoy the lyrics of this song before you listened to it being performed?
2. Did any of the lyrics stand out to you while you were listening to the song?

 Understand

1. What is this song about?
2. Comment on the use of rhyme in this poem. What is the effect of this technique?

 Explore

1. Choose the statement that applies to you and explain your choice.
   (a) The lyrics are better on their own, unaccompanied by music.
   (b) The lyrics are better when they are performed, accompanied by music.
2. Select one part of the song that you liked best. Explain your choice.
3. Who do you think might 'misjudge' the speaker?
4. Do you agree that you should not judge a book by the cover?

 Create

 Design an album cover for The Strypes in the space provided on page 22 of your Portfolio. When you have finished, you should explain your design with reference to the song above. Choose an album name based on the lyrics of the song.

Listen to the following song by The Beatles and gently tap the beat of the song on your lap.

When I'm Sixty-Four

When I get older, losing my hair,
Many years from now,
Will you still be sending me a valentine
Birthday greetings, bottle of wine?

If I'd been out 'till quarter to three,
Would you lock the door?
Will you still need me, will you still feed me,
When I'm sixty-four?

You'll be older too.
And if you say the word
I could stay with you.

I could be handy, mending a fuse,
When your lights have gone.
You can knit a sweater by the fireside,
Sunday mornings go for a ride.

Doing the garden, digging the weeds.
Who could ask for more?
Will you still need me, will you still feed me,
When I'm sixty-four?

Every summer we can rent a cottage in the Isle of Wight,
If it's not too dear.
We shall scrimp and save.
Grandchildren on your knee,
Vera, Chuck and Dave.

Send me a postcard, drop me a line,
Stating point of view.
Indicate precisely what you mean to say,
Yours sincerely, wasting away.

Give me your answer, fill in a form,
Mine for evermore.
Will you still need me, will you still feed me,
When I'm sixty-four?

Focus on ... **rhythm**

Rhythm is the way beats are arranged in a poem or song.

Rhythm gives poetry and songs a beat or sense of timing. It is easier to feel a rhythm than see it written down – this is why it is so important to listen to poetry being read out loud and to practise reading it out loud yourself.

Rhythm can affect the speed or pace of a poem or song. Rhythm can also affect the feeling or mood of a poem or song.

In this song, The Beatles create a regular rhythm. The rhythm quickens and reflects the upbeat mood of the song.

 Form small groups of three or four. One person should read 'When I'm Sixty-Four' out loud. The rest of the group should take turns gently tapping the beat of the song as they listen.

 Discuss

1. What is the song about?
2. Do you like the melody?
3. What is your favourite line **(a)** on paper and **(b)** as it is sung?
4. What is the speed or pace of this song?
5. What feeling is expressed throughout the song?
6. Did you notice the rhythm of the song when you first read it aloud?

Understand

1. What question does the speaker repeat?
2. What sort of things will the couple do as they grow older?
3. Who are Vera, Chuck and Dave?
4. What is your favourite example of rhyme in the song?
5. In your opinion, does this song have a memorable beat?

ABBEY
ROAD
NW8

71

Explore

Compare this song to 'You Can't Judge a Book by the Cover' on page 67.

1. What do the songs have in common?
2. What are the differences between the songs?
3. Which song do you prefer and why?

Investigate

 Work with a partner to find out the following information about 'When I'm Sixty-Four':

◖ when the song was written
◖ the names of each member of The Beatles
◖ which band member sings 'When I'm Sixty-Four'
◖ what instruments are used
◖ the name of the album that features this song
◖ the names of two other songs by The Beatles.

Create

1. Sketch a picture of the couple carrying out one of the activities mentioned in 'When I'm Sixty-Four'.
2. Write the lyrics of a song – you may like to model your lyrics on one of the songs you have read. Carefully consider rhyme and rhythm as you write your lyrics.

Poetry

Look at the title of the poem below. Based on the title alone, do you think that this poem might be serious or lighthearted?

Property for Sale
By Rachel Rooney

Two houses up for sale.
One stick, one straw.
Both self-assembly,
See pig next door.

 **Focus on ... title**

A **title** is the name given to a poem or song.

You should always examine the title of a poem before reading it. What do you expect from the poem based on the title? Return to the title when you have finished reading the poem. Does it make you think differently about what you have read?

 Reread 'Property for Sale'. With a partner, discuss whether you felt differently about the title after reading the poem.

 Understand

1. Can you guess which well-known fairy tale inspired this poem?
2. We are told that both houses are 'self-assembly'. What does this mean?
3. What materials are mentioned in the second line?
4. In Ireland, is it usual to build a house with the materials mentioned in the second line?

Explore

1. Do you think the title, 'Property for Sale' has been well-chosen? Explain your answer.
2. Choose a new title that you feel would suit this poem.
3. In your view, does this poem do a good job of advertising the houses for sale?

Create

1. Advertisements usually persuade consumers to buy something. Imagine you are in charge of advertising each item below. Write a catchy caption to encourage consumers to buy the item. The first one has been done for you.

(a)

Race away in a new car today!

(b)

(c)

(d)

 2. **(a)** In small groups, list as many fairy tales as you can. What do you learn about the story from the titles?

(b) Choose one of the fairy tales that you have listed and give it a new title. For example, Rapunzel could be renamed 'Let Your Hair Down'.

3. Choose a fairy tale or well-known story and rewrite it, changing elements of the plot and/or the outcome.

In the following poem the speaker tells a fictional story about a time when they met a girl with curious features.

The Girl with Many Eyes
By Tim Burton

One day in the park
I had quite a surprise.
I met a girl
who had many eyes.

She was really quite pretty
(and also quite shocking!)
and I noticed she had a mouth,
so we ended up talking.

We talked about flowers,
and her poetry classes,
and the problems she'd have
if she ever wore glasses.

It's great to know a girl
who has so many eyes,
but you really get wet
when she breaks down and cries.

Focus on ... narrative poetry

Narrative poetry is poetry that tells a story.

'The Girl with Many Eyes' is written in narrative form. It contains many of the features of storytelling. The speaker in the poem becomes a narrator, describing events and characters.

 Work with a partner to identify the narrative voice in this poem. Who do you think the person telling the story might be?

Understand

1. In your own words, describe what happens in 'The Girl with Many Eyes'.
2. What did you learn about the girl in this poem?
3. Trace the rhyming scheme in 'The Girl with Many Eyes' and list the words that rhyme.
 4. Work with a partner to put the following images in order to tell the story of 'The Girl with Many Eyes'. Find a quote from the poem to accompany each of the images.

 Explore

 1. Why might the girl break down and cry, in your opinion?
2. Who is the narrator, in your opinion? Try to imagine the person telling the story. Consider their age, gender, physical appearance and characteristics.

 Create

 The narrator says that the girl talked about her poetry classes. Imagine you are the girl described in the poem. Write the poem from her point of view in the space provided on page 23 of your Portfolio.

Something unexpected happens in this narrative poem about a pig. Pay attention to the mood created in this poem as you read it.

The Pig
By Roald Dahl

In England once there lived a big
And wonderfully clever pig.
To everybody it was plain
That Piggy had a massive brain.
He worked out sums inside his head,
There was no book he hadn't read.
He knew what made an airplane fly,
He knew how engines worked and why.
He knew all this, but in the end
One question drove him round the bend:
He simply couldn't puzzle out
What LIFE was really all about.
What was the reason for his birth?
Why was he placed upon this earth?
His giant brain went round and round.
Alas, no answer could be found,
Till suddenly one wondrous night,
All in a flash, he saw the light.
He jumped up like a ballet dancer
And yelled, 'By gum, I've got the answer!
They want my bacon slice by slice
To sell at a tremendous price!
They want my tender juicy chops
To put in all the butchers' shops!
They want my pork to make a roast
And that's the part'll cost the most!
They want my sausages in strings!
They even want my chitterlings!
The butcher's shop! The carving knife!
That is the reason for my life!'

Such thoughts as these are not designed
To give a pig great peace of mind.
Next morning, in comes Farmer Bland,
A pail of pigswill in his hand,
And Piggy with a mighty roar,
Bashes the farmer to the floor…
Now comes the rather grizzly bit
So let's not make too much of it,
Except that you *must* understand
That Piggy *did eat* Farmer Bland,
He ate him up from head to toe,
Chewing the pieces nice and slow.
It took an hour to reach the feet,
Because there was so much to eat,
And when he'd finished, Pig, of course,
Felt absolutely no remorse.
Slowly he scratched his brainy head
And with a little smile, he said,
'I had a fairly powerful hunch
That he might have me for his lunch.
And so, because I feared the worst,
I thought I'd better eat *him* first.'

Focus on ... tone and mood

Tone is a poet's attitude towards the subject matter of a poem. **Mood** is the feeling or atmosphere in a poem.

The poet's tone often determines the dominant mood of a poem. Sometimes the poet's tone is serious, while at other times it is light-hearted. You may notice that the mood in 'The Pig' is playful and that the tone is humorous. Readers can share in this feeling of fun.

Take turns reading this poem stanza by stanza with a partner and pick out the parts that you find humorous. How would you describe the mood in these lines?

 Understand

1. What unexpected thing happens in this poem?
2. How do you know that the pig is clever?
3. We are told that the pig felt 'no remorse'. What does this mean?

 Explore

 1. Do you feel sympathy for the pig at any point in the poem?

 2. Do you think that this is a funny poem?

 Investigate

Roald Dahl is famous for writing many wonderful children's books. Find out more about Roald Dahl's stories by reading reviews online. Choose one of his novels to borrow from your library and enjoy reading it for yourself.

 Create

Write a review of the book you have read by Roald Dahl for your school website. In your review you should:

● name the book and author
● give a brief outline of the story, but do not give away the ending
● share your thoughts or opinions. Did you like the story? Why or why not?
● recommend the book to a particular age group. Who would be interested in reading it?

(For information on reviews see page 53.)

The poet William Butler Yeats was living in London when he wrote the following poem. He longed to escape the busy, dreary streets and live a simple, self-sufficient life on the uninhabited island of Innisfree. Yeats brings to life the beauty of nature on the island.

Read the poem aloud and listen for the parts that bring nature to life.

The Lake Isle of Innisfree
By W. B. Yeats

I will arise and go now, and go to Innisfree,
And a small cabin build there, of clay and wattles made;
Nine bean-rows will I have there, a hive for the honey-bee,
And live alone in the bee-loud glade.

And I shall have some peace there, for peace comes dropping slow,
Dropping from the veils of the morning to where the cricket sings;
There midnight's all a glimmer, and noon a purple glow,
And evening full of the linnet's wings.

I will arise and go now, for always night and day
I hear lake water lapping with low sounds by the shore;
While I stand on the roadway, or on the pavements grey,
I hear it in the deep heart's core.

Focus on ... imagery

Imagery is descriptive language that appeals to our senses (sight, sound, smell, taste and touch).

Every poem contains imagery. When you read a poem, try to imagine what the poet is describing. This technique helps readers to imagine what a person, place or experience is really like. For most of us, it is easy to remember a poem by thinking of the sensory images associated with it.

Yeats creates a wonderful image of Innisfree in the reader's mind. This emphasises one of the main themes in the poem, the beauty of nature.

Poets do not have to describe the sound of something, they only need to suggest it. This is enough for your imagination to take over. You can imagine the many sounds of Innisfree, including the 'bee-loud glade'.

 Listen to 'The Lake Isle of Innisfree' being read and work with a partner to pick out at least two more images from the poem.

Understand

1. What is your impression of Innisfree based on the description in the poem?
2. Choose two images in this poem that appeal to the senses. Explain your choices.
3. What is the mood in this poem?

Explore

 1. How does Yeats feel about Innisfree? Use evidence from the poem to support your answer.
2. Suggest at least one benefit and one drawback of living alone on an uninhabited island.

Create

1. **(a)** Do you have a favourite place where you sometimes long to be? Write about your favourite place. Try to bring the place to life using imagery that appeals to all of the senses.

    (b) Read your description carefully. Does it appeal to all of the senses? Redraft your description. (For information on drafting and redrafting see pages 31–32.)

    (c) Read your second piece to the class. Vary your expression, tone and pace.

Many of you may be familiar with the speaker's feelings in the following poem. The speaker leaves us in no doubt about the cause of his misery!

Homework! Oh, Homework!

By Jack Prelutsky

Homework! Oh, homework!
I hate you! You stink!
I wish I could wash you
away in the sink,
if only a bomb
would explode you to bits.
Homework! Oh, homework!
You're giving me fits.

I'd rather take baths
with a man-eating shark,
or wrestle a lion
alone in the dark,
eat spinach and liver,
pet ten porcupines,
than tackle the homework
my teacher assigns.

porcupines:
rodents with sharp
spikes known as quills

Homework! Oh, homework!
You're last on my list,
I simply can't see
why you even exist,
if you just disappeared
it would tickle me pink.
Homework! Oh, homework!
I hate you! You stink!

Focus on ... repetition

NB
Poets use **repetition** to emphasise their point or to draw attention to an important theme.

In 'Homework! Oh, Homework!' the speaker emphasises their point of view through the use of repetition. In pairs, take turns reading the poem aloud. Spend one minute talking to your partner about the speaker's point of view. Do you agree with what the speaker says?

Discuss

1. How does the speaker feel about homework?
2. Why do you think he feels this way?
3. How do you feel about homework?
4. Can you see any benefits of homework?

Understand

1. Count how many times the poet repeats the word 'homework' in this poem. Why do you think he does this?
2. Besides the word 'homework', does the poet repeat any other words or phrases?

Explore

1. Do you think that this is a memorable poem? What stands out most?
2. The speaker says that he cannot see why homework exists. Give the speaker two reasons why homework is important.

Create

Carry out a class debate on the following motion: *This house believes that school uniforms should be banned.* (For information on debates see pages 47–48.)

Research

In your study of English and in preparation for your first Classroom-Based Assessment you will be required to carry out research.

Why research?

In order to fully inform yourself of a particular subject or topic, you must investigate the topic. This means finding out more about the topic you have chosen. Actively seeking out information is an important part of the learning process.

How do I begin?

Decide which form of research best suits your needs. For example, if you are researching a topic to present to your class, you may wish to find information from sources such as the library or the internet. If you are researching a topic that relates to your classmates, you might use an interview or survey to find out their opinions.

Primary research

Primary research is when you find information for yourself, instead of relying on other sources. Forms of primary research include:

- inviting someone to share their knowledge or experience by writing letters and sending emails
- carrying out an interview
- conducting a survey.

How do I carry out a survey?

1. **Make a list of relevant questions.**

   Work alone or with a group to decide which questions will help you to gather information.

2. **Ask the questions.**

   When you have chosen the questions, present them to the group. The group may fill out a paper or online questionnaire.

3. **Analyse the results.**

   Gather your results. You may wish to convert figures to percentages in order to present your findings later on.

4. **Present your findings.**

   Show your results using a table, graph or chart. You may also wish to quote responses to the questions as part of your presentation.

Secondary research

Secondary research is when you use sources to gather information. Forms of secondary research include:

- gathering official facts and statistics from organisations or groups
- watching documentaries
- reading information in books
- using the internet to find information.

How do I carry out an online search?

When carrying out an online search remember to use specific key words.

- You will have more success when you use **specific search terms.** *Causes of the First World War* is more effective than *Why did the First World War begin?*

- Place an **asterisk at the end of a word** to search for a variation of that key word. *France* First World War* will show variations of the word 'France', such as 'French'.

- Use **quotation marks to search for a phrase** rather than individual key words. *'Hitler's rise to power'* will show results including this entire phrase.

- Include the word **AND** in capital letters to show **two search results**. *Painters AND sculptors* will show results for both key words.

- Include the word **OR** in capital letters to show **two similar results**. *Hotels OR Hostels in Galway* will show both options for accommodation.

- Include the word **NOT** in capital letters to **filter particular results**. *Dublin Restaurants NOT Italian* will show results that do not include Italian restaurants.

Make sure the information you are gathering is from reliable sources. Use more than one source of information to cross-reference, ensuring the details you have found are accurate.

Keep a record of where your information came from, such as webpages or names of books and authors.

When researching, remember ...

1. Be clear about your topic.
Before thinking about the kind of research you will carry out, you must decide on your topic.

2. Make a list/use headings.
Consider the kind of information you would like to find beforehand. Use headings to help you.

RESEARCH

3. Record the most useful information.
Do not copy and paste lots of information. Make a note of the most interesting or useful facts.

4. Save the information as you go along.
You may wish to use images, video links or an exact statistic or quote. Save the details of your sources in a file and remember to save regularly.

5. Use information that is relevant.
Report back to your class when you have completed your research and gathered all of the relevant information. You should arrange your information in a clear and logical way.

Search

GO

Rosa Parks is known as the mother of the civil rights movement. In the past, African-American people were segregated and forced to give up their seats to white passengers on the bus or stand back while white customers were served first at the supermarket. In 1955, Rosa Parks refused to give up her seat to a white man. This sparked huge protests. She, along with many others, had the courage to stand up for what she believed in – equal rights for all. This poem is written in dedication to her.

Rosa Parks
By Jan Dean

she sorts the drawer
knives at the left
forks at the right
spoons in the middle
like neat silver petals
curved inside each other

the queue sorts itself
snaking through the bus
whites at the front
blacks at the back

but people are not knives
not forks
not spoons
their bones are full of stardust
their hearts full of songs
and the sorting on the bus
is just plain wrong

so Rosa says no
and Rosa won't go
to the place for her race

she'll face up to all the fuss
but she's said goodbye
to the back of the bus

Focus on ... theme

The **theme** is the main message or idea explored in a poem. Poems can have more than one theme. Some of the themes in the poetry you will explore in this unit include youth, love and nature.

Sometimes the theme and subject matter can be the same, but this may not always be the case. The subject matter is centred around the topic, events or story of a poem and the theme is explored through the subject matter. For example, Rosa's actions are the subject of the poem 'Rosa Parks', but the theme of justice is also explored.

 Read 'Rosa Parks' aloud with a partner and try to guess some of the other themes explored in this poem. Highlight the words that are emphasised or stressed as you move through the poem. Do these give you an idea of the main message in the poem?

Understand

1. **(a)** How does 'she' sort the drawer?

   (b) Why is this significant?

2. Find the internal rhyme in this poem.

3. The speaker says that 'people are not knives / not forks / not spoons'. What could this mean?

Explore

 1. Based on what you have read in the poem, what sort of person is Rosa Parks?

 2. Do you think the poet admires Rosa Parks? Give reasons for your answer.

3. How do you think Rosa felt when she said 'no'? Write one paragraph explaining your thoughts.

4. Is there a character in a novel you have read or studied who takes action like Rosa? Write about the actions of your chosen character.

Investigate

1. **(a)** Use your research skills to learn more about Rosa Parks and the American civil rights movement. Try to find the following information:
   - the date of Rosa Parks's birth and death
   - where she lived
   - at least one of her achievements
   - images and media links.

 (b) Share the information you have gathered with the class.

Examine this image of the poet Siegfried Sassoon.

Discuss

1. What are your first impressions of this poet?
2. Is this how you would imagine a poet to dress?
3. What sort of issues might be important to someone like this?

Your teacher will read you the poem 'Base Details'. As you listen to the poem being read, write down at least one word or image that stands out to you.

Discuss

 Work in small groups to share your interpretations of this poem. What do you think the poem is about?

Explore

 Now that you have had time to share your first impressions of the poem, return to the word or image that you wrote down as you were listening to the poem. Share your chosen word or image with your classmates and explain why you chose this word or image.

The poem 'Base Details' is about war. As you might have guessed, the poet Siegfried Sassoon was a soldier in the First World War. He saw the horrors of war for himself and knew what it was like to be one of the ordinary soldiers forced to take orders from those in charge. Listen out for words that appear close together and start with the same sound or letter.

Base Details

By Siegfried Sassoon

If I were fierce, and bald, and short of breath,
I'd live with scarlet Majors at the Base,
And speed glum heroes up the line to death.
You'd see me with my puffy petulant face,
Guzzling and gulping in the best hotel,
Reading the Roll of Honour. 'Poor young chap,'
I'd say – 'I used to know his father well;
Yes, we've lost heavily in this last scrap.'
And when the war is done and youth stone dead,
I'd toddle safely home and die – in bed.

Majors:
high-ranking army officers

petulant: sulky

Roll of Honour:
list of soldiers who died in battle

Focus on ... alliteration

Alliteration is a sound effect created when words that begin with the same letter are placed beside or close to one another in a sentence.

Siegfried Sassoon uses alliteration in 'Base Details' to create a particular beat and rhythm and to make certain lines memorable. The following line contains alliteration: 'You'd see me with my **p**uffy **p**etulant face'.

Work in pairs to find the other examples of alliteration in the poem. Read these lines aloud. What do you notice about the sound effect created by this technique?

Share some other examples of alliteration. You may consider some of your favourite childhood stories or rhymes. For what reasons might authors include alliteration in their writing?

Discuss

1. Discuss the impact of alliteration in the poem. What is the effect of this technique?
2. A rhyming couplet is a pair of lines in poetry that rhyme and usually have the same rhythm. Can you find the rhyming couplet in this poem?
3. Did you find the rhyming couplet effective and/or memorable?

Understand

1. **(a)** Make a list of words used to describe the Majors.
   (b) What do these words tell us about the Majors?
2. **(a)** Make a list of words used to describe the soldiers.
   (b) What do these words tell us about the soldiers?

Explore

 1. Does Sassoon resent (hold a grudge against) the Majors? Explain your answer.

 2. Does this poem encourage young men to go to war? Give a reason for your answer.

Create

Imagine you are a soldier in the trenches of the First World War, battling through terrible conditions and watching as some of your fellow soldiers die. Write a diary entry recording your thoughts, feelings and hopes. (For information on diary entries see page 5.)

 'Stopping by Woods on a Snowy Evening' effectively depicts a winter scene. Listen out for 's' sounds as you read the poem.

Stopping by Woods on a Snowy Evening
By Robert Frost

Whose woods these are I think I know.
His house is in the village, though;
He will not see me stopping here
To watch his woods fill up with snow.

My little horse must think it queer
To stop without a farmhouse near
Between the woods and frozen lake
The darkest evening of the year.

He gives his harness bells a shake
To ask if there is some mistake.
The only other sound's the sweep
Of easy wind and downy flake.

The woods are lovely, dark and deep,
But I have promises to keep,
And miles to go before I sleep,
And miles to go before I sleep.

Focus on ... sibilance

Sibilance is a sound effect that occurs when 's' or 'sh' sounds are created in words that are placed close together.

In this poem, sibilance is used to create a peaceful sound. All is calm as the speaker looks on at the undisturbed snow.

Listen to the poem being read aloud. As you listen, underline the 's' sounds that stand out to you.

Work in groups to examine the use of sibilance in 'Stopping by Woods on a Snowy Evening'. Each person should take a turn reading one stanza of the poem. Emphasise all 's' sounds as you read. As a group, decide which stanza contains the best example of sibilance. Share your reasons for choosing this stanza.

 ## Understand

1. What does the speaker stop to look at in the first stanza?
2. How does the horse communicate with the speaker?
3. What time of year is it? Use evidence from the poem to support your answer.
4. Find examples of **(a)** alliteration and **(b)** repetition in the poem.

 ## Explore

1. Choose your favourite image from the poem. Explain your choice in one short paragraph.
2. The speaker tells us he has 'miles to go' before he sleeps. Who could the speaker be and where might he be going?

 ## Create

1. Tell the story from the horse's point of view. You can choose the form that your writing will take. For example, you might like to write a short story or a poem. You should also include an illustration.
2. Write a story set in winter and inspired by one of the following prompts:
   - It was the stormiest night of the year ...
   - The clock struck midnight as everyone rang in the new year. This year it would all be different ...
   - An adventure in the snow.

The following poem tells the story of a classroom in the dead of night. The poet imagines a scenario in which the letters come to life and express their feelings. Look out for the unexpected behaviour of the letters.

The ABC
By Spike Milligan

'Twas midnight in the schoolroom
And every desk was shut,
When suddenly from the alphabet
Was heard a loud 'Tut-Tut!'

Said A to B, 'I don't like C;
His manners are a lack.
For all I ever see of C
Is a semi-circular back!'

'I disagree,' said D to B,
'I've never found C so.
From where I stand, he seems to be
An uncompleted O.'

C was vexed, 'I'm much perplexed,
You criticize my shape.
I'm made like that, to help spell Cat
and Cow and Cool and Cape.'

'He's right,' said E; said F,
'Whoopee!'
Said G, "Ip, 'ip, 'ooray!'
'You're dropping me,' roared H to G.
'Don't do it please I pray!'

'Out of my way,' LL said to K.
'I'll make poor I look ILL.'
To stop this stunt, J stood in front,
And presto! ILL was JILL.

'U know,' said V, 'that W
Is twice the age of me,
For as a Roman V is five
I'm half as young as he.'

X and Y yawned sleepily,
'Look at the time!' they said.
'Let's all get off to beddy byes.'
They did, then 'Z-z-z.'

vexed:
annoyed

perplexed:
confused

Focus on ... personification

Personification is when an object is described as if it has feelings and behaves in a human way.

Before reading 'The ABC', you were asked to look out for the unexpected behaviour of the letters. These are all examples of personification. We see how the letters of the alphabet behave just like people. The poet, Spike Milligan, cleverly brings the letters to life, turning them into characters. For example:

'"I disagree," said D to B'.

Here, Spike Milligan personifies the letter D by giving this letter a voice and an opinion.

 Practise saying your favourite stanza out loud in pairs. Give each letter a distinctive voice.

Understand

1. Find two examples of personification in the 'The ABC'.
2. Describe the setting of the poem.
3. How would you describe the mood of this poem?

Explore

1. 'The ABC' has been described as a fun and playful poem. Do you agree with this description?
2. Do you think that any of the letters display personality traits? For example, you might describe the letter 'F' as energetic and excitable as it says 'Whoopee!' Choose one letter mentioned in the poem and list their characteristics based on the evidence in the poem.

Create

1. Look around your classroom and make a list of the ordinary objects that you see. Choose one item from your list and write one paragraph about life as that object. You should use personification to bring your object to life. Use this example to help you. Can you guess the item being personified?

   They are wearing me out! Every day, they use me to hide their mistakes. I am living in a dark pencil case, squashed between the cranky pencil sharpener and leaky red pen. Soon, I will be gone.

2. Some letters of the alphabet are not mentioned in the poem. Write a stanza involving at least two of the letters that are not included in the poem in the space provided on page 24 of your Portfolio. Try to personify these characters by giving them human qualities.

Apostrophes

An apostrophe is a punctuation mark that looks like this:

Apostrophes are used to indicate belonging.

When using an apostrophe to show that something belongs to someone, you should place the apostrophe before the 's': *Polly's car is purple.*

When using an apostrophe to show that something belongs to more than one person, you should place the apostrophe after the 's' at the end of the plural word: *The boys' faces lit up.*

Some plural words, such as children, sheep and feet do not end in 's'. In this case, you should add an apostrophe and an 's' after the word to indicate ownership: *The men's team will meet at 3 p.m.*

 Remember, an apostrophe should never be used to show that something is plural.

Apostrophes are also used to show where letters are missing.

Sometimes certain words are placed together to form one word, meaning letters are left out. These words are known as contractions. Apostrophes are used to show where letters are left out.

Look at the word 'don't' in the second stanza of 'The ABC' (page 92). This word started off as 'do not'. The poet brings the two words together by dropping the letter 'o' and replacing it with an apostrophe.

Let us look at another example: 'I will' becomes 'I'll'. In this case the letters 'wi' have been removed, so an apostrophe goes in their place.

Its never has an apostrophe to show belonging.

✗ *The monkey used it's hand to peel a banana.*

It's means 'it is'. The monkey did not use 'it is' hand to peel a banana.

✓ *The monkey used its hand to peel a banana.*

 Understand

1. Find the other examples of contractions in the poem 'The ABC' (page 92). Write the contractions as full terms.

2. Look at the examples below and rewrite them as contractions. The first one is done for you.

   (a) Do not = Don't   **(c)** Cannot   **(e)** They are

   (b) We are   **(d)** It is   **(f)** Who is

 When you have finished, turn to your partner and check their answers. Do they match yours? If not, try to work out which answer is right.

 Grammar Primer: pages 22–23

The following poem was written about a woman called Maud Gonne. The poet, W. B. Yeats, was in love with this woman and had been rejected by her many times.

When You are Old
By William Butler Yeats

When you are old and grey and full of sleep,
And nodding by the fire, take down this book,
And slowly read, and dream of the soft look
Your eyes had once, and of their shadows deep;

How many loved your moments of glad grace,
And loved your beauty with love false or true,
But one man loved the pilgrim soul in you,
And loved the sorrows of your changing face;

And bending down beside the glowing bars,
Murmur, a little sadly, how Love fled
And paced upon the mountains overhead
And hid his face amid a crowd of stars.

Focus on ... **lyric poetry**

Lyric poetry is written in a simple style and expresses emotions or personal feelings. Lyric poems usually rhyme, creating rhythm and a musical quality.

'When You are Old' fits into this form of poetry for the following reasons:

- emotions and personal feelings are expressed
- there is a clear rhyming scheme
- the rhythm is easy to detect.

Understand

1. What does Yeats ask the woman to imagine in the first stanza?
2. Apart from 'and', what word is repeated most in the poem? Why do you think Yeats repeats this word?
3. How do you know that 'When You are Old' is a lyric poem?

Explore

1. How do you think Maud Gonne felt as she read this poem?
2. What do you think the poet means when he says that 'one man loved the ... sorrows of your changing face'?
3. In your opinion, what is **(a)** the subject matter and **(b)** the theme of this poem?

Investigate

1. **(a)** Use your research skills to find out more about W. B. Yeats. Find the following information:

   - date of birth and death
   - where he grew up
   - at least one of his achievements
   - when his first poetry collection was published
   - common themes in his poems
   - images and media links.

 (b) Work in groups to compare the information you have gathered. Piece together your research, pictures and video links to create a three-minute presentation. During your presentation, each member of the group should speak for an equal amount of time.

William Wordsworth celebrated nature in many of his poems. As you read the poem, try to spot any comparisons made by the poet.

Daffodils
By William Wordsworth

I wandered lonely as a cloud
That floats on high o'er vales and hills,
When all at once I saw a crowd,
A host, of golden daffodils;
Beside the lake, beneath the trees
Fluttering and dancing in the breeze.

Continuous as the stars that shine
And twinkle on the milky way,
They stretched in never-ending line
Along the margin of a bay:
Ten thousand saw I at a glance,
Tossing their heads in sprightly dance.

sprightly: lively

The waves beside them danced; but they
Out-did the sparkling waves in glee:
A poet could not but be gay,
In such a jocund company:
I gazed – and gazed – but little thought
What wealth the show to me had brought:

gay: cheerful
jocund: merry

For oft, when on my couch I lie
In vacant or in pensive mood,
They flash upon that inward eye
Which is the bliss of solitude;
And then my heart with pleasure fills,
And dances with the daffodils.

oft: often
vacant: emotionless
pensive: reflective
solitude: being alone

Focus on ... simile

Similes compare one thing to another, using the words 'like' or 'as' or 'than'.

- Her eyes shone **like** diamonds.
- Her eyes were as bright **as** diamonds.
- Her eyes sparkled brighter **than** diamonds.

Poets will often use similes to exaggerate or emphasise something.

Did you find any comparisons in 'Daffodils'? Do any of the comparisons that you found include the word 'as'? If so, you have found a simile!

 In pairs, think of an example of each type of simile. Write three comparisons using 'like', 'as' and 'than'.

 Understand

1. Give three examples of nature imagery in the poem 'Daffodils'.
2. How do the daffodils make the speaker feel?
3. Find the similes used in 'Daffodils' and explain the comparisons.

 Explore

 1. What, in your opinion, is the central theme of this poem? Use quotations from the poem to support your answer.
2. Why do you think this poem is famous?
3. Have you ever been cheered up by something in the same way as the speaker in this poem? Write a short paragraph about the thing that never fails to cheer you up.

 Create

1. Create a simile with each of the words below. For example: **Memories** filled her head like a thick fog.
   - Snow
   - Train
   - Wolf
   - Roses
   - Cage
2. 'I saw a crowd, / A host of golden daffodils. / Beside the lake, beneath the trees' Sketch a picture inspired by the nature imagery as depicted in the line above.
3. In the poem 'Daffodils', William Wordsworth's sorrow is relieved by a feeling of inspiration and joy.

   Write a personal essay about a time when you felt either sorrow or joy, in the space provided on pages 25–26 of your Portfolio. Describe the situation and explain how you felt.

Carol Ann Duffy is a Scottish poet who is the first ever female poet laureate. This means she has been appointed as the nation's official poet by the British Government.

The speaker in this poem imagines the dark as various sources of comfort. Look out for the comparisons in the poem.

Don't Be Scared
By Carol Ann Duffy

The dark is only a blanket
for the moon to put on her bed.

The dark is a private cinema
for the movie dreams in your head.

The dark is a little black dress
to show off the sequin stars.

The dark is the wooden hole
behind the strings of happy guitars.

The dark is a jeweller's velvet cloth
where children sleep like pearls.

The dark is a spool of film
to photograph boys and girls,

so smile in your sleep in the dark.
Don't be scared.

Focus on ... **metaphor**

Metaphors describe something as though it is something else.

The poem 'Don't Be Scared' claims that the dark 'is only a blanket / for the moon', 'a little black dress' and 'a jeweller's velvet cloth'. Of course, the dark is none of these things, but by saying one thing is literally something else, the poet is using metaphor.

 Work with a partner to make a list of all the metaphors in 'Don't Be Scared'.

Understand

1. Find the repetition in the poem.
2. Find the simile in the poem.
3. Choose one of the metaphors from the poem and explain its meaning in your own words.

Explore

 1. Do you think this poem is comforting? Give reasons for your answer.
2. 'The dark is a jeweller's velvet cloth.' Explain how the poet makes use of imagery in this line.

Create

1. **(a)** Imagine this poem has been written to convince children that they should be afraid of the dark. The title has been changed to 'Be Very Scared'.

   Rewrite the poem using metaphors that compare the dark to negative, frightening things. For example, you might say:

   The dark is a hood that conceals

   a face they don't want you to see.

   The dark is the depths of the ocean

   taking you away from me.

   Model your new, scary poem on the one you have read. Do not worry if you cannot make it rhyme, some of the best poems do not rhyme anyway!

    (b) Read your poem aloud to a partner in a spooky voice.

The speaker in this poem describes the actions of playground bullies. As you read the poem aloud with your partner, find the parts of the poem where the poet exaggerates his point.

Back in the Playground Blues

By Adrian Mitchell

I dreamed I was back in the playground, I was about four feet high
Yes dreamed I was back in the playground, standing about four feet high
Well the playground was three miles long and the playground was five miles wide

It was broken black tarmac with a high wire fence all around
Broken black dusty tarmac with a high fence running all around
And it had a special name to it, they called it The Killing Ground

Got a mother and a father, they're one thousand years away
The rulers of The Killing Ground are coming out to play
Everybody thinking: 'Who they going to play with today?'

Well you get it for being Jewish
And you get it for being black
Get it for being chicken
And you get it for fighting back
You get it for being big and fat
Get it for being small
Oh those who get it get it and get it
For any damn thing at all.

Sometimes they take a beetle, tear off its six legs one by one
Beetle on its black back, rocking in the lunchtime sun
But a beetle can't beg for mercy, a beetle's not half the fun

I heard a deep voice talking, it had that iceberg sound
'It prepares them for Life' – but I have never found
Any place in my life worse than The Killing Ground.

A note from the poet: Educational Health Warning. None of these poems or any other work by Adrian Mitchell is to be used in connection with any examination or test whatsoever. But I'm glad if people who like them read them aloud, sing them, dance them or act them in schools. And even happier if they choose to learn any of them by heart.

Focus on ... hyperbole

Hyperbole is when a poet uses exaggeration to get their point across.

We know that the playground is not really a 'Killing Ground'. By saying this, the speaker makes his dreadful experience clear.

Practise reading the poem out loud. Find where the poet uses hyperbole.

 In pairs, discuss the reasons the poet chose to describe the playground of his childhood as 'The Killing Ground'. What effect does such exaggeration have on the reader?

 Discuss

1. What feelings do you associate with the word 'playground'?
2. How does the speaker feel about the school playground?
3. What do you think about when you hear the phrase 'The Killing Ground'?
4. Is this somewhere you would like to be?

 Understand

1. How does the speaker describe the playground?
2. Describe the actions of the bullies in the fifth stanza.
3. The speaker hears a deep voice towards the end of the poem.
   (a) What does this person say?
   (b) How is their voice described?
   (c) Who do you think this person might be?

 Explore

1. What does the speaker mean when he says, 'You get it ...'?
2. The speaker tells us that his mother and father are 'one thousand years away'. Do you think this is true?
3. How would you feel if you were in a playground like the one described in the poem?
4. Imagine you are a student at this school. You have witnessed the bullying for long enough and decide to take action. What action would you take?

 Create

Imagine you are the speaker in the poem. You have been subjected to bullying since starting school. Write your diary entry after a particularly bad day at 'The Killing Ground'.

The speaker in this poem is denied access to books simply because she is a girl. In order to survive the harsh reality of her life, the girl uses her imagination to create stories of her own.

Although it is quite long, you will notice that the lines are short. A helpful tip when reading this poem (and most other poems) is to read to a full stop or comma. Do not stop reading at the end of each line.

Tula

By Margarita Engle

Books are door-shaped
portals
carrying me
across oceans
and centuries,
helping me feel
less alone.

But my mother believes
that girls who read too much
are unladylike
and ugly,
so my father's books are locked
in a clear glass cabinet. I gaze
at enticing covers
and mysterious titles,
but I am rarely permitted
to touch
the enchantment
of words.

Poems.
Stories.
Plays.
All are forbidden.
Girls are not supposed to think,
but as soon as my eager mind
begins to race, free thoughts
rush in
to replace
the trapped ones.

I imagine distant times
and faraway places.
Ghosts.
Vampires.
Ancient warriors.
Fantasy moves into
the tangled maze
of lonely confusion.

Secretly, I open
an invisible book in my mind,
and I step
through its magical door-shape
into a universe
of dangerous villains
and breathtaking heroes.

Many of the heroes are men
and boys, but some are girls
so tall
strong
and clever
that they rescue other children
from monsters.

portals:
gateways

enchantment:
magic

Focus on ... enjambment

Enjambment is when a sentence or phrase runs from one line of poetry into the next.

Poets use this technique to control the pace (speed) of a poem for effect or emphasis. By including run-on lines or enjambment, poets often create a feeling of urgency.

Look at how the lines are split in 'Tula'.

 Work in groups to read this poem together. Each person in the group should read to the punctuation mark, then change speaker. Follow carefully, as you will have several chances to read. What do you notice about the use of enjambment throughout the poem?

Discuss

1. How important are books to you?
2. What do you think this poem is about?
3. What might be the poet's message?

Understand

1. How do you know that the girl loves books?
2. What does the girl's mother believe about books?
3. The girl says that 'Secretly, I open an invisible book in my mind'. In your own words, describe what happens next.
4. Write out three examples of enjambment from this poem.

Explore

1. Do you feel sympathy for the speaker? Give reasons for your answer.
2. The speaker tells us that some of the heroes in her stories are girls who 'rescue other children from monsters'. Write a description of a monster likely to feature in one of the speaker's stories.

Create

Write a short story in which you bring one of the speaker's exciting stories to life. Include at least one of the following in your story:

- faraway places
- ghosts
- vampires
- ancient warriors
- dangerous villains
- monsters
- heroes.

In the following poem the poet shares lots of images associated with hot summers, yet he is aware that summer does not last forever. He knows the days will leave, just like his daughter. Dig beneath the surface and you will find quite an emotional poem.

Midsummer, Tobago

By Derek Walcott

Broad sun-stoned beaches.

White heat.
A green river.

A bridge,
scorched yellow palms

scorched:
burned

from the summer-sleeping house
drowsing through August.

drowsing:
dozing

Days I have held,
days I have lost,

days that outgrow, like daughters,
my harboring arms.

harboring:
sheltering

Focus on ... free verse

Free verse is poetry that is written without any set pattern.

Poems written in free verse will often sound like natural speech, as they do not have to rhyme and have no set rhythm. Poets who write in this style do not follow rules.

Notice how Derek Walcott does not follow a particular rhyming scheme. In this poem he expresses his thoughts in a conversational, reflective way.

Understand

1. What time of year is mentioned in this poem?
2. Find the repetition in the poem.
3. How do you know that this poem is written in free verse?

Explore

1. How did this poem make you feel?
2. In your opinion, what is the central theme of the poem?
3. Explain what the speaker means when he mentions his daughter. You should include quotations from the poem in your answer.

Investigate

Find at least two other examples of poems written in free verse. You may wish to search for poems by Emily Dickinson or Langston Hughes, who often write in this style.

Create

1. **(a)** Write a poem of your own in free verse in the space provided on page 27 of your Portfolio. Derek Walcott chose to set his poem during the summer. Set your poem in any one of the four seasons.

   (b) Write a second draft of your poem, aiming to improve on your first attempt, in the space provided on page 83 of your Portfolio.

   (c) When you are happy with your poem, recite it to the class. When you speak, remember to:
   - express yourself clearly – vary your tone
   - speak at the right speed – do not rush
   - control the volume – ensure you can be heard.

Below are the first four verses from Edgar Allan Poe's famous poem 'The Raven'. The speaker hears knocking on his door. The mood is dark and menacing as the speaker's fear becomes apparent. Listen out for vowel sounds as you read the poem.

The Raven
By Edgar Allan Poe

Once upon a midnight dreary, while I pondered, weak and weary,
Over many a quaint and curious volume of forgotten lore—
While I nodded, nearly napping, suddenly there came a tapping,
As of some one gently rapping, rapping at my chamber door.
''Tis some visiter,' I muttered, 'tapping at my chamber door—
                         Only this and nothing more.'

Ah, distinctly I remember it was in the bleak December;
And each separate dying ember wrought its ghost upon the floor.
Eagerly I wished the morrow;—vainly I had sought to borrow
From my books surcease of sorrow—sorrow for the lost Lenore—
For the rare and radiant maiden whom the angels name Lenore—
                         Nameless *here* for evermore.

And the silken, sad, uncertain rustling of each purple curtain
Thrilled me—filled me with fantastic terrors never felt before;
So that now, to still the beating of my heart, I stood repeating
''Tis some visiter entreating entrance at my chamber door—
Some late visiter entreating entrance at my chamber door;—
                         This it is and nothing more.'

Presently my soul grew stronger; hesitating then no longer,
'Sir,' said I, 'or Madam, truly your forgiveness I implore;
But the fact is I was napping, and so gently you came rapping,
And so faintly you came tapping, tapping at my chamber door,
That I scarce was sure I heard you'—here I opened wide the door;—
                         Darkness there and nothing more.

Focus on ... assonance

Assonance is a poetic technique that uses repeated vowel sounds to draw out each word.

In 'The Raven' assonance is used to emphasise the speaker's fear and to create a spooky atmosphere. For example:

*'Once upon a midnight dr**ea**ry, while I pondered, w**ea**k and w**ea**ry'*

 Work with a partner to find the broad vowel sounds in the poem. Practise saying these out loud and elongate the sounds as you do so. What effect does this technique have on the overall mood and atmosphere?

Understand

1. Use a dictionary to find a definition for each of the following words:
   - lore
   - ember
   - entreating
   - chamber
   - maiden
   - implore.
2. What does the speaker hear at the beginning of the poem?
3. What does the speaker find when he opens the door?
4. Identify three feelings experienced by the speaker.
5. Which of the following words best describes the atmosphere created in this poem? Explain your choice.
   - Mysterious
   - Frightening
   - Dark

Explore

1. The speaker describes his feelings of fear as 'fantastic terrors'. What do you think he means by this?
2. Who is Lenore, in your opinion?
3. Imagine you are the speaker in the poem, all alone at night when suddenly you hear a gentle knock on your door. Describe how you would react.

Create

 1. **(a)** Write two more verses to end the poem in the space provided on page 28 of your Portfolio. Who was knocking at the speaker's door? What happens when he peers even closer into the darkness? Try to follow the poem's rhyming scheme and write in a similar style to Edgar Allan Poe.

 (b) Read your ending aloud, emphasising any examples of assonance you have used.

In the following poem Seamus Heaney writes about his childhood ritual of picking blackberries each summer. Heaney relished this activity. Excitedly, he would trek the fields until all his cans were full of berries. The tone of the poem changes as the berries do not stay fresh for long.

As you read the poem, listen out for any words that stand out to you for the sound they create.

Blackberry-Picking
By Seamus Heaney

Late August, given heavy rain and sun
For a full week, the blackberries would ripen.
At first, just one, a glossy purple clot
Among others, red, green, hard as a knot.
You ate that first one and its flesh was sweet
Like thickened wine: summer's blood was in it
Leaving stains upon the tongue and lust for
Picking. Then red ones inked up, and that hunger
Sent us out with milk-cans, pea-tins, jam-pots
Where briars scratched and wet grass bleached our boots.
Round hayfields, cornfields and potato-drills,
We trekked and picked until the cans were full,
Until the tinkling bottom had been covered
With green ones, and on top big dark blobs burned
Like a plate of eyes. Our hands were peppered
With thorn pricks, our palms sticky as Bluebeard's.

We hoarded the fresh berries in the byre.
But when the bath was filled we found a fur,
A rat-grey fungus, glutting on our cache.
The juice was stinking too. Once off the bush,
The fruit fermented, the sweet flesh would turn sour.
I always felt like crying. It wasn't fair
That all the lovely canfuls smelt of rot.
Each year I hoped they'd keep, knew they would not.

Bluebeard:
a pirate who
was known for
killing his wives

byre: cowshed

glutting: filling

cache: store

Focus on ... onomatopoeia

Onomatopoeia is a sound effect created when a word sounds like what it is describing. For example, 'sizzle', 'crackle', 'thud', 'buzz' and 'boom'.

Heaney makes use of onomatopoeia in this poem. Pay attention to the descriptions of the berries in particular.

Listen to the poem being read and use your pencil to underline any onomatopoeic words that you hear.

 Discuss

1. What poetic techniques stood out to you in this poem?
2. Could this poem be a metaphor?

 Understand

1. When would the blackberries ripen and for how long?
2. Where did Heaney trek to find the berries?
3. Choose your favourite example of onomatopoeia from the poem.
4. Find examples of each of the following in this poem:
   - alliteration
   - simile
   - metaphor
   - personification
   - rhyming couplet.

 Explore

 1. What is the tone or feeling in the first stanza?

 2. How does the tone or feeling change in the second stanza?

 3. Do you think the speaker learned his lesson and picked fewer berries the next year?

 Create

 Write a short biography piece about the summers of your childhood. Try to include at least one onomatopoeic word. See if your classmates can spot the examples of onomatopoeia when you read your finished piece.

This poem is also written by Seamus Heaney. The mood is very different to 'Blackberry-Picking'. This poem is called 'Mid-Term Break'. What do you associate with your school holidays?

Mid-Term Break
By Seamus Heaney

I sat all morning in the college sick bay,
Counting bells knelling classes to a close.
At two o'clock our neighbours drove me home.

In the porch I met my father crying –
He had always taken funerals in his stride –
And Big Jim Evans saying it was a hard blow.

The baby cooed and laughed and rocked the pram
When I came in, and I was embarrassed
By old men standing up to shake my hand

And tell me they were 'sorry for my trouble'.
Whispers informed strangers I was the eldest,
Away at school, as my mother held my hand

In hers and coughed out angry tearless sighs.
At ten o'clock the ambulance arrived
With the corpse, stanched and bandaged by the nurses.

Next morning I went up into the room. Snowdrops
And candles soothed the bedside; I saw him
For the first time in six weeks. Paler now,

Wearing a poppy bruise on his left temple,
He lay in the four foot box as in his cot.
No gaudy scars, the bumper knocked him clear.

A four foot box, a foot for every year.

knelling:
ringing slowly
(like funeral bells)

stanched:
stopped the
flow of blood

Focus on ... **symbols**

A **symbol** is something that represents another thing.

You might recognise some of these symbols of Ireland:

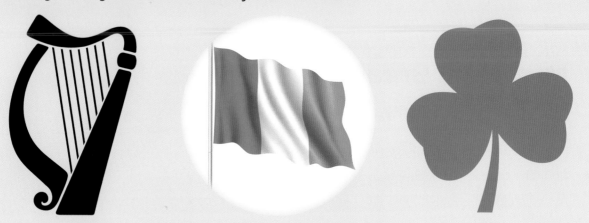

When someone sees these images, they may automatically think of Ireland. In poetry, writers use symbols to enhance their meaning.

 Work in groups to find the symbols Heaney uses in 'Mid-Term Break'. Discuss your choices. What do these words or images symbolise? Why are they important?

Understand

1. Why is the speaker taken home from school unexpectedly?
2. Describe the actions of **(a)** the father, **(b)** the mother and **(c)** the baby in the poem.
3. How does the speaker feel in the third stanza? Why does he feel this way?
4. How long has it been since the speaker last saw his brother?
5. What do the following symbols represent?

Explore

 1. In the first stanza the speaker suggests that tragedy will follow. What are the signs that something bad has happened at the start of the poem?
2. Do you think the title 'Mid-Term Break' is an unusual one for a poem like this? Explain your answer.
3. How did this poem make you feel?

Create

Seamus Heaney's young brother died tragically after being hit by a car. Write a speech encouraging all road users (drivers, pedestrians and cyclists) to behave responsibly and safely on the roads. Choose one of the images below to accompany your speech. (For information on speeches see pages 42–43.)

In 'I, Too', Langston Hughes alludes to the treatment of African Americans who were sold as slaves and subjected to dreadful cruelty. Hughes imagines a more inclusive America where African Americans will be treated equally.

I, Too
By Langston Hughes

I, too, sing America.

I am the darker brother.
They send me to eat in the kitchen
When company comes,
But I laugh,
And eat well,
And grow strong.

Tomorrow,
I'll be at the table
When company comes.
Nobody'll dare
Say to me,
'Eat in the kitchen,'
Then.

Besides,
They'll see how beautiful I am
And be ashamed—

I, too, am America.

Focus on ... **allusion**

Allusion is an indirect or subtle reference to something.

Poets use allusion in their poems when they suggest something rather than say it explicitly. In 'I, Too', Hughes alludes to the inequality of black people in America. He alludes to the years of slavery generations of black people were forced to endure.

Hughes believes that white people will one day see the equal worth of African American citizens. Tomorrow, they will realise what they have done and feel shame and regret.

'They'll see how beautiful I am / And be ashamed'.

 Understand

1. Langston Hughes uses the personal pronoun 'I' several times throughout this poem. How many times does it appear?
2. What happens 'When company comes'?
3. What will happen 'Tomorrow'?

 Explore

1. 'They'll see how beautiful I am / And be ashamed'. In your view, who are 'they' and why should they be ashamed?
2. Is the speaker being vain when he refers to his beauty? Explain your answer.
3. Do you think there is an element of pride in the speaker's tone, especially when he says, 'I, too, am America'?
 4. Choose one image from the poem that you found effective and explain your choice.

 Create

In the poem, 'I, Too', Langston Hughes shares his dream of equality amongst fellow Americans. Tweet your dream for the future. Remember that your tweet should be no more than 280 characters. You can include hashtags and emojis to express your dream. Begin your tweet with 'Tomorrow, ...'.

Language Skills

Pronouns

A noun is a person, animal, place or thing.

Pronouns are words that are used in place of a noun.

Possessive pronouns show ownership.
my, *her*, *his*, *their*

Personal pronouns are used in place of a noun when the noun is a person or thing.
it, *she*, *I*, *you*, *him*, *we*

 Understand

1. **(a)** Identify the nouns and pronouns in the sentences below.
   - **i.** A woman rescued a dog.
   - **ii.** She rescued a dog.
   - **iii.** The woman's family named their dog Benson.
   - **iv.** They named the dog Benson.

   (b) Which of the pronouns you identified in the sentences above is a possessive pronoun?

2. Write out the following passage using pronouns to replace the nouns.

   > Scott ran all the way home from school. Scott was sure that if he hurried, he would be home ahead of his mother and father. The fearful boy could easily delete the voice message before anyone else heard it. The boy raced down the road towards his house and as he did so Scott noticed a bright red car parked outside the house. The car looked identical to Mr O'Brien's, Scott's school principal. It couldn't be ...

3. In the poem 'I, Too' on page 114, the poet uses the personal pronoun 'I' several times. Make a list of all the lines containing this personal pronoun.

 Explore

 1. Write a paragraph about your family. Swap it with your partner when you have finished. Underline all the pronouns in your partner's paragraph. Did you find them all?

 2. Tell a story as a class without using nouns. Use pronouns instead of naming people, animals, places or things. Each student should take a turn contributing one sentence to the story.

 Grammar Primer: pages 24–26

Take turns reading each poem in small groups. Look out for similarities and differences.

Dream Variations
By Langston Hughes

To fling my arms wide
In some place of the sun,
To whirl and to dance
Till the white day is done.
Then rest at cool evening
Beneath a tall tree
While night comes on gently,
  Dark like me—
That is my dream!

To fling my arms wide
In the face of the sun,
Dance! Whirl! Whirl!
Till the quick day is done.
Rest at pale evening ...
A tall, slim tree ...
Night coming tenderly
  Black like me.

Be Like the Bird
By Victor Hugo

Be like the bird, who
Resting in his flight
On a twig too slight
Feels it bend beneath him
Yet sings,
Knowing he has wings.

Focus on ... comparing and contrasting

Often poems are studied together. You should explore the similarities and differences between poems using the following headings:

◖ form   ◖ structure   ◖ language   ◖ theme.

Start up: The language in **both** poems conveys a message of hope.

Back up: In 'Dream Variations' the speaker longs to 'Dance! Whirl! Whirl!', **while** the bird in 'Be Like the Bird' sings out with joy. **Both** poems make use of simile. In 'Be Like the Bird' we are told to 'be like the bird' by believing in ourselves. The speaker in 'Dream Variations' **also** believes in himself, as he is compared to the gentle night which is 'dark like me'.

Sum up: The language in both poems makes them uplifting and hopeful.

Notice how the words in bold compare the similarities and differences in the poems. Can you think of any other words or phrases to use when comparing or contrasting poetry?

 In pairs, discuss the similarities and differences in the poems above.

Understand

1. What does the speaker long to do in 'Dream Variations'?
2. To what does the speaker compare himself in 'Dream Variations'?
3. Why does the bird sing in 'Be Like the Bird'?

Explore

1. What is the message in both poems?
2. The speaker dances in 'Dream Variations' and the bird sings in 'Be Like the Bird'. What do these actions show us?

 3. Which poem do you like best? Give reasons for your answer.

Investigate

1. **(a)** Now that you have studied two poems by Langston Hughes, use your research skills to learn more about the poet. Find the following information:

   - the date of Langston Hughes's birth and death
   - where he lived
   - interesting facts about his life
   - the names of other poems he wrote
   - images and media links.

   (b) Use the information you have gathered on Langston Hughes to make a poster. You may wish to make a traditional poster using your artistic skills or a digital poster using Glogster.

   OR

   Use the information you have gathered to create a Langston Hughes page on Padlet.

Making links between poetry and song

 In pairs, make a list of the ways in which song lyrics and poems are similar. You should consider the poetic techniques that you have learned in this unit.

 Discuss

1. Are the techniques that you have encountered only used in poems or can they be used in other styles of writing?
2. Think about some of your favourite elements of music and songs. Do any of these feature in poetry?

The following song was written by a band called The Velvet Underground. You will notice that the vocalist in the original version is male.

Read the lyrics as if they were a poem.

I Found a Reason

I found a reason to keep livin',
Oh, and the reason dear is you
I found a reason to keep singin'
Wow-woh, and the reason dear is you.

Oh, I do believe
If you don't like things you leave
For someplace you've never gone before.

Honey, I found a reason to keep livin'
And you know the reason dear it's you
And I've walked down life's lonely highways
hand in hand with myself
And I realize
how many paths have crossed between us.

Oh, I do believe
you are what you perceive
What comes is better than what came before.

And you better come, come, come, come to me
Come, come, come to me
Better come, come, come, come to me.

Write down your initial impressions of the song lyrics. Ask yourself, does the song sound like a poem when read aloud?

Now, listen to the song. When your teacher plays the song, make a note of what you like about the sounds. What do you notice as you listen to the lyrics being performed that you might have missed when they were read aloud?

 http://youtu.be/GmmMy-712ZA

 ## Discuss

Do you prefer the lyrics being spoken or sung? Explain your choice.

 ## Understand

1. Find three poetic techniques used to write this song.
2. Do you think this is an uplifting song? Give reasons for your answer.
3. What is the theme of the song, in your opinion?

 ## Investigate

Use your research skills to find and listen to the version of this song by Cat Power. While you are listening, make a list of comparisons between this and the original version by The Velvet Underground. Your instinct will tell you which you prefer, but ask yourself why.

1. Compare and contrast the two songs. You should point out similarities and differences.
2. Which version of the song do you prefer? Give at least two reasons for your answer.
3. How did this song make you feel?
4. Do you think that Cat Power's cover is more or less uplifting than The Velvet Underground's version? Explain your thoughts by referring to what you have heard.

The following song was written by Anthony Newley and Leslie Bricusse. Read the lyrics aloud.

Feeling Good

Birds flyin' high, you know how I feel.

Sun in the sky, you know how I feel.

Breeze driftin' on by, you know how I feel.

It's a new dawn.

It's a new day.

It's a new life for me,

And I'm feelin' good.

Fish in the sea, you know how I feel.

River runnin' free, you know how I feel.

Blossom on the tree, you know how I feel.

It's a new dawn.

It's a new day.

It's a new life for me,

And I'm feelin' good.

Dragonfly out in the sun, you know what I mean.

Butterflies all havin' fun, you know what I mean.

Sleep in peace when day is done, that's what I mean,

And this old world is a new world and a bold world for me.

Stars when you shine, you know how I feel.

Scent of the pine, you know how I feel.

Freedom is mine, and I know how I feel.

It's a new dawn, it's a new day, it's a new life for me,

And I'm feelin' good.

Discuss

1. What is your first impression of this song?
2. What images stand out most to you?

Understand

1. The speaker tells us they are 'feelin' good'. Suggest two other words or phrases they could use to describe how they are feeling.
2. List three examples of nature imagery in this song.
3. Identify the following in the song:
   ◀ tone   ◀ mood   ◀ theme.

 Explore

1. Why do you think the 'birds flyin' high' understand how the speaker feels?
2. Compare this song to one of the poems in this unit.
   (a) What similarities do the poem and song share?
   (b) What are the differences between the poem and song?
   (c) Which do you prefer and why?

 Investigate

'Feeling Good' was made famous when Nina Simone recorded her version of it. Use your research skills to find a recording of her version of the song.

 Create

1. **(a)** Choose a song that you feel has inspiring lyrics. Make a poster with the song lyrics in the centre. Some of the imagery could be represented in drawings or cut-outs placed around the lyrics.

   OR

   Make a poster using Glogster. Choose a template and add the lyrics, theme and images. You have the option of adding media files to your poster.

    (b) Present your poster to the class. Explain your song choice and discuss some of the poetic techniques used. Read the lyrics to the class or play a recording of the song.

Revising poetry and song

Reflect and review

1. Look back at the images on page 65. Now that you have studied poetry and song, would you change any of those images? Think of some alternative images that could be used to illustrate poetry and song.

2. Fill in the unit review on pages 29–30 of your Portfolio.

Language skills

1. **(a)** Rewrite the underlined words in full:
   i. <u>You'll</u> be amazed to discover the truth.
   ii. It <u>doesn't</u> make any sense!
   iii. <u>You've</u> got to hurry up.

   (b) Rewrite the underlined words, this time bringing them together with an apostrophe.
   i. <u>They are</u> arriving at 6 p.m.
   ii. <u>You are</u> the funniest person I have ever met.
   iii. They <u>have not</u> done anything wrong.

Oral assessment

Prepare a two-minute presentation about your favourite poem or poet.
◖ Explain why you have chosen this poem or poet.
◖ Include lots of detail in your presentation, such as background information on the poem or poet.
◖ Prepare your presentation – make use of a slideshow, images or props.
◖ Practise your presentation, focusing on the delivery of your message.
◖ Deliver your presentation in front of your classmates.

OR

Choose your favourite poem from this unit. Learn the poem by heart and recite it for your classmates. Explain why this poem is the one you liked best of all.

Written assessment

1. **(a)** Choose a poem that you have studied in First Year that you really loved. Write a letter to the poet in praise of the poem you have chosen in the space provided on pages 31–32 of your Portfolio.

   (b) Redraft your letter in the space provided on pages 84–85 of your Portfolio.

Unit 3

Fiction

Why study this area?

Fiction allows us to enter different worlds. Stories can transport us to other times and places, sometimes real and sometimes imaginary. In order to fully understand fiction, we must first look at its features.

Learning intentions

- Read fluently, for understanding and pleasure.
- Understand the techniques used in story writing.
- Appreciate and compare different styles of writing.
- Recognise the features you enjoy in fiction and use these in your own writing.
- Use a dictionary and a thesaurus.
- Identify and use the correct verb and tense in context.

💬 Discuss

1. Which of the images above best represents fiction, in your opinion?
2. What is your favourite childhood story?
3. What book are you reading currently?
4. What types of books do you generally like to read?
5. Have you ever heard the expression 'don't judge a book by its cover'? What do you think this means?
6. Would you choose a book to read based only on its cover?
7. What kinds of details do you look for on a book cover?
8. Would you be put off reading a book if it did not have certain details or images on the cover?

🚀 Explore

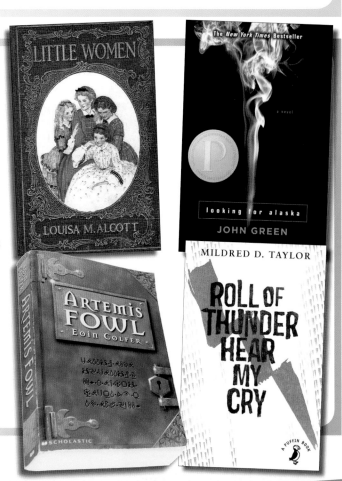

1. Rank the book covers from one to four, one being the book you would most like to read. Remember, judge the book only by its cover.

   (a) Explain why you ranked each book where you did.

   (b) Which element of the covers stood out to you more, the images or the text?

   (c) Can you guess what each of these books is about?

 2. Fill in the reading profile on page 33 of your Portfolio.

Introducing fiction

Fiction is telling a story. Think of all the ways you can tell a story. Can you tell a story without using words? Without using pictures? Only using your hands or body?

 In order to start writing stories, you need to look at the main features of story writing. These are like ingredients in a recipe.

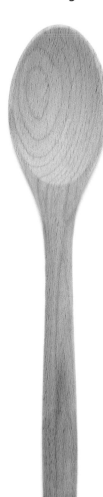

The main ingredients you will need to get started on your own short story are:

(plot structure
(setting
(character.

Of course, ingredients are not everything – you have to know what to do with them. Writers use many methods and narrative techniques in order to use these ingredients properly. Two that will be dealt with in this unit are:

(openings
(narrative voice.

You may have already come across them in stories you have read, and you will find plenty of examples in this unit. Look out for the **Focus on …** boxes, which are used every time you are introduced to a new feature of fiction. When you see these boxes, add the definition to the glossary on pages 1–2 of your Portfolio.

When you have been shown an example of each feature of fiction you will have a writing activity. At the end of the unit you will use what you have learned to create your own short story.

 **Create**

Read the following story that is only six words long.

For sale: baby shoes, never worn.

Come up with your own story using only six words.

Stories come in all shapes, sizes and formats. For example, cartoons and images can tell a story, or even inspire one.

Look at the following two cartoons from the *New Yorker* magazine and think about the story each cartoon is telling. What message are they each trying to convey?

"Over, damn you, over!"

💬 **Discuss**

1. When it comes to story writing we can get inspiration from anywhere. How would you use one of these cartoons to start your own story?
2. Discuss some ideas for a story you might like to write. You can take inspiration from things you have read or seen or from objects lying around.

Focus on ... openings

The **opening** is the beginning of a piece of writing.

The first few lines of a story tell us a lot about its world. A good opening grabs our attention and motivates us to read on. It gives us a glimpse into the world of the story and the people in it.

A good opening:

- hooks the reader and grabs their attention
- may be dramatic or exciting
- is clear and understandable and uses descriptive language
- is an interesting introduction to the world of the story.

Read the following openings from *1984* by George Orwell, *Pride and Prejudice* by Jane Austen and *The Kite Runner* by Khaled Hosseini.

1984

It was a bright cold day in April, and the clocks were striking thirteen.

Pride and Prejudice

It is a truth universally acknowledged, that a single man in possession of a good fortune, must be in want of a wife.

The Kite Runner

I became what I am today at the age of twelve, on a frigid overcast day in the winter of 1975. I remember the precise moment, crouching behind a crumbling mud wall, peeking into the alley near the frozen creek. That was a long time ago, but it's wrong what they say about the past, I've learned, about how you can bury it. Because the past claws its way out. Looking back now, I realize I have been peeking into that deserted alley for the last twenty-six years.

Discuss

1. When and where do you think each story takes place? How do you know?
2. What kind of people live in each of these worlds?
3. Are they positive or negative worlds?

 Explore

1. Would you like to live in any of these worlds? Why or why not?
 2. Which one of these openings makes you want to read on the most? Explain your choice.

 Investigate

The genre of a book is the category it falls into. Read back over each of the openings and match them to the appropriate genre.

◖ Bildungsroman

◖ Romance

◖ Dystopian/Fantasy

> *Bildungsroman:*
> *a novel that traces a*
> *character's development*
> *from childhood to adulthood*

 Create

 Write an opening sentence for a story then swap it with a partner. Discuss each other's work. Did your opening grab your partner's attention?

The following openings from *Divergent* by Veronica Roth and *Fangirl* by Rainbow Rowell give the reader a lot of information in a few short lines. Think back to the features of a good opening and decide whether these openings include any of these features.

Divergent

There is one mirror in my house. It is behind a sliding panel in the hallway upstairs. Our faction allows me to stand in front of it on the second day of every third month, the day my mother cuts my hair.

Fangirl

There was a boy in her room.

Cath looked up at the number painted on the door, then down at the room assignment in her hand.

Pound hall, 913.

 Understand

1. What do you learn about the narrator in the first extract?
2. Where does the second extract take place?

 Explore

1. Why do you think the author began *Fangirl* with the short statement 'There was a boy in her room'?
 2. Which world would you prefer to live in, the one described in *Divergent* or the one in *Fangirl*? Explain your choice.
 3. What kind of challenges do you imagine that the narrators in each of the extracts face?

 Create

 Work with a partner to design a book cover for either *Divergent* or *Fangirl* based only on these openings. Decide on an image to use and explain your choice.

Present tense and past tense

Look at the two openings on page 130 again. One is written in the present tense and one is written in the past tense. Can you guess which is which?

The present tense describes things that are happening right now, in the present moment.

James waits for the bus. He is tired from a long day at the office.

The present tense also describes things that happen on a regular basis.

She goes swimming every day after school.

The past tense describes things that have already happened. It is a finished action in the past.

Johnny painted his walls red to match his favourite team's colours.

I spent all of last summer at the beach.

You may choose to write a story in either the present or the past tense, just make sure to stick to the same tense and do not mix them up.

Stories are commonly written in the past tense, as the action has already taken place and the narrator is now looking back. Some writers choose to write in the present tense, as it brings the reader into the moment straight away. This can be another way to hook your reader.

 Understand

1. Change the following sentences from the present tense into the past tense.
   (a) The police are investigating the murder of a local woman.
   (b) Every day she runs five miles in preparation for the big race.
   (c) The room is small and cramped. It barely fits a bed and a desk.
   (d) 'How dare you?' she screams.
   (e) She creeps into the room and everything goes silent.

2. Rewrite the extract from *Divergent* on page 130 in the past tense.

3. Rewrite the extract from *Fangirl* on page 130 in the present tense.

  Create

 1. **(a)** Choose one of the extracts from *Divergent* or *Fangirl* on page 130 and write your own paragraph following on from the opening lines in the space provided on page 34 of your Portfolio. You do not need to finish the story, just write the next part.

(b) Redraft your paragraph in the space provided on page 86 of your Portfolio. (For information on drafting and redrafting see pages 31–32.)

 Grammar Primer: pages 27–28

Read the following opening from Siobhán Parkinson's novel *Bruised*.

Bruised

My grandmother died.

I know this is not what you would call a dramatic opening. It's what *happens* to grandparents. They get old (jeez, they *are* old to start with, or they wouldn't *be* grandparents, would they?); they die. (My grandfather died too, actually, but that's another story.)

Mr O'Connell, who is my Creative Writing teacher, which is to say he's my English teacher, but he's into Creative Writing (capital letters deliberate) – he would say, *Not intriguing enough, Jonathan. You need to* hook *your reader.*

But, frankly, I couldn't be bothered with the hooking part. See, I don't think you need to start on the premise that your reader (if you have one) is a *fish.*

There used to be a song about that, Gramma used to sing it, about how uneducated fish are, how they can't write their name or read a book – which may or may not have been put in for the rhyme with *brook.* That's where the illiterate fish in question lives, allegedly. Come to think of it, maybe it was the other way round. Maybe *brook* was put in to rhyme with *book,* I mean, because you would think *river,* wouldn't you, in association with fish, not bloody babbling *brook,* like a feckin' poem.

 Understand

1. What features of a good opening do you see in this piece?

2. **(a)** 'That's where the illiterate fish in question lives, allegedly.' What does the word 'allegedly' mean? Choose one from the following options:

   i. In a happy, content way

   ii. According to claims, but without any proof

   iii. Studious or hard-working

   (b) Write a sentence in your copy using the word 'allegedly'.

 Explore

1. What does Mr O'Connell mean by 'hook your reader'?
2. Why do you think the author put 'Creative Writing' in capital letters?
3. When do you usually use capital letters? (See page 10 for a reminder.)

 Investigate

 Look back at the section on paragraphs on pages 23–24. Work with a partner or in a group to summarise each paragraph in this extract from *Bruised* in one sentence by putting the main idea or point into your own words.

Use a dictionary

A **dictionary** lists all of the words in a language in alphabetical order and explains their meaning. You may have a small pocket dictionary, your teacher might have a large English dictionary in the classroom or you may use a dictionary app or website. Once you know the alphabet, you can use a dictionary. Dictionaries are great for understanding words, checking spelling and building your vocabulary.

In order to use a dictionary, you need to know the first three letters of the word.

1. If you want to look up the word 'controversy', you would start by going to the 'C' section of the dictionary.

2. Then you look at the second letter, 'O', which is much further down the alphabet, so you need to keep going to near the end of the Cs.

3. When you have found the words that begin with 'CO' you would look at the next letter, 'N'. Again, it is further down the alphabet so you keep looking past words that start COD ... COL ... COM ... until you come to CON. Keep going until you have found your word.

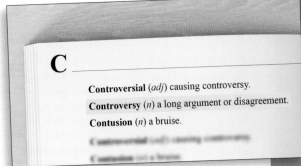

Beside the word you might see a small 'n', 'v' or 'adj'. These stand for noun, verb or adjective. For example, 'controversy' is a noun.

As well as giving the meaning of the word, some dictionaries give an alternative word that means the same thing. This is called a **synonym**. If you are looking for more synonyms then you must use a **thesaurus**. A thesaurus can be used in the same way as the dictionary, but instead of offering definitions, it only offers synonyms.

If you do not have a dictionary to hand, you will have to use your own knowledge to make an educated guess about a word's meaning. Look at the sentences before and after, and make a guess based on the context in which the word is being used.

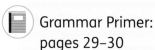 Grammar Primer: pages 29–30

Understand

1. Use a dictionary to look up the meaning of the following words:
   - omission
   - primitive
   - repository
   - uncharted
   - catastrophe
   - inextricably.

2. Come up with a synonym for each of the following words:
   - fast
   - happy
   - shout
   - sad
   - speak
   - wash.

Discuss

1. Look at the title of the extract on page 134. Based on this title, can you guess where and when this story will take place?

2. Have you read any other stories or seen any films with a similar setting?

Read the following extract from *The Hitchhiker's Guide to the Galaxy* by Douglas Adams. Douglas Adams was a science fiction writer born in 1952. This story was originally a radio comedy broadcast, but it was adapted into a novel and later a film.

The Hitchhiker's Guide to the Galaxy

Far out in the uncharted backwaters of the unfashionable end of the Western Spiral Arm of the Galaxy lies a small unregarded yellow sun.

Orbiting this at a distance of roughly ninety-two million miles is an utterly insignificant little blue-green planet whose ape-descended life forms are so amazingly primitive that they still think digital watches are a pretty neat idea.

This planet has – or rather had – a problem, which was this: most of the people living on it were unhappy for pretty much of the time. Many solutions were suggested for this problem, but most of these were largely concerned with the movements of small green pieces of paper, which is odd because on the whole it wasn't the small green pieces of paper that were unhappy.

And so the problem remained; lots of the people were mean, and most of them were miserable, even the ones with digital watches.

Many were increasingly of the opinion that they'd all made a big mistake in coming down from the trees in the first place. And some said that even the trees had been a bad move, and that no one should ever have left the oceans.

And then, one Thursday, nearly two thousand years after one man had been nailed to a tree for saying how great it would be to be nice to people for a change, a girl sitting on her own in a small café in Rickmansworth suddenly realized what it was that had been going wrong all this time, and she finally knew how the world could be made a good and happy place. This time it was right, it would work, and no one would have to get nailed to anything.

Sadly, however, before she could get to a phone to tell anyone about it, a terrible, stupid catastrophe occurred, and the idea was lost forever.

This is not her story.

But it is the story of that terrible stupid catastrophe and some of its consequences.

It is also the story of a book, a book called The Hitchhiker's Guide to the Galaxy *– not an Earth book, never published on Earth, and until the terrible catastrophe occurred, never seen or even heard of by any Earthmen.*

Nevertheless, a wholly remarkable book.

In fact it was probably the most remarkable book ever to come out of the great publishing corporations of Ursa Minor *– of which no Earthman had ever heard either.*

Not only is it a wholly remarkable book, it is also a highly successful one – more popular than The Celestial Home Care Omnibus, *better selling than* Fifty-Three More Things to do in Zero Gravity, *and more controversial than Oolon Colluphid's trilogy of philosophical blockbusters* Where God Went Wrong, Some More of God's Greatest Mistakes *and* Who is this God Person Anyway?

In many of the more relaxed civilizations on the Outer Eastern Rim of the Galaxy, the Hitchhiker's Guide has already supplanted the great Encyclopaedia Galactica as the standard repository of all knowledge and wisdom, for though it has many omissions and contains much that is <u>apocryphal</u>, *or at least wildly inaccurate, it scores over the older, more pedestrian work in two important respects.*

Ursa Minor:
a constellation of stars in the northern sky, also known as the Little Bear

First, it is slightly cheaper; and secondly it has the words Don't Panic *inscribed in large friendly letters on its cover.*

But the story of this terrible stupid Thursday, the story of its extraordinary consequences, and the story of how these consequences are inextricably intertwined with this remarkable book begins very simply.

It begins with a house.

Understand

1. Which planet orbits the sun at a distance of roughly ninety-two million miles?

   (a) Mercury **(b)** Mars **(c)** Earth

2. What was the major cause of unhappiness for the people on this planet?

3. 'They'd all made a big mistake in coming down from the trees in the first place.' Explain what this line means to you.

4. Match the following words with the correct definition.

Controversial	Leaving something or someone out
Omission	Replaced
Supplanted	Causing debate or issue

5. The word 'apocryphal' is underlined. Reread the sentence it appears in and the sentences that come before and after. Can you guess what this word means?

   (a) Untrue **(b)** Humorous **(c)** Authentic or real

   Verify your answer by checking in the dictionary.

Explore

 1. The author uses humour in this extract. Can you find any examples of this?

 2. What kind of person would this book appeal to?

 3. Do you feel this is a good opening to a story? Would you want to read more?

Create

 1. *'Not only is it a wholly remarkable book, it is also a highly successful one – more popular than* <u>The Celestial Home Care Omnibus</u>, *better selling than* <u>Fifty-Three More Things to do in Zero Gravity</u>, *and more controversial than Oolon Colluphid's trilogy of philosophical blockbusters* <u>Where God Went Wrong</u>, <u>Some More of God's Greatest Mistakes</u> *and* <u>Who is this God Person Anyway?</u>'

   Can you come up with some space-related titles for popular books, television shows or films? For example, *Keeping Up with the Extra-Terrestrials, Lord of the Saturn Rings.*

 2. Carry out a class debate on the following motion: *This house believes that the government should allocate more money towards space exploration.*
   (For information on debates see pages 47–48.)

Focus on ... plot

Plot is the sequence of events in a piece of fiction that make up the story.

It is essential to plan where a story is going. This is where you need to do some rough work. Make sure you know how your story will end before you start writing.

Most stories can be broken down into four main steps that make up the plot structure.

1. **Situation:** the scene is set, the characters are introduced and the setting is established.
2. **Complication:** there is a clear problem or conflict that must be overcome.
3. **Problem or crisis point:** the problem or conflict comes to a head.
4. **Resolution:** the problem or conflict is dealt with.

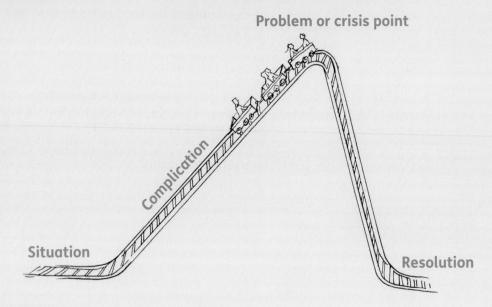

For example:

Cinderella

1. **Situation:** Cinderella is a poor, unfortunate girl surrounded by horrible stepsisters and a cruel stepmother who will not let her attend the ball.
2. **Complication:** after making a wish to her fairy godmother, Cinderella goes to the ball but has to leave abruptly as the clock strikes midnight. The prince is left longing to know more about his mystery princess.
3. **Problem or crisis point**: on fleeing the ball, Cinderella leaves behind a glass slipper, the only clue to her true identity.
4. **Resolution:** the prince scours the kingdom in order to find the owner of the slipper, and eventually finds his princess.

In order to understand plot structure, it may help to break stories down into pictures or images. A comic strip is a story told in the form of a cartoon in which scenes or stages of the story are captured in frames. Frames are pictures of a scene or action, which, when put together in sequence, describe the plot of a story.

Each image represents an action or a situation. You can add speech to the frame if you want your characters to have a conversation. You can focus on just one character in a frame if you would like this character to be the main focus.

 **Discuss**

Can you think of any well-known stories, fairy tales or nursery rhymes? Name one, and summarise its plot in a few sentences.

 Understand

 1. In groups or pairs, choose one of the stories you just discussed with your classmates and reduce it down to four main steps (situation, complication, problem or crisis point, resolution).

2. **(a)** Consider the well-known story of 'The Tortoise and the Hare'. Can you sort the frames into the correct order?

   1. Situation
   2. Complication
   3. Problem or crisis point
   4. Resolution

(b) Sort the frames showing the story of 'Goldilocks and the Three Bears' into the correct order.

 Investigate

Find out all you can about the recent viral phenomenon the **Mannequin Challenge**. Find some interesting videos of mannequin challenges online and discuss the stories behind the videos.

 Create

 1. A freeze frame is where you imagine someone is taking a picture of you and you hold still in a particular pose, like you have seen in the mannequin challenge videos. In groups, choose a story that everyone has read and decide on a scene or image from the story. Arrange yourselves into freeze frame depicting this scene. Show your classmates and see if they can guess the story.

 2. (a) Use the comic strip template on page 35 of your Portfolio to create your own story. Fill in all four frames. Remember to use the four stages in the plot structure.

 (b) Write a story based on your comic strip in the space provided on pages 36–37 of your Portfolio. Remember to:

◖ have an opening that hooks your reader

◖ choose a tense (e.g. past or present) and stick with it.

Ray Bradbury was a science fiction author who published the following short story in May 1950. He originally set the story in what was then the future (1985), but it was later adapted for modern audiences.

August 2026: There Will Come Soft Rains

In the living room the voice-clock sang, *Tick-tock, seven o'clock, time to get up, time to get up, seven o'clock!* as if it were afraid that nobody would. The morning house lay empty. The clock ticked on, repeating and repeating its sounds into the emptiness. *Seven-nine, breakfast time, seven-nine!*

In the kitchen the breakfast stove gave a hissing sigh and ejected from its warm interior eight pieces of perfectly browned toast, eight eggs sunnyside up, sixteen slices of bacon, two coffees, and two cool glasses of milk.

'Today is August 4, 2026,' said a second voice from the kitchen ceiling, 'in the city of Allendale, California.' It repeated the date three times for memory's sake. 'Today is Mr. Featherstone's birthday. Today is the anniversary of Tilita's marriage. Insurance is payable, as are the water, gas, and light bills.'

Somewhere in the walls, relays clicked, memory tapes glided under electric eyes.

Eight-one, tick-tock, eight-one o'clock, off to school, off to work, run, run, eight-one! But no doors slammed, no carpets took the soft tread of rubber heels. It was raining outside. The weather box on the front door sang quietly: 'Rain, rain, go away; rubbers, raincoats for today …' And the rain tapped on the empty house, echoing.

Outside, the garage chimed and lifted its door to reveal the waiting car. After a long wait the door swung down again.

At eight-thirty the eggs were shrivelled and the toast was like stone. An aluminum wedge scraped them into the sink, where hot water whirled them down a metal throat which digested and flushed them away to the distant sea. The dirty dishes were dropped into a hot washer and emerged twinkling dry.

Nine-fifteen, sang the clock, *time to clean.*

Out of warrens in the wall, tiny robot mice darted. The rooms were acrawl with the small cleaning animals, all rubber and metal. They thudded against chairs, whirling their mustached runners, kneading the rug nap, sucking gently at hidden dust. Then, like mysterious invaders, they popped into their burrows. Their pink electric eyes faded. The house was clean.

Ten o'clock. The sun came out from behind the rain. The house stood alone in a city of rubble and ashes. This was the one house left standing. At night the ruined city gave off a radioactive glow which could be seen for miles.

Ten-fifteen. The garden sprinklers whirled up in golden founts, filling the soft morning air with scatterings of brightness. The water pelted windowpanes, running down the charred west side where the house had been burned evenly free of its white paint. The entire west face of the house was black, save for five places. Here the silhouette in paint of a man mowing a lawn. Here, as in a photograph, a woman bent to pick flowers. Still farther over, their images burned on wood in one titanic instant, a small boy, hands flung into the air; higher up, the image of a thrown ball, and opposite him a girl, hands raised to catch a ball which never came down.

The five spots of paint—the man, the woman, the children, the ball—remained. The rest was a thin charcoaled layer.

The gentle sprinkler rain filled the garden with falling light.

Until this day, how well the house had kept its peace. How carefully it had inquired, 'Who goes there? What's the password?' and, getting no answer from lonely foxes and whining cats, it had shut up its windows and drawn shades in an old-maidenly preoccupation with self-protection which bordered on a mechanical paranoia.

It quivered at each sound, the house did. If a sparrow brushed a window, the shade snapped up. The bird, startled, flew off! No, not even a bird must touch the house!

The house was an altar with ten thousand attendants, big, small, servicing, attending, in choirs. But the gods had gone away, and the ritual of the religion continued senselessly, uselessly.

Twelve noon.

A dog whined, shivering, on the front porch.

The front door recognized the dog voice and opened. The dog, once huge and fleshy, but now gone to bone and covered with sores, moved in and through the house, tracking mud. Behind it whirred angry mice, angry at having to pick up mud, angry at inconvenience.

For not a leaf fragment blew under the door but what the wall panels flipped open and the copper scrap rats flashed swiftly out. The offending dust, hair, or paper, seized in miniature steel jaws, was raced back to the burrows. There, down tubes which fed into the cellar, it was dropped into the sighing vent of an incinerator which sat like evil Baal in a dark corner.

Baal: an evil spirit or god

The dog ran upstairs, hysterically yelping to each door, at last realizing, as the house realized, that only silence was here.

It sniffed the air and scratched the kitchen door. Behind the door, the stove was making pancakes which filled the house with a rich baked odor and the scent of maple syrup.

The dog frothed at the mouth, lying at the door, sniffing, its eyes turned to fire. It ran wildly in circles, biting at its tail, spun in a frenzy, and died. It lay in the parlor for an hour.

Two o'clock, sang a voice.

Delicately sensing decay at last, the regiments of mice hummed out as softly as blown gray leaves in an electrical wind.

Two-fifteen.

The dog was gone. In the cellar, the incinerator glowed suddenly and a whirl of sparks leaped up the chimney.

Two thirty-five.

Bridge tables sprouted from patio walls. Playing cards fluttered onto pads in a shower of pips. Martinis manifested on an oaken bench with egg-salad sandwiches. Music played.

But the tables were silent and the cards untouched. At four o'clock the tables folded like great butterflies back through the paneled walls.

. . . .

Four-thirty.

The nursery walls glowed.

Animals took shape: yellow giraffes, blue lions, pink antelopes, lilac panthers cavorting in crystal substance. The walls were glass. They looked out upon color and fantasy.

Hidden films clocked through well-oiled sprockets, and the walls lived. The nursery floor was woven to resemble a crisp, cereal meadow. Over this ran aluminum roaches and iron crickets, and in the hot still air butterflies of delicate red tissue wavered among the sharp aroma of animal spoors! There was the sound like a great matted yellow hive of bees within a dark bellows, the lazy bumble of a purring lion. And there was the patter of okapi feet and the murmur of a fresh jungle rain, like other hoofs, falling upon the summer-starched grass. Now the walls dissolved into distances of parched weed, mile on mile, and warm endless sky. The animals drew away into thorn brakes and water holes.

It was the children's hour.

okapi: a type of giraffe

. . . .

Five o'clock. The bath filled with clear hot water.

Six, seven, eight o'clock. The dinner dishes manipulated like magic tricks, and in the study a *click*. In the metal stand opposite the hearth where a fire now blazed up warmly, a cigar popped out, half an inch of soft gray ash on it, smoking, waiting.

Nine o'clock. The beds warmed their hidden circuits, for nights were cool here.

Nine-five. A voice spoke from the study ceiling:

'Mrs. McClellan, which poem would you like this evening?'

The house was silent.

The voice said at last, 'Since you express no preference, I shall select a poem at random.' Quiet music rose to back the voice. 'Sara Teasdale. As I recall, your favorite …

'There will come soft rains and the smell of the ground,
And swallows circling with their shimmering sound;

And frogs in the pools singing at night,
And wild plum trees in tremulous white;

Robins will wear their feathery fire,
Whistling their whims on a low fence-wire;

And not one will know of the war, not one
Will care at last when it is done.

Not one would mind, neither bird nor tree,
if mankind perished utterly;

And Spring herself, when she woke at dawn
Would scarcely know that we were gone.'

The fire burned on the stone hearth and the cigar fell away into a mound of quiet ash on its tray. The empty chairs faced each other between the silent walls, and the music played.

. . . .

At ten o'clock the house began to die.

The wind blew. A failing tree bough crashed through the kitchen window. Cleaning solvent, bottled, shattered over the stove. The room was ablaze in an instant!

'Fire!' screamed a voice. The house lights flashed, water pumps shot water from the ceilings. But the solvent spread on the linoleum, licking, eating, under the kitchen door, while the voices took it up in chorus: 'Fire, fire, fire!'

The house tried to save itself. Doors sprang tightly shut, but the windows were broken by the heat and the wind blew and sucked upon the fire.

The house gave ground as the fire in ten billion angry sparks moved with flaming ease from room to room and then up the stairs. While scurrying water rats squeaked from the walls, pistoled their water, and ran for more. And the wall sprays let down showers of mechanical rain.

But too late. Somewhere, sighing, a pump shrugged to a stop. The quenching rain ceased. The reserve water supply which had filled baths and washed dishes for many quiet days was gone.

The fire crackled up the stairs. It fed upon Picassos and Matisses in the upper halls, like delicacies, baking off the oily flesh, tenderly crisping the canvases into black shavings.

Now the fire lay in beds, stood in windows, changed the colors of drapes!

And then, reinforcements.

From attic trapdoors, blind robot faces peered down with faucet mouths gushing green chemical.

The fire backed off, as even an elephant must at the sight of a dead snake. Now there were twenty snakes whipping over the floor, killing the fire with a clear cold venom of green froth.

But the fire was clever. It had sent flames outside the house, up through the attic to the pumps there. An explosion! The attic brain which directed the pumps was shattered into bronze shrapnel on the beams.

The fire rushed back into every closet and felt of the clothes hung there.

The house shuddered, oak bone on bone, its bared skeleton cringing from the heat, its wire, its nerves revealed as if a surgeon had torn the skin off to let the red veins and capillaries quiver in the scalded air. Help, help! Fire! Run, run! Heat snapped mirrors like the brittle winter ice. And the voices wailed, Fire, fire, run, run, like a tragic nursery rhyme, a dozen voices, high, low, like children dying in a forest, alone, alone. And the voices fading as the wires popped their sheathings like hot chestnuts. One, two, three, four, five voices died.

In the nursery the jungle burned. Blue lions roared, purple giraffes bounded off. The panthers ran in circles, changing color, and ten million animals, running before the fire, vanished off toward a distant steaming river …

Ten more voices died. In the last instant under the fire avalanche, other choruses, oblivious, could be heard announcing the time, playing music, cutting the lawn by remote-control mower, or setting an umbrella frantically out and in the slamming and opening front door, a thousand things happening, like a clock shop when each clock strikes the hour insanely before or after the other, a scene of maniac confusion, yet unity; singing, screaming, a few last cleaning mice darting bravely out to carry the horrid ashes away! And one voice, with sublime disregard for the situation, read poetry aloud in the fiery study, until all the film spools burned, until all the wires withered and the circuits cracked.

The fire burst the house and let it slam flat down, puffing out skirts of spark and smoke.

In the kitchen, an instant before the rain of fire and timber, the stove could be seen making breakfasts at a psychopathic rate, ten dozen eggs, six loaves of toast, twenty dozen bacon strips, which, eaten by fire, started the stove working again, hysterically hissing!

The crash. The attic smashing into kitchen and parlor. The parlor into cellar, cellar into sub-cellar. Deep freeze, armchair, film tapes, circuits, beds, and all like skeletons thrown in a cluttered mound deep under.

Smoke and silence. A great quantity of smoke.

Dawn showed faintly in the east. Among the ruins, one wall stood alone. Within the wall, a last voice said, over and over again and again, even as the sun rose to shine upon the heaped rubble and steam:

'Today is August 5, 2026, today is August 5, 2026, today is …'

Understand

1. What tense is the story written in?
   (a) Past   (b) Present   (c) Future
2. Was the house aware that no one was living there? How do you know?
3. How long has the house been empty?
4. (a) Use the following words in sentences:
   - drapes
   - vanished
   - perished.

   (b) Find a synonym for each of the words listed above.

Explore

1. What do you think happened to the people who owned the house?
2. Suggest an alternative title for this story and explain your choice.
 3. Literary devices are not just limited to poetry. They can also make fiction more interesting. Identify one of the following devices in this story and explain why it is effective (see Unit 2 for explanations of these devices).
   - Personification
   - Simile
   - Onomatopoeia
4. When does the problem or crisis point occur in this story? Map out the plot structure using the diagram on page 136 to help you.

Investigate

An atomic bomb is an explosive device that gains its destructive power from nuclear reactions. In August 1945 the United States dropped two atomic bombs on the Japanese cities of Hiroshima and Nagasaki. Around 200,000 people were killed as a result of these bombings. Find out more about these places in the aftermath of these attacks. Below are some headings to get you started.
   - Level of damage
   - Short-term effects
   - Death and injury
   - Long-term effects

Create

1. Draw your future house then present your design to a partner.
2. Write a blog post for parents discussing the dangers of young people's dependence on technology, and offering advice on how best to guide them. Use the title 'Your teen and technology'. (For information on blogs see page 11.)
3. Can you imagine losing everything you own, including your home? Write a diary entry from the perspective of someone who has lost everything. (For information on diary entries see page 5.)
4. Carry out a class debate on the following motion: *This house believes that smartphones are not making us smarter.* (For information on debates see pages 47–48.)

Verbs

Verbs are action words.

Verbs are important as they help bring your writing to life.

◖ *Mark plays rugby.*

In this sentence, Mark is doing the action. He is playing rugby.

◖ *Kate texted Jon to ask what time they were meeting.*

In this sentence Kate is the subject of the verb and the person doing the action. The action in this case is texting.

What action will Tom do in the sentence below?

Tom will walk the dog tomorrow.

 Understand

1. Find the verbs in the sentences below.
   - **(a)** Alan and Hayley raced home from school.
   - **(b)** Sean eats his dinner at 6 p.m. every day.
   - **(c)** The dog barked all night long.
   - **(d)** My granny hummed the song, as she didn't know the lyrics.
   - **(e)** Holly put the rubbish in the bin.
   - **(f)** Fred teased his sister so much that she cried.
   - **(g)** The cat meowed until Dad gave up and eventually fed her.
   - **(h)** The girls laughed after they read the text.

2. Identify the verbs in the first four paragraphs of 'There Will Come Soft Rains' on page 139? (Hint: the first paragraph contains the verbs 'sang', 'ticked' and 'repeating'.)

 Grammar Primer: pages 31–32

The following short story was written by Brendan Behan (1923–1964), an Irish playwright, writer and poet who wrote in both English and Irish.

The Confirmation Suit

For weeks it was nothing but simony and sacrilege, and the sins crying to heaven for vengeance, the big green Catechism in our hands, walking home along the North Circular Road. And after tea, at the back of the brewery wall, with a butt too, to help our wits, what is a pure spirit, and don't kill that, Billser has to get a drag out of it yet, what do I mean by apostate, and hell and heaven and despair and presumption and hope. The big fellows, who were now thirteen and the veterans of last year's Confirmation, frightened us, and said the Bishop would fire us out of the Chapel if we didn't answer his questions, and we'd be left wandering around the streets, in a new suit and top-coat with nothing to show for it, all dressed up and nowhere to go. The big people said not to mind them; they were only getting it up for us, jealous because they were over their Confirmation, and could never make it again. At school we were in a special room to ourselves, for the last few days, and went round, a special class of people. There were worrying times too, that the Bishop would light on you, and you wouldn't be able to answer his questions. Or you might hear the women complaining about the price of boys' clothes.

'Twenty-two and sixpence for tweed, I'd expect a share in the shop for that. I've a good mind to let him go in jersey and pants for that.'

'Quite right, ma'am,' says one to another, backing one another up, 'I always say what matter if they are good and pure'. What had that got to do with it, if you had to go into the Chapel in a jersey and pants, and every other kid in a new suit, kid gloves and tan shoes and a scoil cap. The Cowan brothers were terrified. They were twins, and twelve years old, and every old one in the street seemed to be wishing a jersey and pants on them, and saying their poor mother couldn't be expected to do for two in the one year, and she ought to go down to Sister Monica and tell her to put one back. If it came to that, the Cowans agreed to fight it out, at the back of the brewery wall, whoever got best, the other would be put back.

I wasn't so worried about this. My old fellow was a tradesman, and made money most of the time. Besides, my grandmother, who lived at the top of the next house, was a lady of capernosity and function. She had money and lay in bed all day, drinking porter or malt, and taking pinches of snuff, and talking to the neighbours that would call up to tell her the news of the day. She only left her bed to go down one flight of stairs and visit the lady in the back drawing-room, Miss McCann.

Miss McCann worked a sewing-machine, making habits for the dead. Sometimes girls from our quarter got her to make dresses and costumes, but mostly she stuck to the habits. They were a steady line, she said, and you didn't have to be always buying patterns, for the fashions didn't change, not even from summer to winter. They were like a long brown shirt, and a hood attached, that was closed over the person's face before the coffin lid was screwn down. A sort of little banner hung out of one arm, made of the same material, and four silk rosettes in each corner, and in the middle, the letters I.H.S., which mean, Miss McCann said; 'I Have Suffered.'

My grandmother and Miss McCann liked me more than any other kid they knew. I like being liked, and could only admire their taste.

simony:
buying and selling of church offices

apostate:
a person who rejects their religious faith

capernosity:
abandoning a religious group or faith

My Aunt Jack, who was my father's aunt as well as mine, sometimes came down from where she lived, up near the Basin, where the water came from before they started getting it from Wicklow. My Aunt Jack said it was much better water, at that. Miss McCann said she ought to be a good judge. For Aunt Jack was funny. She didn't drink porter or malt, or take snuff, and my father said she never thought much about men, either. She was also very strict about washing yourself very often. My grandmother took a bath every year, whether she was dirty or not, but she was in no way bigoted in the washing line in between times.

Aunt Jack made terrible raids on us now and again, to stop snuff and drink, and make my grandmother get up in the morning, and wash herself, and cook meals and take food with them. My grandmother was a gilder by trade, and served her time in one of the best shops in the city, and was getting a man's wages at sixteen. She liked stuff out of the pork butchers, and out of cans, but didn't like boiling potatoes, for she said she was no skivvy, and the chip man was better at it. When she was left alone it was a pleasure to eat with her. She always had cans of lovely things and spicy meat and brawn, and plenty of seasoning, fresh out of the German man's shop up the road. But after a visit from Aunt Jack, she would have to get up and wash for a week, and she would have to go and make stews and boil cabbage and pig's cheeks. Aunt Jack was very much up for sheep's heads too. They were so cheap and nourishing.

brawn: *meat from a pig or calf's head, preserved in jelly*

But my grandmother only tried it once. She had been a first-class gilder in Eustace Street, but never had anything to do with sheep's heads before. When she took it out of the pot, and laid it on the plate, she and I sat looking at it, in fear and trembling. It was bad enough going into the pot, but with the soup streaming from its eyes, and its big teeth clenched in a very bad temper, it would put the heart crossways in you. My grandmother asked me, in a whisper, if I ever thought sheep could look so vindictive, but that it was more like the head of an old man, and would I for God's sake take it up and throw it out of the window. The sheep kept glaring at us, but I came the far side of it, and rushed over to the window and threw it out in a flash. My grandmother had to drink a Baby Power whiskey, for she wasn't the better of herself.

Afterwards she kept what she called her stock-pot on the gas. A heap of bones, and as she said herself, any old muck that would come in handy, to have boiling there, night and day, on a glimmer. She and I ate happily of cooked ham and California pineapple and sock-eye salmon, and the pot of good nourishing soup was always on the gas even if Aunt Jack came down the chimney, like the Holy Souls at midnight. My grandmother said she didn't begrudge the money for the gas. Not when she remembered the looks that sheep's head was giving her. And all she had to do with the stock-pot was to throw in another sup of water, now and again, and a handful of old rubbish the pork butcher would send over, in the way of lights or bones. My Aunt Jack thought a lot about barley, too, so we had a package of that lying beside the gas, and threw a sprinkle in any time her foot was heard on the stairs. The stock-pot bubbled away on the gas for years after, and only when my grandmother was dead did someone notice it. They tasted it, and spat it out just as quick, and wondered what it was. Some said it was paste, and more that it was gold size, and there were other people and they maintained that it was glue. They all agreed on one thing, that it was dangerous tack to leave lying around, where there might be young children, and in the heel of the reel, it went out the same window as the sheep's head.

Miss McCann told my grandmother not to mind Aunt Jack but to sleep as long as she liked in the morning. They came to an arrangement that Miss McCann would cover the landing and keep an eye out. She would call Aunt Jack in for a minute, and give the signal by banging the grate, letting on to poke the fire, and have a bit of a conversation with Aunt Jack about dresses and costumes, and hats and habits. One of these mornings, and Miss McCann delaying a fighting action, to give my grandmother time to hurl herself out of bed and into her clothes and give her face the rub of a towel, the chat between Miss McCann and Aunt Jack came to my Confirmation suit.

When I made my first Communion, my grandmother dug deep under the mattress, and myself and Aunt Jack were sent round expensive shops, I came back with a rig that would take the sight of your eye. This time, however, Miss McCann said there wasn't much stirring in the habit line, on account of the mild winter, and she would be delighted to make the suit, if Aunt Jack would get the material. I nearly wept, for terror of what these old women would have me got up in, but I had to let on to be delighted, Miss McCann was so set on it. She asked Aunt Jack did she remember my father's Confirmation suit. He did. He said he would never forget it. They sent him out in a velvet suit, of plum colour, with a lace collar. My blood ran cold when he told me.

The stuff they got for my suit was blue serge, and that was not so bad. They got as far as the pants, and that passed off very civil. You can't do much to a boy's pants, one pair is like the next, though I had to ask them not to trouble themselves putting three little buttons on either side of the legs. The waistcoat was all right, and anyway the coat would cover it. But the coat itself, that was where Aughrim was lost.

serge:
a heavy fabric

Aughrim:
*a battle in 1691
where the Irish
were defeated*

The lapels were little wee things, like what you'd see in pictures like *Ring* magazine of John L. Sullivan, or Gentleman Jim, and the buttons were the size of saucers, or within the bawl of an ass of it, and I nearly cried when I saw them being put on, and ran down to my mother, and begged her to get me any sort of a suit, even a jersey and pants, than have me set up before the people in this get-up. My mother said it was very kind of Aunt Jack and Miss McCann to go to all this trouble and expense, and I was very ungrateful not to appreciate it. My father said that Miss McCann was such a good tailor that people were dying to get into her creations, and her handiwork was to be found in all the best cemeteries. He laughed himself sick at this, and said if it was good enough for him to be sent down to North William Street in plum-coloured velvet and lace, I needn't be getting the needle over a couple of big buttons and little lapels. He asked me not to forget to get up early the morning of my Confirmation, and let him see me, before he went to work: a bit of a laugh started the day well. My mother told him to give over and let me alone, and said she was sure it would be a lovely suit, and that Aunt Jack would never buy poor material, but stuff that would last forever. That nearly finished me altogether, and I ran through the hall up to the corner, fit to cry my eyes out, only I wasn't much of a hand at crying. I went more for cursing, and I cursed all belonging to me, and was hard at it on my father, and wondering why his lace collar hadn't choked him, when I remembered that it was a sin to go on like that, and I going up for Confirmation, and I had to simmer down, and live in fear of the day I'd put on that jacket.

The days passed, and I was fitted and refitted, and every old one in the house came up to look at the suit, and took a pinch of snuff, and a sup out of the jug, and wished me long life and the health to wear and tear it, and they spent that much time viewing it round, back, belly and sides, that Miss McCann hadn't time to make the overcoat, and like an answer to a prayer, I was brought down to Talbot Street, and dressed out in a dinging overcoat, belted, like a grown-up man's. And my shoes and gloves were dear and dandy, and I said to myself that there was no need to let anyone see the suit with its little lapels and big buttons. I could keep the topcoat on all day, in the chapel, and going round afterwards.

The night before Confirmation day, Miss McCann handed over the suit to my mother, and kissed me, and said not to bother thanking her. She would do more than that for me, and she and my grandmother cried and had a drink on the strength of my having grown to be a big fellow, in the space of twelve years, which they didn't seem to consider a great deal of time. My father said to my mother, and I getting bathed before the fire, that since I was born Miss McCann thought the world of me. When my mother was in hospital, she took me into her place till my mother came out, and it near broke her heart to give me back.

In the morning I got up, and Mrs Rooney in the next room shouted in to my mother that her Liam was still stalling, and not making any move to get out of it, and she thought she was cursed; Christmas or Easter, Communion or Confirmation, it would drive a body into Riddleys, which is the mad part of Grangegorman, and she wondered she wasn't driven out of her mind, and above in the puzzle factory years ago. So she shouted again at Liam to get up, and washed and dressed.

And my mother shouted at me, though I was already knotting my tie, but you might as well be out of the world, as out of fashion, and they kept it up like a pair of mad women, until at last Liam and I were ready and he came in to show my mother his clothes. She hanselled him a tanner, which he put in his pocket and Mrs Rooney called me in to show her my clothes. I just stood at her door, and didn't open my coat, but just grabbed the sixpence out of her hand, and ran up the stairs like the hammers of hell. She shouted at me to hold on a minute, she hadn't seen my suit, but I muttered something about it not being lucky to keep a Bishop waiting, and ran on.

The Church was crowded, boys on one side and the girls on the other, and the altar ablaze with lights and flowers, and a throne for the Bishop to sit on when he wasn't confirming. There was a cheering crowd outside, drums rolled, trumpeters from Jim Larkin's band sounded the Salute. The Bishop came in and the doors were shut. In short order I joined the queue to the rails, knelt and was whispered over, and touched on the cheek. I had my overcoat on the whole time, though it was warm, and I was in a lather of sweat waiting for the hymns and the sermon.

The lights grew brighter and I got warmer, was carried out fainting. But though I didn't mind them loosening my tie, I clenched firmly my overcoat, and nobody saw the jacket with the big buttons and the little lapels.
When I went home, I got into bed, and my father said I went into a sickness just as the Bishop was giving us the pledge. He said this was a master stroke, and showed real presence of mind.

Sunday after Sunday, my mother fought over the suit. She said I was liar and a hypocrite, putting it on for a few minutes every week, and running into Miss McCann's and out again, letting her think I wore it every week-end. In a passionate temper my mother said she would show me up, and tell Miss McCann, and up like a shot with her, for my mother was always slim, and light on her feet as a feather, and in next door. When she came back she said nothing, but sat at the fire looking into it. I didn't really believe she would tell Miss McCann. And I put on the suit and thought I would go in and tell her I was wearing it this week-night, because I was going to the Queen's with my brothers. I ran next door and upstairs, and every step was more certain and easy that my mother hadn't told her. I ran, shoved in the door, saying: 'Miss Mc., Miss Mc., Rory and Sean and I are going to the Queen's...' She was bent over the sewing-machine and all I could see was the top of her old grey head, and the rest of her shaking with crying, and her arms folded under her head, on a bit of habit where she had been finishing the I.H.S. I ran down the stairs and back into our place, and my mother was sitting at the fire, sad and sorry, but saying nothing.

I needn't have worried about the suit lasting forever. Miss McCann didn't. The next winter was not so mild, and she was whipped before the year was out. At her wake people said how she was in a habit of her own making, and my father said she would look queer in anything else, seeing as she supplied the dead of the whole quarter for forty years, without one complaint from a customer.

At the funeral, I left my topcoat in the carriage and got out and walked in the spills of rain after her coffin. People said I would get my end, but I went on till we reached the graveside, and I stood in my Confirmation suit drenched to the skin. I thought this was the least I could do.

Understand

1. Who is the narrator?
2. How does the narrator feel about making his confirmation?
3. Why did the narrator faint in church?

Explore

 1. What impression do you get of the narrator's grandmother?

2. 'My blood ran cold when he told me.' What does the narrator mean by this?

 3. Why does his father find the situation so amusing?

 4. Do you feel sorry for Miss McCann? Explain your answer.

5. What is the climax of the story? How is it resolved?

6. Identify some features of good storytelling in this story.

Create

1. Design a poster advertising the confirmation suit. How would you make it more appealing for people to buy?

 2. Carry out a class debate on the following motion: *This house believes that we are what we wear.* (For information on debates see pages 47–48.)

3. Have you ever had to wear something to spare someone else's feelings? Write a diary entry describing how it made you feel and what you did about it. (For information on diary entries see page 5.)

Focus on ... **setting**

Setting is the time, place and type of world in which a story takes place.

When you start your story it is not enough to just mention the location, you should also try to bring the place to life for your reader. You can do this by appealing to as many of the five senses as you can in your descriptions.

Discuss

1. Can you list the five senses?
2. Which sense(s) do each of the following descriptions appeal to?
   (a) The strong aroma of coffee filled the corridor.
   (b) I walked carefully, letting the sun wash over me like hot water from a shower.
   (c) Bright and vivid colours danced in front of my eyes.
   (d) The leaves crackled underfoot, while the wind howled and shrieked.
   (e) Mary tasted the salt on the wind even before the blue waves came into view.

Create

Choose one of these images and write five sentences describing the setting. Remember to appeal to all five senses in order to bring your setting to life.

Read the following extract from *The Hobbit* by J. R. R. Tolkien.

The Hobbit

In a hole in the ground there lived a hobbit. Not a nasty, dirty, wet hole, filled with the ends of worms and an oozy smell, nor yet a dry, bare, sandy hole with nothing in it to sit down on or to eat: it was a hobbit-hole, and that means comfort.

Did you notice how many of the five senses the author appeals to in his description of this setting?

 Sight: 'dirty', 'filled with the ends of worms'

Smell: 'oozy smell'

 Taste: 'nothing in it … to eat'

 Touch: 'wet', 'dry, bare, sandy', 'comfort'

Read the following extracts from 'The Sentinel' by Arthur C. Clarke and pay particular attention to his description of the setting in each.

The Sentinel

Extract 1

The next time you see the full moon high in the south, look carefully at its right-hand edge and let your eye travel upward along the curve of the disk. Round about two o'clock you will notice a small, dark oval: anyone with normal eyesight can find it quite easily. It is the great walled plain, one of the finest on the Moon, known as the Mare Crisium – the Sea of Crises. Three hundred miles in diameter, and almost completely surrounded by a ring of magnificent mountains, it had never been explored until we entered it in the late summer of 1996.

Extract 2

One could never grow tired of those incredible mountains, so much more rugged than the gentle hills of Earth. We never knew, as we rounded the capes and promontories of that vanished sea, what new splendors would be revealed to us. The whole southern curve of the Mare Crisium is a vast delta where a score of rivers once found their way into the ocean, fed perhaps by the torrential rains that must have lashed the mountains in the brief volcanic age when the Moon was young. Each of these ancient valleys was an invitation, challenging us to climb into the unknown uplands beyond. But we had a hundred miles still to cover, and could only look longingly at the heights which others must scale.

Extract 3

We kept Earth-time aboard the tractor, and precisely at 22.00 hours the final radio message would be sent out to Base and we would close down for the day. Outside, the rocks would still be burning beneath the almost vertical sun, but to us it was night until we awoke again eight hours later. Then one of us would prepare breakfast, there would be a great buzzing of electric razors, and someone would switch on the short-wave radio from Earth. Indeed, when the smell of frying sausages began to fill the cabin, it was sometimes hard to believe that we were not back on our own world – everything was so normal and homely, apart from the feeling of decreased weight and the unnatural slowness with which objects fell.

Understand

1. Where does 'The Sentinel' take place?
2. What are the 'new splendors' to be explored in extract 2?
3. What senses are referred to in extract 3?
4. Why was the writer experiencing a feeling of 'decreased weight and unnatural slowness'?

Investigate

1. *Mare* is the Latin word for sea. Can you think of any words relating to the sea that start with 'mar'?
2. The English language is full of words that have come from Latin and Greek. Can you think of any others?
3. *Aqua* is Latin for water. Think of all the words that begin with 'aqua' – aquamarine, aquarium, aquatic. What do they have in common?
4. Make a list of all the words you can think of that start with the letters below. When you cannot think of any more, use your dictionary to help you.
   - Bio (from the Greek *bios*, meaning life)
   - Aud (from the Latin *audio*, meaning hear)
   - Civ (from the Latin *civis*, meaning citizen)
   - Phon (from the Greek *phone*, meaning sound)
   - Photo (from the Greek *phos*, meaning light)

Explore

1. Do you think the narrator enjoys the sights in extract 2? How do you know?
2. What word would you use to describe the narrator's attitude towards the landscape? Explain your choice.
3. On Earth, if the sun is 'almost vertical', what time of the day is it?
4. What objects do you feel helped the narrator feel at home in the cabin?
5. Compare and contrast the three extracts from 'The Sentinel' using the questions below to guide you.
   - Which is the most descriptive?
   - What kind of language is used in each?
   - Is there a particular mood or atmosphere evident?
6. Make a list of five things that you would bring with you on an exploration of space. Remember, they must be small and portable. Give reasons for choosing each.

The following extract is from a story called 'The Golden Shroud' by Margo Lanagan. It is loosely based on the fairy tale Rapunzel. In this extract the prince arrives at the tower. He believes his true love is being held captive, but she is nowhere to be seen.

The Golden Shroud

I could not leave it, yet I could not carry such a weight – I had tried, marvelling, laughing, often enough. She herself had kept it coiled on bed or wall, roaming from its weight only so far, like a tied dog. It was a cruelty to her, even as, pegged through on the sill, it had made our meeting possible; it had been my ladder to her and my line. *You can reel me in like a fish*, I had laughed to her. And unsmiling she replied, *Only if you are there below*.

I knelt and attacked the gold, unplaiting from the thick head-end, where the witch's sword or scissors had hacked. The stuff fell apart, slithered side to side, transformed it seemed into other matter: cascading water, rippling cloth-of-gold. Strands of it wandered in the air and at the edges. I fought it and wept; I was in a welter of goldness, up to my knees, bogged in beauty. Perhaps if I dug far enough I would find her, curled delicate as an ear under all this richness.

I did not, do I need say? The hair was spread, lacquering path and field like a syrup, materials for a thousand gorgeous bird-nests, and she was gone. It was only as I loosed the ribbon at the narrower plait-end, and unworked the last several yards from there more easily, that cold realization came, and cooled my tears and my sweat, and sat in my heart like stone.

lacquering: hard, glossy coating

I lay in the slippery whorl of her hair, the spread sun on the ground, trailing and looping out into the green. I smelt, I felt, the grass through the perfumed strands pillowing my cheek. What had the old witch done: had she killed her? Had she worse? Had she found worse than this tower and this tether of hair?

whorl: pattern of spirals

I could not take all the hair, and I could not leave. I sat up and dashed the last cold tears from my eyes, and of one of the several strands caught in my fingers I chose the strongest and brightest. Back through the labyrinth and tangle I followed it; I found one end, and from there looped it loose around three fingers, and wound it up, the full length, becoming a brighter and solider ribbon, knuckle to knuckle, fattening, gleaming, scented with her loveliness.

When I had all of the strand, I bound it into itself and tucked it, narrow and bright as a bracelet made to the measure of her small wrist, into my belt-satchel with all the gifts I had brought her: the foods from the palace, a piece of fine lace I had bought her at market, the jewelled comb.

'Well, this is pretty.' The voice was cold and clear as October mornings.

I sprang to my feet. 'I did not hear you.'

'Ah, but I heard *you*.'

Never had there been a crueller contrast than the sunlit spillage about my feet with the tall woman in the edge of the shadowed wood, white-faced above her black riding-garb, her hand like a knot of bones in her stallion's reins, himself night-black and leering.

'I heard you long ago,' she said, 'when first you threatened to besmirch my lily. I heard you scrambling and your fondling fingers. I knew exactly and from the beginning what you sought. And that is all that matters: that you should not have it.'

besmirch: *damage or spoil*

'Why not?' said I. 'Why should I not have her, as my wedded wife? I am a prince, one day to be king of all lands east of here. Am I not man enough to husband her?'

She had been surveying the hair, but she looked up at me, and gave a faint snort. 'That girl is part of such machinations, boy, your courtly politics are but a May dance, but a nodding daffy-dilly, beside them. Tut-tut! Such a mess you have made.' She shook her head over the hair again. 'It will be much less easy to bear away now.'

machinations: *schemes or plans*

In the instant I glanced down at the hair myself, she was dismounted and at me. In three strides only she covered that impossible distance — I counted them even as they took no time at all. She pressed some rasping cloth or spell to my nose and mouth, that caught in my throat and closed it; she was muttering in my ear her witch-language; she was strong, all iron and leather. But I barely had time to realise I could not fight her before I was gone insensible.

Discuss

Share what you know about the fairy tale Rapunzel.

Understand

1. How does the prince feel about the princess?
2. Remember, literary devices can be found in fiction as well as poetry. What literary devices can you find in this story?
3. What does 'before I was gone insensible' mean?

Explore

1. Pick a sentence that you feel is descriptive and explain why you think it is effective.
2. Can you name any films based on the fairy tale Rapunzel?
3. Compare this extract to the original fairy tale under the headings below.

◀ Title   ◀ Characters   ◀ Setting

Create

Write your own opening to this story, describing the prince's arrival at the tower, in the space provided on page 38 of your Portfolio. Set the scene for your reader.

Focus on ... **character**

A **character** is a person who appears in a story.

As in real life, we form opinions of characters based on their actions and behaviour. When creating characters, you can say a lot about their appearance and personality by describing how they act.

When describing characters you should remember to show, not tell. It is more interesting when you figure things out about characters yourself, without being told by the author.

Look at this description of a character from the novel *Of Mice and Men* by John Steinbeck.

Of Mice and Men

This room was swept and fairly neat, for Crooks was a proud, aloof man. He kept his distance and demanded that other people keep theirs. His body was bent over to the left by his crooked spine, and his eyes lay deep in his head, and because of their depth seemed to glitter with intensity. His lean face was lined with deep black wrinkles, and he had thin, pain-tightened lips which were lighter than his face.

 Discuss

1. Why do you think people called Crooks by that name?
2. Do you know anyone with a nickname? Why do they have this nickname?
3. Can you think of any fictional characters who are known by their nickname?

Understand

Fill in the profile for Crooks on page 39 of your Portfolio using the information you have learned from reading the passage.

 Explore

1. 'He kept his distance and demanded that other people keep theirs.' What does this tell you about Crooks?

  Investigate

Find out if there are other characters in *Of Mice and Men* who have nicknames and share your findings with the class.

  Create

 1. Write a short diary entry from the perspective of Crooks after a hard day, in the space provided on page 39 of your Portfolio. (For information on diary entries see page 5.)

2. **(a)** Choose a character from a story you have read in class. As a group, try to answer the questions below.

   ◖ How might this character say 'How are you?'
   ◖ What would his/her favourite film be?
   ◖ What kind of music does he/she listen to?
   ◖ What would he/she have for breakfast?
   ◖ Who is his/her hero?
   ◖ Does he/she have any hobbies?
   ◖ Who would play him/her in a film?

    (b) Work in pairs to come up with some more questions to ask this character. Take turns playing the part of the interviewee and the character, and try to answer the questions the way you think the character would. (For information on interviews see page 56.)

Clothing often tells us a lot about a character. Think back to 'The Confirmation Suit' and how important the outfit was to the story.

Read the following two character descriptions of Miss Hilly from the novel *The Help* by Kathryn Stockett and Miss Havisham from the novel *Great Expectations* by Charles Dickens.

The Help

Miss Hilly got a round face and dark brown hair in the beehive. Her skin be olive color, with freckles and moles. She wear a lot a red plaid. And she getting heavy in the bottom. Today, since it's so hot, she wearing a red sleeveless dress with no waist to it. She one a those grown ladies that still dress like a little girl with big bows and matching hats and such.

Great Expectations

She was dressed in rich materials – satins, and lace, and silks – all of white. Her shoes were white. And she had a long white veil dependent from her hair, and she had bridal flowers in her hair, but her hair was white. Some bright jewels sparkled on her neck and on her hands, and some other jewels lay sparkling on the table. Dresses, less splendid than the dress she wore, and half-packed trunks, were scattered about. She had not quite finished dressing, for she had but one shoe on – the other was on the table near her hand …

 Understand

Describe the outfits worn by each of these women in your own words.

 Explore

 1. What do you learn about the women from how they are dressed?
2. Compare and contrast the two descriptions. Make a list of the similarities and the differences.
3. Which character would you rather read more about, Miss Hilly or Miss Havisham?
4. What have you learned about the setting of each of these stories?
 5. If each of these was the opening of a story, would they be effective?

 Investigate

Find out more about these two novels and decide which one you would prefer to read.

 Create

 Draw a portrait of one of the characters described in these extracts then swap your picture with a partner and explain your drawing.

The following short story, written by Irish author Claire Keegan, takes place over the summer months in rural Ireland.

Sisters

It is customary for the Porters to send a postcard to say when they will be arriving. Betty waits. Each time the dog barks she finds herself going to the window at the foot of the stairs, looking out through the maidenhair fern to see if the postman is cycling up the avenue. It is almost June. The chill has slackened off; plums are getting plumper on the trees. The Porters will soon come, demanding strange food, fresh handkerchiefs, hot-water bottles, ice.

Louisa, Betty's sister, went away to England when she was young and married Stanley Porter, a salesman who fell for her, he said, because of the way her hair fell down her back. Louisa always had beautiful hair. When they were young, Betty brushed it every night, one hundred strokes, and secured the gold braid with a piece of satin ribbon.

Betty's own hair is, and always has been, an unremarkable brown. Her hands were always her best feature, white, lady-like hands that played the organ on Sundays. Now, after years of work, her hands are ruined, the skin on her palms is hard and masculine, the knuckles enlarged; her mother's wedding band cannot be removed.

Betty lives in the homestead, the big house, as it is called. It once belonged to a Protestant landlord who sold up and moved away after a childless marriage ended. The Land Commission, who bought the estate, knocked down the three-storey section of the house and sold the remaining two-storey servants' quarters and the surrounding seventy acres to Betty's father for a small sum when he married. The house looks too small for the garden and too close to the yard, but its ivy-covered walls look handsome nonetheless. The granite archway leads to a yard with stables, a barn and lofty sheds, coach houses, kennels and a spout-house. There's a fine walled orchard at the back in which the landlord grazed an Angus bull to keep the children out, seeing as he had none of his own. The place has a history, a past. People said Parnell had a tooth pulled in the parlour. The big kitchen has a barred window, an Aga and the deal table Betty scrubs on Saturdays. The white, marble fireplace in the parlour suits the mahogany furniture. A staircase curves on to a well-lighted landing with oak doors opening into three large bedrooms overlooking the yard, and a bathroom Betty had plumbed in when her father became ill.

Betty, too, had wanted to go to England, but she stayed back to keep house. Their mother died suddenly when Betty and Louisa were small. She went out to gather wood one afternoon and dropped dead coming back through the meadow. It seemed natural for Betty, being the eldest, to step into her mother's shoes and mind her father, a humoursome man given to violent fits of temper. She hadn't an easy life. There were cattle to be herded and tested, pigs to fatten, turkeys to be sent off on the train to Dublin before Christmas. They cut the meadow in summer and harvested a field of oats in autumn.

Her father gave instructions and did less and less, paid a man to come in and do the hardest work. He criticised the veterinary bills, insulted the priest who came to anoint him when he was ill, belittled Betty's cooking and claimed that nothing was as it should have been. Nothing was the way it used to be, he meant. He hated change. Towards the end he'd put on his black overcoat and walk the fields, seeing how tall the grass was in the meadow, counting the grains of corn on the stalks, noting the thinness of a cow or the rust on a gate. Then he would come inside just before dark and say, 'Not much time left. Not much time.'

'Don't be morbid,' Betty used to answer, and continued on; but last winter her father took to his bed, and for the three days preceding his death he lay there roaring and kicking his feet, calling for 'Buttermilk! Buttermilk!' When he died on a Tuesday night, by willing himself to die, Betty was more relieved than sorry.

Betty kept track of Louisa's progress through the years; her wedding, which she did not attend, the birth of her children, one boy and one girl, what Louisa had wanted. She sent a fruit cake through the post every Christmas, home-made fudge at Easter, and remembered the children's birthdays, put pound notes she could not spare in cards.

Betty had been too busy for marriage. She had once walked out with a young Protestant man named Cyril Dawe her father disapproved of. Nothing ever came of it. The time for marriage and children passed for Betty. She became used to attending to her father's needs in the big house, quelling his temper, making his strong tea, ironing his shirts and polishing his good shoes on a Saturday night.

After his death she managed to live by renting out the land and cautiously spending the savings her father had left in the Allied Irish Bank. She was fifty years old. The house was hers, but a clause was put in her father's will that gave Louisa right of residence for the duration of her lifetime. Her father had always favoured Louisa. She had given him the admiration he needed, whereas Betty only fed and clothed and pacified him.

When June passes without word from the Porters, Betty becomes uneasy. She pictures the lettuce and the scallions rotting in the vegetable patch, toys with the notion of renting a guest house by the sea, of going off to Ballymoney or Cahore Point; but in her heart she knows she won't. She never goes anywhere. All she ever does is cook and clean and milk the cow she keeps for the house, attends mass on Sundays. But she likes it this way, likes having the house to herself, knowing things are as she left them.

An overwhelming sense of freedom has accompanied the days since her father's death. She pulls weeds, keeps the gardens tidy, goes out with the secateurs on Saturdays to cut flowers for the altar. She does the things she never had time to do before: she crochets, blues the lace curtains, replaces the bulb in the Sacred Heart lamp, scrapes the moss off the horse trough and paints the archway gate. She can make jam later on when the fruit ripens. She can pit the potatoes and pickle the tomatoes in the greenhouse. Nothing, really, will go to waste if the Porters do not come. She is getting used to this idea of living through the summer alone, is humming a tune softly and weighing candied peel on the scales, when the postman wheels the bicycle up to the door.

'They're coming on the ninth off the evening ferry, Miss Elizabeth,' he says. 'They're coming as far as Enniscorthy on the bus. You'll have to send a car.' He puts the card on the dresser and slides the kettle over on the hot plate to make himself some tea. 'Not a bad day.'

Betty nods. She has only four days to get the house ready. They could have given her more notice. It seems strange, their not bringing the car, Stanley's big company car that he always takes such pride in.

The next morning she throws out her father's old vests she's used as dusters, carries the empty stout bottles up the wood and dumps them under the bushes. She takes out rugs and beats them with more vigour than is necessary, raises a flurry of dust. She hides old bedspreads at the back of the wardrobe, turns the mattresses and puts the good sheets on the beds. She always keeps good bed-linen in case she'll get sick and she wouldn't want the doctor or the priest saying her sheets are patched. She takes all the cracked and chipped plates off the dresser and arranges the good willow-pattern dinner set on the shelves. She orders bags of flour and sugar and wheaten meal from the grocer, gets down on her knees and polishes the floor until it shines.

They arrive in the avenue on a hot Friday evening. Betty takes off her apron when the taxi beeps the horn and rushes out into the avenue to greet them.

'Oh Betty!' Louisa says, as if she's surprised to see her there.

She embraces Louisa, who looks as young as ever in her white summer two-piece, her hair hanging in gold waves down her back. Her bare arms are brown with the sun.

Her son, Edward, has grown tall and lanky, a hidden young man who prefers to stay indoors; he extends a cold palm, which Betty shakes. There is little feeling in his handshake. The girl, Ruth, skips down to the old tennis court without so much as a word of hello.

'Come back here and kiss your Aunt Betty!' Louisa screams.

'Where's Stanley?'

'Oh he's busy, had to work, you know,' Louisa says. 'He may follow on later.'

'Well, you're looking great, as usual.'

Louisa's prominent white teeth are too plentiful for her smile. She accepts but does not return the compliment. The taxi-man is taking suitcases off the roof-rack. There is an awful lot of luggage. They've brought a black Labrador and books and pillows and wellingtons, a flute, raincoats, a chessboard and woolly jumpers.

'We brought cheese,' Louisa says, and hands Betty a slab of pungent Cheddar.

'How thoughtful,' Betty says, and sniffs it.

Louisa stands at the front gates and gazes out towards Mount Leinster with its ever-lighted mast, and the lush deciduous forest in the valley.

'Oh, Betty,' she says, 'it's so lovely to be home.'

'Come on in.'

Betty has the table set; two kettles stand boiling on the Aga, their spouts expelling pouty little breaths of steam. A pool of evening sunlight falls through the barred window over the cold roast chickens and potato salad.

'Poor Coventry was put in a cage for the entire journey,' Louisa says, referring to the dog. He has slumped down in front of the dresser and Betty has to slide him across the lino to get the cupboard doors open.

'Any beetroot, Aunt Elizabeth?' Edward asks.

Betty has taken great care washing the lettuce but now finds herself hoping an earwig won't crawl out of the salad bowl. Her eyesight isn't what it used to be. She scalds the teapot and cuts a loaf of brown bread into thin, dainty slices.

'I need the toilet!' Ruth announces.

'Take your elbows off the table,' Louisa instructs, and removes a hair from the butter dish.

There is too much pepper in the salad dressing and the rhubarb tart could have used more sugar, but all that's left is a few potato skins, chicken bones, greasy dishes.

When evening falls, Louisa says she'd like to sleep with Betty.

'It'll be like old times,' she says. 'You can brush my hair.'

She has developed an English accent, which Betty doesn't care for. Betty does not want Louisa in her bed. She likes being sprawled out on her double mattress, waking and sleeping when she feels like it, but she can't say no. She puts Edward in her father's room and Ruth in the other and helps Louisa drag her luggage up the stairs.

Louisa pours two measures of duty-free vodka into glasses and talks about the improvements she has made to the house in England Betty has never seen. She describes the satin floor-length curtains in the living room, which cost £25 a yard, the velvet headboards, the dishwasher that sterilises the dishes and the tumble dryer that means she doesn't have to race out to the line every time a drop of rain falls.

'No wonder Stanley's working,' Betty says, and sips the vodka. She doesn't care for the taste; it reminds her of the holy water she drank as a child, thinking it would cure her stomach aches.

'Don't you miss Daddy?' Louisa says suddenly. 'He always had such a warm welcome for us.'

Betty gives her a straight look, feels the ache in her arms after the four days' work.

'Oh. I don't mean you –'

'I know what you mean,' Betty says. 'No, I don't really miss him. He was so contrary towards the end. Going out to the fields and talking about death. But then, you brought out the sweeter side of him.'

Her father used to hold Louisa in a tight embrace when she arrived home, then stood back to look at her. He used to tell Betty to keep fig rolls in the house because she had a taste for figs. Nothing was ever too good for Louisa.

Now she unpacks her clothes, holding them up for Betty to admire. There's a linen dress with pink butterflies swooping towards the tail, a glittery scarf, a burgundy lace slip, a cashmere jacket, leather peep-toe shoes. She takes the cap off a bottle of American perfume and holds it out for Betty to sniff, but she does not spray a sample on her wrist. Louisa's clothes have the luxurious feel of money. The hems are deep, the linings satin, her shoes have leather insoles. She takes a covetous pride in her belongings, but then Louisa has always been the fashionable one.

Before she went to England Louisa got a job housekeeping for a rich woman in Killiney. Once, Betty took the train to Dublin to spend a day with her. When Louisa saw her at Heuston station with her country suit and her brown handbag, she whipped the handbag from her hands, fast as greased lightning, and said 'Where do you think you're going with that old thing?' and pushed it down in her shopping bag.

Now she sits at the dressing table, singing an old Latin hymn while Betty brushes her hair. Betty listens to her girlish voice and, catching a glimpse of their reflection in the mirror, realises that nobody would ever suspect they were sisters. Louisa with her gold hair and emerald earrings, looking so much younger than her years: Betty with her brown hair and her man's hands and the age showing so plainly on her face.

'Chalk and cheese' was the phrase their mother used.

Discuss

Imagine if Betty could go back in time and change her actions. What do you think she would do differently?

Understand

1. Betty lives in 'the big house'. Describe her house in your own words.
2. How does Betty feel since the death of her father?
3. The sisters are described as 'chalk and cheese'. What does this suggest about them?

Explore

1. What words would you use to describe Louisa? Explain your choice.
2. What words would you use to describe Betty? Explain your choice.
3. Why do you think Louisa and Betty are so different from one another?
4. **(a)** This story uses both the past and the present tense. Find an example of a sentence that is written in **(i)** the past tense and **(ii)** the present tense.

   (b) Why does the story change tenses?
 5. Is the setting clearly described by the author? Where exactly does the story take place and how does she bring it to life?
6. Choose one description that you think describes the setting of this story well and explain why you like it.

Create

1. Write your own ending to the story. What do you think might happen next, based on what you have learned about Louisa and Betty?
2. In pairs, assume the roles of Louisa and Betty. How would you express your feelings towards your sister? Act out the conversation you might have.
3. Prepare a two-minute oral presentation on the topic of family and make your presentation to your classmates. (For information on how to make a presentation see page 22.)
 4. Research and organise a class debate on the following motion: *This house believes that children should have to care for their elderly parents.* (For information on debates see pages 47–48.)

In Neil Gaiman's graphic novel *Coraline*, Coraline, a young girl, is bored at home and is fed up with her parents ignoring her. She finds a hidden door in her new house that leads to an alternate world. There are similarities with her world, but it seems a lot more appealing to Coraline.

Coraline

Understand

1. Explain what is happening in each frame in your own words.
2. From the images in the bottom three frames, how can you tell that Coraline is going through the door?

 Explore

Identify three details from the frames to suggest that what lies beyond the door is a mystery.

 Create

1. Imagine what happens when Coraline goes through the door. Create five questions that you would ask the author about what happens next.
2. Write a paragraph continuing the story after Coraline goes through the door. Use the following headings to help you:
   ◖ setting
   ◖ problem or crisis that might occur
   ◖ a character she might meet.

Focus on ... narrative voice

The **narrative voice** is the voice or perspective a story is told through.

In Unit 1 you learned about personal writing. Personal writing is always written in the first person (I), meaning that you are talking about yourself (I saw, I experienced). This is called a first-person narrative. For example:

> 'August 25, 1991
>
> Dear Friend,
>
> I am writing to you because she said you listen and understand.'
>
> (Stephen Chbosky, *Perks of Being a Wallflower*)

This is written in the form of a letter, and the first word is 'I'. We call this a first-person narrative, meaning the narrator is a character within the story.

In third-person narratives the story is told by an unknown narrator who is not involved in the story. For example:

> 'Vincent Sheils had two main claims to fame. He could put his left leg behind his head and stick the big toe into his right ear. And he'd once met Muhammad Ali.'
> (Roddy Doyle, 'Vincent')

This extract is written about a person named Vincent Sheils. Vincent himself is not telling the story.

Explore

 Work in pairs to list the advantages and disadvantages in using a first-person narrative voice and a third-person narrative voice.

Read the following short story by Tobias Wolff.

Powder

Just before Christmas my father took me skiing at Mount Baker. He'd had to fight for the privilege of my company, because my mother was still angry with him for sneaking me into a nightclub during his last visit, to see Thelonious Monk.

He wouldn't give up. He promised, hand on heart, to take good care of me and have me home for dinner on Christmas Eve, and she relented. But as we were checking out of the lodge that morning it began to snow, and in this snow he observed some rare quality that made it necessary for us to get in one last run. We got in several last runs. He was indifferent to my fretting. Snow whirled around us in bitter, blinding squalls, hissing like sand, and still we skied. As the lift bore us to the peak yet again, my father looked at his watch and said, 'Criminy. This'll have to be a fast one.'

By now I couldn't see the trail. There was no point in trying. I stuck to him like white on rice and did what he did and somehow made it to the bottom without sailing off a cliff. We returned our skis and my father put chains on the Austin-Healey while I swayed from foot to foot, clapping my mittens and wishing I was home. I could see everything. The green tablecloth, the plates with the holly pattern, the red candles waiting to be lit.

We passed a diner on our way out. 'You want some soup?' my father asked. I shook my head. 'Buck up,' he said. 'I'll get you there. Right, doctor?'

I was supposed to say, 'Right, doctor,' but I didn't say anything.

A state trooper waved us down outside the resort. A pair of sawhorses were blocking the road. The trooper came up to our car and bent down to my father's window. His face was bleached by the cold. Snowflakes clung to his eyebrows and to the fur trim of his jacket and cap.

'Don't tell me,' my father said.

The trooper told him. The road was closed. It might get cleared, it might not. Storm took everyone by surprise. So much, so fast. Hard to get people moving. Christmas Eve. What can you do.

My father said, 'Look. We're talking about five, six inches. I've taken this car through worse than that.'

The trooper straightened up. His face was out of sight but I could hear him. 'The road is closed.'

My father sat with both hands on the wheel, rubbing the wood with his thumbs. He looked at the barricade for a long time. He seemed to be trying to master the idea of it. Then he thanked the trooper, and with a weird, old-maidy show of caution turned the car around. 'Your mother will never forgive me for this,' he said.

'We should have left before,' I said. 'Doctor.'

He didn't speak to me again until we were in a booth at the diner, waiting for our burgers. 'She won't forgive me,' he said. 'Do you understand? Never.'

'I guess,' I said, but no guesswork was required; she wouldn't forgive him.

'I can't let that happen.' He bent toward me. 'I'll tell you what I want. I want us all to be together again. Is that what you want?'

'Yes, sir.'

He bumped my chin with his knuckles. 'That's all I needed to hear.'

When we finished eating he went to the pay phone in the back of the diner, then joined me in the booth again. I figured he'd called my mother, but he didn't give a report. He sipped at his coffee and stared out the window at the empty road. 'Come on, come on,' he said, though not to me. A little while later he said it again. When the trooper's car went past, lights flashing, he got up and dropped some money on the check. 'Okay. Vamanos.'

The wind had died. The snow was falling straight down, less of it now and lighter. We drove away from the resort, right up to the barricade. 'Move it,' my father told me. When I looked at him he said, 'What are you waiting for?' I got out and dragged one of the sawhorses aside, then put it back after he drove through. He pushed the door open for me. 'Now you're an accomplice,' he said. 'We go down together.' He put the car into gear and gave me a look. 'Joke, son.'

Down the first long stretch I watched the road behind us, to see if the trooper was on our tail. The barricade vanished. Then there was nothing but snow: snow on the road, snow kicking up from the chains, snow on the trees, snow in the sky; and our trail in the snow. Then I faced forward and had a shock. The lay of the road behind us had been marked by our own tracks, but there were no tracks ahead of us. My father was breaking virgin snow between a line of tall trees. He was humming 'Stars Fell on Alabama'. I felt snow brush along the floorboards under my feet. To keep my hands from shaking I clamped them between my knees.

My father grunted in a thoughtful way and said, 'Don't ever try this yourself.'

'I won't.'

'That's what you say now, but someday you'll get your license and then you'll think you can do anything. Only you won't be able to do this. You need, I don't know—a certain instinct.'

'Maybe I have it.'

'You don't. You have your strong points, but not this. I only mention it because I don't want you to get the idea this is something just anybody can do. I'm a great driver. That's not a virtue, okay? It's just a fact, and one you should be aware of. Of course you have to give the old heap some credit, too. There aren't many cars I'd try this with. Listen!'

I did listen. I heard the slap of the chains, the stiff, jerky rasp of the wipers, the purr of the engine. It really did purr. The old heap was almost new. My father couldn't afford it, and kept promising to sell it, but here it was.

I said, 'Where do you think that policeman went to?'

'Are you warm enough?' He reached over and cranked up the blower. Then he turned off the wipers. We didn't need them. The clouds had brightened. A few sparse, feathery flakes drifted into our slipstream and were swept away. We left the trees and entered a broad field of snow that ran level for a while and then tilted sharply downward. Orange stakes had been planted at intervals in two parallel lines and my father steered a course between them, though they were far enough apart to leave considerable doubt in my mind as to exactly where the road lay. He was humming again, doing little scat riffs around the melody.

'Okay then. What are my strong points?'

'Don't get me started,' he said. 'It'd take all day.'

'Oh, right. Name one.'

'Easy. You always think ahead.'

True, I always thought ahead. I was a boy who kept his clothes on numbered hangers to insure proper rotation. I bothered my teachers for homework assignments far ahead of their due dates so I could draw up schedules. I thought ahead, and that was why I knew that there would be other troopers waiting for us at the end of our ride, if we even got there. What I did not know was that my father would wheedle and plead his way past them—he didn't sing 'O Tannenbaum', but just about—and get me home for dinner, buying a little more time before my mother decided to make the split final. I knew we'd get caught; I was resigned to it. And maybe for this reason I stopped moping and began to enjoy myself.

Why not? This was one for the books. Like being in a speedboat, only better. You can't go downhill in a boat. And it was all ours. And it kept coming, the laden trees, the unbroken surface of snow, the sudden white vistas. Here and there I saw hints of the road, ditches, fences, stakes, but not so many that I could have found my way. But then I didn't have to. My father was driving. My father in his forty-eighth year, rumpled, kind, bankrupt of honor, flushed with certainty. He was a great driver. All persuasion, no coercion. Such subtlety at the wheel, such tactful pedalwork. I actually trusted him. And the best was yet to come — switchbacks and hairpins impossible to describe. Except maybe to say this: if you haven't driven fresh powder, you haven't driven.

Understand

1. Is this first-person or third-person narrative?
2. In the case of each of the following, write the letter corresponding to the correct answer in your copy.
   (a) At what time of year is this story set?
      i. winter   **ii.** summer   **iii.** autumn
   (b) The boy's parents are:
      i. married   **ii.** living together   **iii.** separated
   (c) The boy's father is:
      i. 49   **ii.** 48   **iii.** 47
   (d) An Austin-Healy is a type of:
      i. motorbike   **ii.** snowplough   **iii.** car
3. What do you learn about the narrator's father in the first few lines?
4. What words would you use to describe the boy's father, based on his actions and behaviour?

Explore

1. What kind of mood is created in this passage? Does it change at all? Give reasons for your answer.
 2. What impression do you get of the relationship between the narrator's mother and father?
3. What do you gain from hearing the story from the boy's perspective?
4. How would the story differ if it were told from the father's point of view?

Create

 1. **(a)** Reread the paragraph starting 'When we finished eating he went to the pay phone ...' up until 'Okay. Vamanos.' Rewrite this paragraph, imagining that the father is the narrator of the story, in the space provided on page 40 of your Portfolio.

    (b) Insight is when we gain a deeper understanding into someone or something. What kind of insight might we get into the father's character from writing this passage from his point of view? Write a few sentences reflecting on this in the space provided on page 40 of your Portfolio.
2. Imagine you are the boy's mother. Write the phone conversation that might have taken place between you and the boy's father.
3. Think of a time when you broke the rules. How did you feel? Scared? Excited? Write a personal essay describing your feelings. (For information on personal essays see pages 28–29.)

Writing fiction checklist

Opening	✓ Dramatic and exciting ✓ Attention grabbing ✓ Clear introduction of setting
Plot structure	✓ Situation ✓ Complication ✓ Problem or crisis point ✓ Resolution
Setting	✓ Brings the scene to life ✓ Appeals to all five senses ✓ Explains where and when the story takes place
Character	✓ Show, do not tell ✓ Behaviour and actions ✓ Clothing and appearance ✓ Interesting characters make interesting stories
Narrator	✓ Who is telling the story ✓ First-person narrative (I) ✓ Third-person narrative (he/she/they) ✓ Allows us insight into the character telling their story

Revising fiction

Reflect and review

1. Look back at the images at the top of page 125.
   (a) Which image best represents the unit, in your opinion?
   (b) Which image least represents the unit, in your opinion?
   (c) Think of some alternative images that could be used to represent this unit now that you have completed it.
2. Fill in the unit review on page 41 of your Portfolio.

Language skills

1. Find synonyms for the following words:
   ◖ neat
   ◖ money
   ◖ method.

2. Change the following sentences by inserting synonym(s) where possible.
   (a) 'Tidy up your desk!' shouted the teacher.
   (b) We had such a fantastic time at the show.
   (c) 'I don't believe you,' she answered in an angry voice.
   (d) Their house will be big, with a long garden and stunning flowers.

3. Identify the verbs in the following sentences, then name the tense.
   (a) The teacher explained that we should edit our work.
   (b) I walk into my driveway and a huge black car drives in behind me.
   (c) The dog barked loudly at the robber.
   (d) I live beside the sea and walk on the beach every day.

4. Look up the following words in your dictionary then put each into a sentence:
   ◖ haphazard
   ◖ tenuous.

Oral assessment

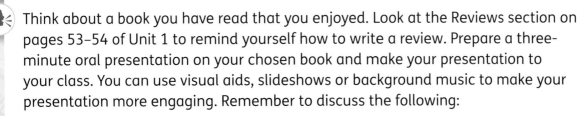

Think about a book you have read that you enjoyed. Look at the Reviews section on pages 53–54 of Unit 1 to remind yourself how to write a review. Prepare a three-minute oral presentation on your chosen book and make your presentation to your class. You can use visual aids, slideshows or background music to make your presentation more engaging. Remember to discuss the following:

◖ what the story is about (no spoilers!)
◖ favourite character and why
◖ strengths and weaknesses
◖ recommendations.

Written assessment

1. **(a)** Write a short story in the space provided on pages 42–43 of your Portfolio inspired by one of the following:

   ◖ 'You just don't get it!' Write a story featuring this line.
   ◖ Write a story beginning with the line: 'I knew straight away that it had been a mistake, but there was no going back.'
   ◖ Write a story featuring two characters in a car.
   ◖ My favourite time of the day.
   ◖ At the beach.

   (b) Use the writing fiction checklist on page 171 to help you to edit the first draft of your story. When you are happy with your story, write your second draft in the space provided on pages 87–89 of your Portfolio.

Unit 4

Stage and Screen

Why study this area?

In Unit 3 the focus was on stories, and how stories can be brought to life using many techniques. In this unit, we will be focusing on drama, television and film. Even if you have limited experience of the theatre, it is vital to gain an understanding of this genre so you can appreciate and evaluate the drama on your course. Most people have a favourite film, and in this unit we will discover how some of the best film and television productions were created. Studying this unit will give you a chance to be a part of the artistic process, from the production team to acting.

Learning intentions

◖ Discuss reactions to pieces of theatre and film.

◖ Read and actively engage with scripts.

◖ Participate in group reading and improvisation activities.

◖ Present views and opinions in a clear way.

◖ Understand and use key terms referring to stage and screen.

◖ Write, direct and perform your own work.

◖ Analyse moving images and production techniques.

◖ Recognise and learn how to use adverbs.

 Discuss

1. Look at the images above. Which image best represents stage and which image best represents screen, in your opinion?

2. Name some plays you have seen or heard of.

3. Name some films you have seen recently.

4. Some stories have been made into both plays and films. Can you name any?

5. Some plays or films are based on novels. Can you name any?

6. Think of some stories that have both novel and film versions. Which one was better, in your opinion?

7. Why was the novel/film version better?

8. What are the main differences between plays and films?

9. What are the main similarities between plays and films?

Introducing stage and screen

There are many similarities, but also many differences between stories that take place on stage and stories that are shown on screen.

In stage productions, stories are written in the form of scripts. Actors are given these scripts and they act the story out on stage, under the guidance of the director and with the support of the production team. The final performance takes place in front of a live audience and cannot be edited. This is called a **play**.

On screen, stories are written as screenplays, and again actors act out the story as characters, under the guidance of a director. The story is produced in front of a camera, not on a stage. Unlike a stage production, actors have many opportunities to get it right, as each scene is filmed again and again, from different viewpoints and angles. The material is then edited together and the result is a **film**.

In this unit we will see how stories can be brought to life on the stage or screen. You will encounter a variety of performances for both stage and screen over the course of your Junior Cycle. You may not be familiar with many plays, but you may have been involved in some other form of artistic performance (music or dance) or seen a musical or pantomime.

There are many different techniques that are used to help create a play or a film. Look out for the Focus on ... boxes, which are used every time you are introduced to a new technique or term. When you see these boxes, be sure to add the definition to the glossary on pages 1–2 of your Portfolio.

Explore

1. Think of a film or play you have seen recently. Write a paragraph describing your chosen film or play under one of the following headings.

   ◖ Actors
   ◖ Setting
   ◖ Director
   ◖ Characters
   ◖ Stage directions
   ◖ Camera
   ◖ Scene

   ◖ Script
   ◖ Production
   ◖ Narrator
   ◖ Costumes
   ◖ Lighting
   ◖ Sound effects

2. 'I regard the theatre as the greatest of all art forms, the most immediate way in which a human being can share with another the sense of what it is to be a human being.' (Oscar Wilde)

   Even if you have little experience of the theatre, do you agree with this quote?

Investigate

1. Think of your favourite actor. Find out what plays and/or films they have appeared in throughout their career.

2. Look up the following titles and find out which are plays, which are films and which are both.

   ◖ *The Importance of Being Earnest*
   ◖ *Pitch Perfect*
   ◖ *Macbeth*
   ◖ *The Beauty Queen of Leenane*
   ◖ *X-Men: Apocalypse*

   ◖ *Mrs Doubtfire*
   ◖ *All My Sons*
   ◖ *Romeo and Juliet*
   ◖ *Les Miserables*

Create

Write a paragraph about your own experience of either theatre or film. Complete the following sentences to get you started:

◖ The first film/play I saw was ...
◖ My favourite play/film is ...
◖ I like going to the theatre/cinema because ...

Read the following blog post by Scottish acting coach Mel Churcher.

The differences between stage and screen acting

Screen acting and theatre acting have differences.

Here are my big three:

The first and most important is often the last one that actors think about and yet the most crucial: In theatre, there is an audience. In film, at the moment of acting, there is no audience. Sounds obvious. Yet understanding this will have a deep, subtle effect on your work. On stage, you always share with people out there in the darkness. There is interplay between you and the audience – the observers and the observed. When filming, you are surrounded by technicians, but they are not your audience. Only a few key people like the director, the producer, script supervisor and sound crew are even wearing headphones to hear what you are saying! The camera, certainly, isn't your audience. It's a recording device that will document your acting life. (Which will be cut and pasted at your director's discretion and shown on a screen much later if you are lucky.) You must open yourself up to it, to be minutely scrutinised by it, but you 'share' with it at your peril. Once you help us to understand your subtext or the story, you will seem false. You have to find your 'real' life and surroundings within this weird world full of cameras, microphones and people – to be a child again and believe, in the moment of acting, that there is no one else there but the other roles inhabiting this 'reality' with you. You need to think hard at every moment and drive what you (in the role) need. But not add anything else. The camera will see your thoughts. Thinking (without 'showing') is enough and you have to trust it. You mustn't add 'sub-titles'. All you can do is 'be in the moment' of acting. We will see genuine emotion. Your eyes literally shine with all the thoughts that light them up. Too often, this light dims when an actor is speaking learnt text. All the thoughts, memories and pictures in your head need to be as specific and extra-ordinary as they are in life. You need life and humour in your eyes. You must be as multi-dimensional and interesting as real complex human beings are – as you are!

Next – film is shot out of order. You may bury your lover before you've met them or murder your boss before the interview. Each scene is done from many different angles (or set-ups). The bigger the production, the more set-ups there will be. Each set-up can involve many takes and each take needs to be fresh and spontaneous. So film takes tremendous imagination and focus, not to mention, stamina.

Which brings me to rehearsal. Or rather the lack of it. There's not much rehearsal for film well, not as we know it in theatre. And, until you arrive on set for shooting, you may never have rehearsed with, or even met, the actors with whom you are going to play the scene. You need to do a tremendous amount of preparation before you get to that set. But it must be the right kind. It is you as if you were in that situation or living in that time. And that 'as if' could mean a complete change of physicality, depending on the life you've led in the role. You might be a medieval peasant or an astronaut. Who am I and Where am I? must take the life you've led and the period into account. And you have to reach it organically through research, physical work and specific imagination. At a deep level, you have to, truly, inhabit that imagined world. What do I want in the role? Your needs must be powerful and strong. These needs may be hidden to the other characters (that's sub-text), but strong needs must drive you. Beware of deciding how you get what you want or how you say the lines. If you plot a course or decide how to play the scene, you will not be open to react in the moment. Turn off the director in your head. You don't know what the others will bring yet. You need to stay open to all possibilities. When you were a child, you didn't say, 'Now, I'm going to show you a character called Superman, who can fly'. You said, 'I'm Superman! I can fly' and you must think like that with your roles.

Discuss

1. Have you ever been to the theatre or have you ever been part of a stage production? Share your experiences.
2. Can you think of a particular performance by an actor that impressed you?

Understand

In the case of each of the following, write the letter corresponding to the correct answer in your copy.

1. What is Mel Churcher's profession?
   (a) Costume designer   **(b)** Director   **(c)** Acting coach

2. What type of text is this?
   (a) Blog post   **(b)** Interview   **(c)** Diary

3. What two forms of performance are being compared?
   (a) Theatre and film   **(b)** Theatre and dance   **(c)** Film and music

Explore

1. What are the three main differences between acting in a film and in a play?
 2. Do you think Mel Churcher is an experienced acting coach? How do you know?
3. If you were an actor, which type of production would you prefer to act in – stage or film? Explain your choice.
4. What do you think is the biggest challenge facing actors moving from one type of acting to the other?

Create

 Assume the role of a well-known actor in a film or play you have seen. Write a blog detailing your imagined experiences of the filming, rehearsing and performing of your film/play in the space provided on page 44 of your Portfolio. (For information on blogs see page 11.)

Stage

The following is an extract from Act Two of *Pygmalion* by George Bernard Shaw. Professor Henry Higgins is a speech and language expert. He met Eliza Doolittle the previous day selling flowers on a street corner. He took notes on her accent, which he regards as common and uneducated. The next day she tracks him down at his home.

Pay attention to the words in *italics*. These are instructions from the playwright, explaining how the action should play out.

Pygmalion

Next day at 11 a.m. Higgins's laboratory in Wimpole Street. It is a room on the first floor, looking on the street, and was meant for the drawing room. The double doors are in the middle of the back wall; and persons entering find in the corner to their right two tall file cabinets at right angles to one another against the wall. In this corner stands a flat writing-table, on which are a phonograph, a laryngoscope, a row of tiny organ pipes with a bellows, a set of lamp chimneys for singing flames with burners attached to a gas plug in the wall by an indiarubber tube, several tuning-forks of different sizes, a life-size image of half a human head, shewing in section the vocal organs, and a box containing a supply of wax cylinders for the phonograph.

Further down the room, on the same side, is a fireplace, with a comfortable leather-covered easy-chair at the side of the hearth nearest the door, and a coal-scuttle. There is a clock on the mantelpiece. Between the fireplace and the phonograph table is a stand for newspapers.

On the other side of the central door, to the left of the visitor, is a cabinet of shallow drawers. On it is a telephone and the telephone directory. The corner beyond, and most of the side wall, is occupied by a grand piano, with the keyboard at the end furthest from the door, and a bench for the player extending the full length of the keyboard. On the piano is a dessert dish heaped with fruit and sweets, mostly chocolates.

The middle of the room is clear. Besides the easy-chair, the piano bench, and two chairs at the phonograph table, there is one stray chair. It stands near the fireplace. On the walls, engravings; mostly Piranesis and mezzotint portraits. No paintings.

Pickering is seated at the table, putting down some cards and a tuning-fork which he has been using. Higgins is standing up near him, closing two or three file drawers which are hanging out. He appears in the morning light as a robust, vital, appetizing sort of man of forty or thereabouts, dressed in a professional-looking black frock-coat with a white linen collar and black silk tie. He is of the energetic, scientific type, heartily, even violently interested in everything that can be studied as a scientific subject, and careless about himself and other people, including their feelings. He is, in fact, but for his years and size, rather like a very impetuous baby 'taking notice' eagerly and loudly, and requiring almost as much watching to keep him out of unintended mischief. His manner varies from genial bullying when he is in a good humor to stormy petulance when anything goes wrong: but he is so entirely frank and void of malice that he remains likeable even in his least reasonable moments.

bellows: tool that emits air when squeezed

shewing: showing

coal-scuttle: container for coal

Piranesis: a famous artist

mezzotint: a type of print

genial: good-natured

malice: spite

Higgins: [*as he shuts the last drawer*] Well, I think that's the whole show.

Pickering: It's really amazing. I haven't taken half of it in, you know.

Higgins: Would you like to go over any of it again?

Pickering: [*rising and coming to the fireplace, where he plants himself with his back to the fire*] No, thank you: not now. I'm quite done up for this morning.

Higgins: [*following him, and standing beside him on his left*] Tired of listening to sounds?

Pickering: Yes. It's a fearful strain. I rather fancied myself because I can pronounce twenty-four distinct vowel sounds; but your hundred and thirty beat me. I can't hear a bit of difference between most of them.

Higgins: [*chuckling, and going over to the piano to eat sweets*] Oh, that comes with practice. You hear no difference at first; but you keep on listening, and presently you find they're all as different as A from B. [*Mrs Pearce looks in: she is Higgins's housekeeper*] What's the matter?

Mrs Pearce: [*hesitating, evidently perplexed*] A young woman asks to see you, sir.

Higgins: A young woman! What does she want?

Mrs Pearce: Well, sir, she says you'll be glad to see her when you know what she's come about. She's quite a common girl, sir. Very common indeed. I should have sent her away, only I thought perhaps you wanted her to talk into your machines. I hope I've not done wrong; but really you see such queer people sometimes – you'll excuse me, I'm sure, sir –

Higgins: Oh, that's all right, Mrs Pearce. Has she an interesting accent?

Mrs Pearce: Oh, something dreadful, sir, really. I don't know how you can take an interest in it.

Higgins: [*to Pickering*] Let's have her up. Shew her up, Mrs Pearce [*he rushes across to his working table and picks out a cylinder to use on the phonograph*].

Mrs Pearce: [*only half resigned to it*] Very well, sir. It's for you to say. [*She goes downstairs*].

Higgins: This is rather a bit of luck. I'll shew you how I make records. We'll set her talking: and I'll take it down first in Bell's Visible Speech; then in broad Romic; and then we'll get her on the phonograph so that you can turn her on as often as you like with the written transcript before you.

Mrs Pearce: [*returning*] This is the young woman, sir.

The flower girl enters in state. She has a hat with three ostrich feathers, orange, sky-blue, and red. She has a nearly clean apron and the shoddy coat has been tidied a little. The pathos of this deplorable figure, with its innocent vanity and consequential air, touches Pickering, who has already straightened himself in the presence of Mrs Pearce. But as to Higgins, the only distinction he makes between men and women is that when he is neither bullying nor exclaiming to the heavens against some featherweight cross, he coaxes women as a child coaxes its nurse when it wants to get anything out of her.

pathos:
something that makes you sad or feel pity

deplorable:
shockingly bad; disgraceful

consequential:
significant or important

Higgins: [*brusquely, recognizing her with unconcealed disappointment, and at once, babylike, making an intolerable grievance of it*] Why, this is the girl I jotted down last night. She's no use: I've got all the records I want of the Lisson Grove lingo; and I'm not going to waste another cylinder on it. [*To the girl*] Be off with you: I don't want you.

The flower girl: Don't you be so saucy. You ain't heard what I come for yet. [*To Mrs Pearce, who is waiting at the door for further instructions*] Did you tell him I come in a taxi?

Mrs Pearce: Nonsense, girl! what do you think a gentleman like Mr Higgins cares what you came in?

The flower girl:	Oh, we are proud! He ain't above giving lessons, not him: I heard him say so. Well, I ain't come here to ask for any compliment; and if my money's not good enough I can go elsewhere.
Higgins:	Good enough for what?
The flower girl:	Good enough for ye-oo. Now you know, don't you? I'm come to have lessons, I am. And to pay for 'em te-oo: make no mistake.
Higgins:	[*stupent*] Well!!! [*Recovering his breath with a gasp*] What do you expect me to say to you?
The flower girl:	Well, if you was a gentleman, you might ask me to sit down, I think. Don't I tell you I'm bringing you business?
Higgins:	Pickering: shall we ask this baggage to sit down or shall we throw her out of the window?
The flower girl:	[*running away in terror to the piano, where she turns at bay*] Ah-ah-oh-ow-ow-ow-oo! [*Wounded and whimpering*] I won't be called a baggage when I've offered to pay like any lady.

Motionless, the two men stare at her from the other side of the room, amazed.

Pickering:	[*gently*] What is it you want?
The flower girl:	I want to be a lady in a flower shop stead of sellin' at the corner of Tottenham Court Road. But they won't take me unless I can talk more genteel. He said he could teach me. Well, here I am ready to pay him – not asking any favor – and he treats me zif I was dirt.
Mrs Pearce:	How can you be such a foolish ignorant girl as to think you could afford to pay Mr Higgins?
The flower girl:	Why shouldn't I? I know what lessons cost as well as you do; and I'm ready to pay.
Higgins:	How much?

stupent: confused or shocked

The flower girl:	[*coming back to him, triumphant*] Now you're talking! I thought you'd come off it when you saw a chance of getting back a bit of what you chucked at me last night. [*Confidentially*] You'd had a drop in, hadn't you?
Higgins:	[*peremptorily*] Sit down.
The flower girl:	Oh, if you're going to make a compliment of it –
Higgins:	[*thundering at her*] Sit down.
Mrs Pearce:	[*severely*] Sit down, girl. Do as you're told.
The flower girl:	Ah-ah-ah-ow-ow-oo! [*She stands, half rebellious, half-bewildered*].
Pickering:	[*very courteous*] Won't you sit down? [*He places the stray chair near the hearthrug between himself and Higgins*].
The flower girl:	[*coyly*] Don't mind if I do. [*She sits down. Pickering returns to the hearthrug*].
Higgins:	What's your name?
The flower girl:	Liza Doolittle.
Higgins:	[*declaiming gravely*]

> Eliza, Elizabeth, Betsy and Bess.
>
> They went to the woods to get a bird's nes':

Pickering:	They found a nest with four eggs in it:
Higgins:	They took one apiece, and left three in it.

They laugh heartily at their own fun.

Liza:	Oh, don't be silly.
Mrs Pearce:	[*placing herself behind Eliza's chair*] You mustn't speak to the gentleman like that.
Liza:	Well, why won't he speak sensible to me?
Higgins:	Come back to business. How much do you propose to pay me for the lessons?
Liza:	Oh, I know what's right. A lady friend of mine gets French lessons for eighteen pence an hour from a real French gentleman. Well, you wouldn't have the face to ask me the same for teaching me my own language as you would for French; so I won't give more than a shilling. Take it or leave it.
Higgins:	[*walking up and down the room, rattling his keys and his cash in his pockets*] You know, Pickering, if you consider a shilling, not as a simple shilling, but as a percentage of this girl's income, it works out as fully equivalent to sixty or seventy guineas from a millionaire.
Pickering:	How so?
Higgins:	Figure it out. A millionaire has about £150 a day. She earns about half-a-crown.
Liza:	[*haughtily*] Who told you I only –
Higgins:	[*continuing*] She offers me two-fifths of her day's income for a lesson. Two-fifths of a millionaire's income for a day would be somewhere about £60. It's handsome. By George, it's enormous! it's the biggest offer I ever had.
Liza:	[*rising, terrified*] Sixty pounds! What are you talking about? I never offered you sixty pounds. Where would I get –
Higgins:	Hold your tongue.
Liza:	[*weeping*] But I ain't got sixty pounds. Oh –
Mrs Pearce:	Don't cry, you silly girl. Sit down. Nobody is going to touch your money.

peremptorily: with arrogance, or in a self-assured way

183

Higgins: Somebody is going to touch you, with a broomstick, if you don't stop snivelling. Sit down.

Liza: [*obeying slowly*] Ah-ah-ah-ow-oo-o! One would think you was my father.

Higgins: If I decide to teach you, I'll be worse than two fathers to you. Here [*he offers her his silk handkerchief*]!

Liza: What's this for?

Higgins: To wipe your eyes. To wipe any part of your face that feels moist. Remember: that's your handkerchief; and that's your sleeve. Don't mistake the one for the other if you wish to become a lady in a shop.

Liza, utterly bewildered, stares helplessly at him.

Mrs Pearce: It's no use talking to her like that, Mr. Higgins: she doesn't understand you. Besides, you're quite wrong: she doesn't do it that way at all [*she takes the handkerchief*].

Liza: [*snatching it*] Here! You give me that handkerchief. He gev it to me, not to you.

Pickering: [*laughing*] He did. I think it must be regarded as her property, Mrs Pearce.

Mrs Pearce: [*resigning herself*] Serve you right, Mr Higgins.

Pickering: Higgins: I'm interested. What about the ambassador's garden party? I'll say you're the greatest teacher alive if you make that good. I'll bet you all the expenses of the experiment you can't do it. And I'll pay for the lessons.

Liza: Oh, you are real good. Thank you, Captain.

Higgins: [*tempted, looking at her*] It's almost irresistible. She's so deliciously low – so horribly dirty –

Liza: [*protesting extremely*] Ah-ah-ah-ah-ow-ow-oo-oo!!! I ain't dirty: I washed my face and hands afore I come, I did.

Pickering: You're certainly not going to turn her head with flattery, Higgins.

Mrs Pearce: [*uneasy*] Oh, don't say that, sir: there's more ways than one of turning a girl's head; and nobody can do it better than Mr. Higgins, though he may not always mean it. I do hope, sir, you won't encourage him to do anything foolish.

Higgins: [*becoming excited as the idea grows on him*] What is life but a series of inspired follies? The difficulty is to find them to do. Never lose a chance: it doesn't come every day. I shall make a duchess of this draggletailed guttersnipe.

> follies: mistakes

Focus on ... stage directions

Stage directions are instructions written in a script that describe how the stage should look and how the actors should speak and behave.

Anything written in italics or in brackets is not said by the characters, but is included by the playwright in order to give instructions. We learn a lot about the characters in this scene from Shaw's stage directions.

Understand

1. Some of the equipment found in Mr Higgins's workroom is very obscure. Match each piece of equipment to the correct definition.

Phonograph	A flame burning within a tube and adjusted as to set the air within the tube in vibration, causing sound.
Laryngoscope	Two-pronged steel device used by musicians.
Tuning fork	A record player, able to record and produce sound.
Singing flame	An instrument for examining the larynx.

2. Based on the stage directions at the start of the scene, draw a labelled diagram of the laboratory.
3. What is Mr Higgins's major interest?
4. What simile is used to describe Mr Higgins in the opening stage directions?
5. What does the flower girl want from Mr Higgins?
6. What bet does Mr Higgins make with Mr Pickering?

Explore

1. What kind of person is Eliza Doolittle, in your opinion?
2. Mr Higgins has a lot to say in this scene. Choose three adjectives that you would use to describe him and explain your choices.
3. Choose one piece of stage direction and explain what it tells you about a particular character.

Create

1. Read the script on page 45 of your Portfolio and add your own stage directions in the spaces provided.
2. In groups of five, find a space in the classroom and assign each character (Mr Higgins, Mr Pickering, Mrs Pearse and Eliza Doolittle) to a person in the group. Do a read through of the script, using the space around you and any props that you have to hand. The member of the group who is not playing a character should observe the scene. This person should offer advice and instructions to the actors while they read the script. For example: How should a line be read? Any emotion? What kind of voice? What kind of facial expressions would you make? Should the actor move while speaking? In what way?

Adverbs

Adverbs are used to describe verbs (action words). They usually end in –ly.

Adverbs help to add more description and detail to your sentences.

She danced gracefully/beautifully/ awkwardly.

They spoke quietly/loudly/softly/ suddenly/nervously.

He ran quickly/hurriedly/ frantically/slowly.

Some adverbs do not end in -ly.
fast, never, better, often, almost

 Understand

1. Can you find any adverbs in the extract from *Pygmalion* on pages 183–184?
2. Add adverbs to the following sentences.
   (a) Tom ran to the shop.
   (b) The baby slept all night.
   (c) They looked at the stars.
   (d) Yasmin tiptoed along the corridor.
   (e) Helen spoke to the principal.
   (f) Kevin laughed at the joke.
   (g) The dogs barked at the stranger.
   (h) The teacher shouted across the yard.

 Grammar Primer: pages 33–34

The following extract is from *A Shop Selling Speech* by Sabrina Mahfouz. There is a lot of dialogue between the characters. Pay close attention to who is speaking, what they are saying and what this tells you about them.

The play is set in Cairo, Egypt. The characters in this scene are three robbers (Sara, Mahmoud and Sherif) and five workers (Fatima, Sahmia, Noura, Mo and Ahmed). It is set in a shop where speech tokens are sold. In this world, speech is not free and you must have a token to express yourself.

A Shop Selling Speech

Setting

The setting is a shop.

The time is the present day, whenever that may be, in Cairo, Egypt.

Events that are referred to throughout the play are not necessarily events of a particular date. History does have a tendency to repeat itself.

A dash (–) at the end of a sentence indicates that what follows should be overlapping, quick-paced.

Sara   Take me to the tokens.

Fatima *tries to get her mobile phone out.*

Sara   No, no phones. Mahmoud, Sherif, collect all of their phones now.

Mahmoud *and* **Sherif** *collect all the phones from the workers, who are very nervous.*

Sara   Take me to the tokens, *yalla.*

Fatima   I, I don't know where they are. Only my father knows. He owns the shop. I need to phone him.

Sara   I don't believe you. Your eyes are hard. Where are they, Hard-Eyes?

Fatima   Only my father knows –

Sara   I don't believe you –

Mahmoud   Neither do I –

Sherif   Or I –

Sara   Hard-Eyes is a liar –

Mahmoud   Liar –

Sherif   Liar –

Fatima *puffs up her chest, becoming angry.*

Fatima   I am not. And my name is Fatima. And ... and you don't scare me. We've all seen enough people with guns to know that you're all full of empty words and no action so –

Sara *puts the gun to* **Fatima***'s head. The workers gasp.* **Noura** *covers her eyes.* **Mo** *puts his arms around her.*

Sara   I am a woman of impeccable actions, my dear, do not test me.

Mahmoud   I have seen her slice the head from a chicken with her fingernails –

Sara *smiles and moves the gun away from* **Fatima***'s head and sits down on the desk/counter.* **Fatima** *remains standing.* **Sherif** *and* **Mahmoud** *flank* **Sara***.*

Sara	So, Fatima. If your father owns this shop, you must know where he keeps the speech tokens. This is a shop selling speech; I did come to the right place?
Fatima	Yes, it is. But no, I can't help you. All I know is that there is a safe, somewhere. My father is the only one who knows the code and the location.
Sara	Dubious and dubiouser my dear. But whatever the truth, it seems that *you* are the best way to access what I want.
	Now, for all of you. I just want to make it clear what we're doing here. We are not your regular, selfish robbers, we're not animals –
Sherif	We are not animals. We are doing righteous work –
Mahmoud	We are fighting for freedom –
Sara	For the right to speak –
Sherif	To speak loudly –
Mahmoud	To speak freely –
Sara	About freedom –
Sherif	(*looks up*) About heaven –
Mahmoud	(*looks towards* **Sara**) About love –
Sara	For too long, the right to speak has been given to the few and we are here to change that, to take it to the masses, to dance with words in the streets –

She twirls around and **Mahmoud** *and* **Sherif** *act as her 'dance' partners.*

The workers start to look at them differently – they're not really as scared any more. They begin to get restless. **Sahmia** *stands up, followed by the others.*

Sahmia	You speak quite a lot already, don't you, so what's the problem?

Sara *stops 'dancing' and twirls the gun to point at* **Sahmia**.

Sara	You are very mouthy for one who has a gun pointed at her head.
Sahmia	I've been in the front line too many times at too many protests to be scared of a little gun like that.

Sara   Ahh, a protestor, people. We have a protestor in the house –

Sahmia   An activist, actually and I have seen more deaths than all of you have had hot dinners –

Mahmoud   I don't think you know how much I like to eat –

Sara   A fighter, I like her. OK, OK. I feel I must win you all over with more than a gun, because you are also the workers, the masses. I want you to *want speech to be free*. You must want it, otherwise there's no point to anything, is there? Hard-Eyes, when does your father return?

Fatima   My name is Fatima. He probably won't come back for at least an hour, the traffic is a never-ending centipede in this city.

Sara   So, we wait.

Sherif   Excuse me sister.
              May I say that
              we Egyptians have waited for too long,
              always for someone
              to come back from somewhere
              to sort something out.
              Let's find and open the safe ourselves!

Sara   No. We wait. We do it as we planned.

Sherif   I am ready for the plan to change. I don't want to wait.

Sara   I said, we wait.

Sherif   Forgive me, sister, but I say you're wrong.

Sara *stares at him. Considers his rebellion. She aims her gun at him and snatches whatever weapon he has and hands it to* **Mahmoud**.

As she says the following, she ties **Sherif**'s *hands with cable ties from her pocket.*

Sara   Sherif, I am not your sister. I am your boss. I have been kind to you because you're always polite and quiet and your father knew my father. But I will not tolerate this sort of behaviour.

              Hard-Eyes, pass me some masking tape.

Sherif   Think about what you're doing here, sister –

Sara   Hard-Eyes?

Sherif   I am on your side –

Fatima   I don't think we have _

Sara   Stop lying, Hard-Eyes.

Fatima *passes* **Sara** *masking tape or similar.* **Sara** *starts taping up* **Sherif**'s *mouth as he struggles, but not too much to slow her down.*

Fatima   Are you sure he can breathe?

Sara   Would you like to swap places with him, Hard-Eyes? He wanted to destroy your shop. But I will swap him for you if you wish. Do you?

Fatima   No, no, I –

Sara   Right then. He'll remain here as a reminder to you all
              of how crazy I am,
              how much I believe in my plan,
              how very determined I am.

              Thank you for your assistance, Hard-Eyes. It would have been impossible without you.

She throws the tape back to **Fatima. Sherif** *is now tied up in some way/place.*

Sara Everyone listen.
I will tell you all how I plan
to give speech new homes in the mouths
of those held down on the ground for so long.
I will hope that you join my fight.
First, we must all remind ourselves what we are fighting against.
Peasants of the Shop Selling Speech, let me present –

The following is a quick-paced interruption, the first time the workers start to relax slightly as a group, maybe ironically emboldened by the fact that the group of robbers has lost cohesion. **Sara** *is surprised by the interruption, but interested to see where it goes.*

Sahmia We are not peasants, we're working here to make money to do things with our lives, to make our country great –

Noura I'm making money to get out of this country –

Mo Me too, I hate it here –

Ahmed Ah man, don't say that –

Mo I do –

Noura Mo, why do you hate it here?

Mo I hate it here because ... I'm scared all the time. I'm bored.
Everybody just smokes and gossips
and thinks that because they went out on the streets a few times
and it went on the news that they've lived a life,
but this isn't a life, this is just the same as before,
boring boring –

Sahmia So you think we shouldn't have went on the streets? Left things as they were?
Dictatorships and darkness and damning existences for the non-elites –

Ahmed Sahmia, I don't think he's saying that, you know, he's just frustrated, like most of us –

Mo No, I am saying that: it was a waste of time and now things are worse –

Sahmia Both of you bring shame to this country, *wallahi.*

Ahmed Come on, Sahmia, I was there, I fought –

Sahmia From your open-plan living room with your iPod in your ears! Not there, where it mattered –

Ahmed It mattered where I was too, I made things possible, don't try to make out like you're the only one who knows what they –

Noura What were you trying to do? I still don't know –

Mo I don't know –

Noura I just want to be in America –

Mo Me too! We could –

Sara Enough! We won't be saying that again today. You are not in America. And allahamdullah, because if you were, you would probably all have your own guns and I wouldn't be standing here right now.

Back to my plan.
While we wait for the patriarch to return
with the keys to the castle,
we remind ourselves of the mess freedom is in,
you awaken your senses and believe in me and my gun.
Let's begin! Let's show what is being shown to the people of Egypt.

wallahi:
(Arabic)
I swear by God

allahamdullah:
(Arabic)
praise God

patriarch:
male head
of a family

She presses play or makes actions indicating a show/screening is about to begin and a pre-recorded infomercial begins on a screen – or this could be acted out in a very over-the-top, cheesy way:

Man	(*voice recording*) Hello, people of Egypt. We, your democratically elected, well-connected, never knowingly rejected Government, would like to inform you of a new system being introduced to ensure everyone in this country gets their voice heard –
Woman	(*voice recording*) Yes, because we've heard that you weren't being heard and we heard how absurd this was from those who are better at words than us and so we bring you –
Both/Crowd	(*voice recording*) Speech tokens!
Man	(*voice recording*) Machines have been installed on the corners of all major streets!

The workers begin to briefly talk over the infomercial, overlapping each other:

Sahmia	The streets that we fought for –
Mo	The streets I don't want to walk down –
Noura	The streets that whistle at me and grab my sleeves –
Mo	I won't let anyone do that to –
Ahmed	The streets that don't see me –
Sara	The streets that we plan to make free –

They turn their attention back to the screen.

Woman	(*voice recording*) Oh my, they are so new and shiny! And look, the loudspeakers are the most modern in the Middle East! How do they work, I hear you say –
Man	(*voice recording*) Easy-peasy! Buy a speech token, stick it in the machine and there you have it, one two three – your voice will be heard for a maximum of sixty seconds per day. Free to say what you want to say!
Woman	(*voice recording*) I say the best thing is, nobody will be arrested or tortured or exiled or killed for their loudspeaker words, which is quite revolutionary.
Man	(*voice recording*) Quite revolutionary, indeed.
Both/Crowd	(*voice recording*) Buy your free speech now from recommended retailers!

The show ends. **Fatima** *claps. Nobody else joins in. They look a bit surprised.*

Sara	Thoughts, workers?
Fatima	I think this solution –
Sahima	I do not see that this government has created any solutions of any consequence –
Ahmed	But you had no solutions either, did you? Do you? If you'd have worked with us more, we could have helped you, the international community was waiting, was there –
Sahmia	The international community made the mess in the first place –

Ahmed They made Facebook too though, man, you got to work together –

Sahmia *huffs and turns away from* **Ahmed**. **Sara** *stops their conversation, stands in front of the workers, gun by her side.*

Sara How do you get the tokens to put into the machine, Fatima?

Fatima You have to buy them.

Sara From shops like this?

Fatima Yes.

Ahmed Also, there's an app that rewards you with them the less you go online, which is kind of a contradiction, I suppose, but –

Noura Yeah and I got one for baking cakes for this charity thing once but then when I put it in the machine it didn't work and I was shouting and shouting but nobody could hear me –

Sahmia Like you'd have anything to say anyway –

Mo Hey –

Sara So, Fatima. The only people in this country –
this revolutionised, game-changing country –
who have access to 'free' speech are ...
those who can pay for it
or those who are rewarded it by someone who the government approves of
for doing something the government approves of?

Fatima Yeah, I suppose.

Sara And still you don't see?

Fatima See what?

Focus on ... **props**

Props are moveable objects used in plays and films in order to help tell the story.

Props help the audience to better understand the story, as well as the characters. For example, in *A Shop Selling Speech* Sara has a gun to show that she is dangerous and threatening, and that the shop is under attack. Interesting props add to the entertainment value of a performance.

Understand

1. In the case of each of the following, write the letter corresponding to the correct answer in your copy.

    (a) Who are the robbers?
      i. Sahmia, Mo and Sara
      ii. Sherif, Fatima and Sara
      iii. Sara, Sherif and Mahmoud

    (b) What does the word 'dubious' mean?
      i. Irritating
      ii. Doubtful
      iii. Evil

2. List three props that are used in this scene.

Explore

1. Which one of the following words would you use to describe Sara? Explain your choice.
    ◀ Strong
    ◀ Intelligent
    ◀ Passionate
    ◀ Selfish
    ◀ Controlling

2. What kind of relationship do you think Sara has with Mahmoud?

3. Why does Sara decide to tie Sherif up?

4. Explain, in your own words, how the speech tokens work.

5. What do you learn about the characters based on their dialogue?

6. Choose one of the following words that you feel best completes the sentence: This is a play about ...
    ◀ freedom.
    ◀ human rights.
    ◀ equality.

    Explain your choice.

Investigate

Work with a partner to come up with three basic human rights. Use your research skills to find a place where these human rights are denied. Share your findings with the class.

Create

1. Design a poster advertising *A Shop Selling Speech*. You may want to include:
   ◖ images
   ◖ details about the play
   ◖ reviews or ratings.

 2. Carry out a class debate on one of the following motions:
   ◖ *This house believes that young people have the right to say and post what they want online.*

   OR

   ◖ *This house believes that everyone has the right to free speech.*

   (For information on debates see pages 47–48.)

 3. **(a)** Write a dialogue between two characters who are speaking freely about something they are passionate about in the space provided on page 46 of your Portfolio. For example:

   James: Rugby is too physical and too rough to be played by girls ... they would have to change the game completely to suit the players.

   Beth: I can't believe what I'm hearing! Of course it can be played by girls. Look at the Irish women's team and their huge success internationally.

   If you need help, use one of the following images to inspire you.

 (b) List some props that you would include to help bring your scene to life in the space provided on page 46 of your Portfolio.

Often, plays are adapted from novels. *Noughts & Crosses* is a novel by Malorie Blackman which has been adapted into a play by Dominic Cooke.

In this story, two young people, Callum and Sephy, struggle to maintain their close friendship across a racial divide. 'Noughts' are seen as second-class citizens, in a world run by the privileged 'Crosses'.

Callum and several other Noughts have just joined Sephy's school, which was previously only attended by Crosses.

In this scene, Callum's family discuss the events of the day over dinner.

Noughts & Crosses

Scene 5

Callum's house. At the dinner table.

Ryan	Are you OK, son? I went down to Heathcroft as soon as I heard what was going on, but the police wouldn't let me in.
Callum	Why not?
Ryan	I had 'no official business on the premises' – unquote.
	Pause.
	So how was school? How were your lessons, son?
Callum	It was fine, Dad.
	(Aside) Except that the teachers totally ignored us, and the Crosses used any excuse to bump into us and knock our books on the floor, and even the dinner ladies made sure they served everyone else in the queue before us.
Jude	You were on the telly. So was your little friend. The whole world heard what she said.
Callum	She didn't mean it like that.
Jude	She didn't mean it? That's what she told you, was it? How can you not mean to say something like that?
Meggie	I see Miss Sephy is turning out to be just like her mother.
Ryan	You're better off without that job.
Meggie	You don't have to tell me twice. I admit I miss the money but wouldn't go back for all the stars in space. Anyone who can put up with that stuck-up cow Mrs Hadley is a saint as far as I'm concerned.
Callum	You were friends once.
Meggie	Friends? We were never friends. She patronized me and I put up with it 'cause I needed a job – that's all.
Callum	*(Aside)* That wasn't how I remembered it.

Ryan clicks the remote control.

Ryan	Shush, everyone. The news is on.

*The **news reporter**, a Cross, enters the McGregors' kitchen, perhaps sitting at the table. When reading the news, the reporter speaks directly to the other characters on stage. This convention is used whenever the TV is watched. There is no TV set or video screen on stage.*

Reporter   (*To the family*) Today Kamal Hadley, Deputy Prime Minister, declared that there would be no hiding place, no safe haven for those noughts misguided enough to join the Liberation Militia.

(*To offstage*) Is it true, Mr Hadley, that your government's decision to allow selected noughts in our schools was a direct result of pressure from the Liberation Militia?

*Kamal enters the kitchen. The **reporter** turns to him.*

Kamal   Not at all. This government does not allow itself to be whitemailed by illegal terrorist groups. We acted on a Pangean Economic Community directive that the government had been on the verge of implementing anyway. Our decision to allow the crème-de-la-crème of nought youth to join our educational institutions makes sound social and economic sense.

Callum   (*Aside*) Pompous twit!

Kamal   The Liberation Militia are misguided terrorists and we will leave no stone unturned in our efforts to bring them to justice.

Jude   Long live the Liberation Militia!

Ryan   Too right, son.

Meggie   Shhh.

*Jude and **Ryan** look at each other.*

Reporter   There have been unconfirmed reports that the car bomb found outside the International Trade Centre last month was the work of the Liberation Militia. What attempts are being made to find those responsible?

Kamal   Our highest priority is to bring them to justice. Political terrorism which results in the death or serious injury of even one Cross always has been and always will be a capital crime. Those found guilty will suffer the death sentence …

*Sephy enters with her own remote, which she clicks. The **reporter** and **Kamal** leave the stage.*

Sephy   Politics, politics, politics. I've grown up with it rammed down my throat. I'm not interested in being caught up with it in any manner, shape or form, whether Dad is on the telly or not.

Focus on ... staging

<u>**Staging** is the way a play is presented on stage.</u>

Some details of a story are hard to portray on stage. We have already looked at props, now we must look at all the other elements that make the scene a reality on the stage. The director must carefully consider the use of the space and sometimes approach things in a creative and different way.

For example, read the stage direction at the bottom of page 195 beginning with the line: 'The news reporter, a Cross, enters the McGregors' kitchen, perhaps sitting at the table …' This is a technique used by the director or the playwright to deal with difficult props and complex scene changes on stage.

Discuss

1. Can you name anywhere in the world today where people are divided based on their skin colour?
2. Can you name any other stories, where two characters from completely different worlds try to build an unlikely relationship?
3. Having read this extract, would you prefer to read the novel or watch a stage performance of *Noughts & Crosses*?

Understand

1. Where does this scene from *Noughts & Crosses* take place?
2. Is each of the following characters a Nought or a Cross?
   - Callum
   - Sephy
   - Kamal Hadley
   - Meggie
3. What is Sephy's father's profession?
   (a) News reporter
   (b) President of the Liberation Militia
   (c) Deputy First Minister
4. Callum and his family are watching the broadcast live on television, but the audience see Kamal and the reporter standing on the stage beside them. What stage direction does the playwright use to show that the news broadcast is over?

Explore

1. Why doesn't Callum tell his Dad the truth about what happened at school?
2. What does the stage direction [Aside] mean? Why is this used?
 3. What kind of person do you imagine Mrs Hadley to be?
4. Why do you think the director chose not to put a television screen on the stage?
5. If you were directing this scene, what props would you include? Explain your choice.

 Investigate

1. Segregation has been a part of life for people all over the world for many years. In South Africa, for example, a policy called **Apartheid** existed from 1948 to 1991 (think back to the extract from Nelson Mandela's autobiography *Long Walk to Freedom* on page 20).

   (a) Find out as much as you can about this system and how it affected the people of South Africa.

   (b) Compare what school was like for children during that time in South Africa to your experience of school today.

 Create

 1. In pairs, write a paragraph stating how you would stage this scene if it were a film.

 2. 'Jude and Ryan look at each other.'
   Callum's father and brother seem to share similar political views. Work in pairs to write a dialogue that might take place between them about their views. When you have finished, act out your dialogue.

3. Write a letter to the president of Ireland, describing a form of discrimination that you feel exists today. Explain how you think this problem could be solved. (For information on formal letters see pages 35–36.)

William Shakespeare 1564—1616

William Shakespeare was born in Stratford-upon-Avon, England, in 1564. He is best known for his plays, but he was also an actor and poet. He wrote 39 plays and over 150 sonnets (a particular form of poetry).

Shakespeare's work was originally performed during the Elizabethan period in England. This was a period in the sixteenth century when England was under the rule of Queen Elizabeth I. It became a celebrated period in English history, as the country enjoyed success in both exploration and literature, giving rise to a new sense of national identity. Over 400 years later, Shakespeare's work is still studied and enjoyed by many people.

Understanding Shakespeare

Since Shakespeare wrote his plays over 400 years ago, some of the language is different to our modern English.

Some words are different. For example:

- thou/thee = you
- thy = your.

Some verbs have extra letters. For example:

- didst = did
- hath/hast = have/has
- wilt = will
- doth/dost = do/does
- speakst = speak
- thinkst = think.

Some words are combined. For example:

- 'twas = it was
- 'tis = it is
- is't = is it?

 Discuss

1. Can you name any of Shakespeare's plays or poems?
2. Can you name any films that are based on Shakespeare's plays?

 Understand

Using the information above as a guide, translate the following sentences into Shakespearean English:

1. Do you think of me?
2. Did you speak?
3. It was you!

 Investigate

1. Find out three interesting facts about William Shakespeare.
2. Name a famous English explorer from the Elizabethan period.
3. Find out the names of some other famous playwrights or poets of this time.

The following extract is from *Twelfth Night* by William Shakespeare.

In this extract Olivia is disappointed as she is in love with Cesario, who does not return her feelings (Cesario is actually a girl in disguise). Meanwhile, Malvolio, her uptight and strict servant, openly pines for Olivia, but she is distracted by her own unrequited love.

Others in the household decide to teach Malvolio a lesson and leave a forged letter for him to find, pretending that Olivia wants him to dress up in bizarre costume and act rudely towards the other servants in order to fully express his feelings and therefore win her over.

Twelfth Night

Act 3, Scene 4

OLIVIA's garden.

Enter OLIVIA and MARIA

OLIVIA (*aside*) I have sent after him, he says he'll come.
How shall I feast him? What bestow of him?
For youth is bought more oft than begged or borrowed.
I speak too loud.
(*To Maria*) Where's Malvolio? He is sad and civil,
And suits well for a servant with my fortunes.
Where is Malvolio?

MARIA He's coming, madam, but in very strange manner.
He is sure possessed, madam.

OLIVIA Why, what's the matter, does he rave?

MARIA No, madam, he does nothing but smile. Your ladyship were best to have some guard about you if he come, for sure the man is tainted in's wits.

OLIVIA Go call him hither.

As MARIA goes to call him, enter MALVOLIO, cross-gartered and wearing yellow stockings

I am as mad as he,
If sad and merry madness equal be.
How now, Malvolio!

MALVOLIO Sweet lady, ho, ho!

OLIVIA Smil'st thou? I sent for thee upon a sad occasion.

MALVOLIO Sad, lady? I could be sad. This does make some obstruction in the blood, this cross-gartering, but what of that? If it please the eye of one, it is with me as the very true sonnet is, 'Please one, and please all.'

OLIVIA	Why, how dost thou, man? What is the matter with thee?
MALVOLIO	Not black in my mind, though yellow in my legs. It did come to his hands, and commands shall be executed. I think we do know the sweet roman hand.
OLIVIA	Wilt thou go to bed, Malvolio?
MALVOLIO	'To bed? Ay, sweetheart, and I'll come to thee.'

He kisses his hand

OLIVIA	God comfort thee. Why dost thou smile so, and kiss thy hand so oft?
MARIA	How do you, Malvolio?
MALVOLIO	At your request? Yes, nightingales answer daws.
MARIA	Why appear you with this ridiculous boldness before my lady?
MALVOLIO	'Be not afraid of greatness' – 'twas well writ.
OLIVIA	What mean'st thou by that, Malvolio?
MALVOLIO	'Some are born great,' –
OLIVIA	Ha?
MALVOLIO	'Some achieve greatness' –
OLIVIA	What sayst thou?
MALVOLIO	'And some have greatness thrust upon them.'
OLIVIA	Heaven restore thee.
MALVOLIO	'Remember who commended thy yellow stockings' –
OLIVIA	'Thy yellow stockings'?
MALVOLIO	'And wished to see thee cross-gartered.'
OLIVIA	'Cross-gartered'?
MALVOLIO	'Go to, thou art made, if thou desir'st to be so.'
OLIVIA	Am I made?
MALVOLIO	'If not, let me see thee a servant still.'
OLIVIA	Why, this is very midsummer madness.

Enter a Servant

SERVANT	Madam, the young gentleman of the Count Orsino's is returned. I could hardly entreat him back. He attends your ladyship's pleasure.
OLIVIA	I'll come to him.

Exit Servant

> Good Maria, let this fellow be looked to. Where's my cousin Toby? Let some of my people have a special care of him, I would not have him miscarry for the half of my dowry.

Exeunt OLIVIA and MARIA, severally

---

sweet roman hand: handwriting

daws: jackdaws, a type of bird considered to be of low intelligence

cross-gartered: a garter is a band worn around the leg to hold up stockings, 'cross' suggests cross-dressing, or wearing clothes associated with the opposite gender

Focus on ... costume

A **costume** is the clothing worn by an actor when playing a role.

Costumes can tell us a lot about characters and can be an important part of telling the story. For example, a costume can tell us whether a character is rich or poor, or what time period a play is set in. Malvolio's bizarre costume shows the audience how much he loves Olivia, as he is willing to make himself look ridiculous to win her affections.

 Understand

In the case of each of the following, write the letter corresponding to the correct answer in your copy.

1. Malvolio is described as:
   - **(a)** mad.
   - **(b)** sad.
   - **(c)** witty.
2. Maria says that Malvolio:
   - **(a)** rants and raves.
   - **(b)** smiles all the time.
   - **(c)** cries all the time.
3. What strange clothing does Malvolio wear in order to prove his love?
   - **(a)** Orange socks
   - **(b)** A red hat
   - **(c)** Yellow stockings

 Explore

 1. Do you think that Olivia will return Malvolio's feelings? Explain your answer.
2. Without costumes, do you think this scene would have the same impact?
3. Would you like to read the rest of this play? Give reasons for your answer.

 Investigate

Find some images of Malvolio's costume in a production of your choice. Bring the pictures to class to discuss with your classmates.

 Create

1. Write the letter that Malvolio thought was from Olivia. Include all the strange things you want him to do. (For information on personal letters see pages 33–34.)
 2. In pairs, decide what kind of costume you would give Olivia if you were working in the wardrobe department. You can present the information either in a poster or by explaining your choice orally to your class.

Screen

So far, we have looked at areas of production that are common to both stage and screen. In film, costumes, movement, characters and props are all used in similar ways as on stage. Films also have production teams, who are tasked with similar jobs as in theatre.

Even though there are many similarities between screen production and stage production, the big difference is the camera. Scenes are captured with the use of cameras and the addition of sounds, light and special effects. Cameras can shoot images in a variety of ways, called shots. A few basic examples are:

- **close-up:** the camera is very near to the subject
- **long:** the subject seems far away from the camera
- **establishing:** the camera takes a wide shot, or moves so that the viewer can get a whole picture of where the scene takes place.

A shot continues until the camera cuts to a different angle or scene. These shots can then be edited and enhanced until the desired effect is achieved.

 Discuss

1. Think about something you watched on television or in the cinema recently. Were there any props? What costumes did the actors wear?

2. Can you think of any novels that have been made into plays or screenplays or both? (Think back to some of the extracts in this unit.)

Many actors have performed both on stage and on screen. Read the following extract from an interview with actor Saoirse Ronan, where she describes her own experiences of acting.

Saoirse Ronan on how *Brooklyn* is her own Irish-American journey

At just 12 years old, Saoirse Ronan was nominated for an Oscar, 10 years later she captivates in *Brooklyn*. Sheryl Garratt discusses her coming-of-age performance in a very personal film.

Saoirse Ronan has beautiful pale-blue eyes. Every director she has worked with has chosen to focus on this at some point, because they express so much. As Ian McEwan said of her breakthrough role in the film of his novel *Atonement*, 'She gives us thought processes right on screen, even before she speaks, and conveys so much with her eyes.' Which makes it all the more distressing when, during our meeting, they suddenly fill with tears.

I am telling her how much I enjoyed her latest film, *Brooklyn*, which went to Sundance Film Festival early this year as a small indie vying for attention and came out as an Oscar contender. Ronan ends up apologising for getting emotional. 'I've never worked as hard as that, and I definitely needed a bit of emotional support because it's too close to home,' she says.

'For people to respond to it as well as they have – I have to say it's a dream.' She has not seen the film, she admits later. 'I can't. Just talking about it, you can see I'm a basket case. In a couple of years, or when I have kids or something, we'll all sit and watch it together.'

Adapted by Nick Hornby from Colm Tóibín's novel, and directed by John Crowley, *Brooklyn* tells the story of Eilis Lacey, a shy Irish teenager who is forced to leave her family to look for opportunity in New York in the 1950s, and eventually blossoms there.

Her own parents, Paul and Monica, left Ireland for New York during the recession of the 1980s, in much the same circumstances. Ronan, their only child, was born in New York in 1994, although she has few memories of living there – her father's work as an actor brought the family back to Ireland when she was three.

'I only realised in retrospect that it is essentially their story,' she says. 'They had nothing, and they were illegal for a few years so they couldn't leave because they wouldn't be allowed back in. My dad started out in construction, then he became a bartender, and eventually he was discovered by another Irish actor in the bar.

My mum was a nanny, and she was adamant that she was going to have me there so I wouldn't ever have to go through the tough time that they had in order to get their visas.'

Ronan has dual US/Irish citizenship. 'I'm blessed in that I can just move to New York or LA if I want.

Even when it comes to work, I don't have to worry about visas. So thanks, Mum! She came to see the film at Sundance, and for me she was the most important critic, because I wanted her to feel like it had authentically portrayed her struggle.'

Her childhood, she says, was far from theatre brat, although she was sometimes called in if her father was in something where a baby or toddler was required.

Her first brush with Hollywood was meeting Brad Pitt at the age of two: her father was working with him on the IRA drama *The Devil's Own*. 'I'm sure Brad remembers it really well,' she says drily when I ask about this. 'It's one of the anecdotes he'll bring out at a party.'

At home, she liked putting on shows. 'I was convinced that I was going to be Jean Butler from Riverdance when I grew up.' When she was seven, she did a few hours' work on a film, although she was not keen at first. 'They needed a kid to dress up as a clown for this weird, arty flashback. And I loved being on a film set. I think Dad kind of saw that in me, and he mentioned it to his agent.'

Her proper acting debut was in an Irish television show called *The Clinic*, in 2003. 'I was so nervous beforehand, but as soon as I got on set I felt completely at home. I've always been a bit of a perfectionist, and I liked the challenge of somebody asking you to do something and then trying to do it.

And it was the atmosphere of being on a set: there are so many people there. There was a scene where the fire alarm goes off and everything's a bit manic, and I loved watching the other actors pretend to be scared and stressed, and following suit.'

She was 11 when she made her first film, *I Could Never Be Your Woman*, in which she played Michelle Pfeiffer's daughter with an impeccable American accent.

She worked with a dialect coach, who later mentioned her to *Atonement* director Joe Wright, leading her to play Briony Tallis, an imaginative 13-year-old whose incomplete understanding of events one summer's day destroys lives.

Wright wanted a specific walk for Briony, and a particular voice, and even now Ronan says the walk and the talk are her first ways into a character. 'Even for a 12-year-old, it was very thought-provoking. There was so much emotion that you had to think about and calculate.'

'We had the best crew and the best cast, and I was really looked after by the likes of James [McAvoy], Benedict [Cumberbatch] and Keira [Knightley]. I was in heaven. That's when I knew I loved being an actor. And that hasn't gone away yet. I just like pretending, and I like making that seem real. If you can hold on to that kind of childlike fascination with the imaginary world when you're older, it's the best.'

 Understand

1. Why did Saoirse's family move back to Ireland when she was young?
2. How old was Saoirse when she made her first film?
3. Name one other actor that Saoirse has worked with.
4. What are Saoirse's 'first ways into a character'?
5. Identify some of the features of a typical interview in this piece.

Explore

1. What evidence from Saoirse's childhood would suggest that she was destined to be a star?

2. What evidence from the extract suggests that Saoirse has a good sense of humour?

3. Two of the films mentioned in the interview, *Atonement* and *Brooklyn*, were based on novels.

   (a) What challenges do you think directors face when trying to recreate a story for the screen?

   (b) What advantages do you think a director has over a writer? (Hint: what kind of features can you have in a film that you cannot have in a novel?)

   (c) What advantages do you think a writer has over a director? (Hint: is there anything that you can describe in writing that would be difficult to portray on screen?)

Create

Imagine you were interviewing Saoirse Ronan. Is there anything you would like to know more about or any questions that were not asked in the interview on pages 204–205? Write the dialogue between you (the interviewer) and Saoirse (the interviewee).

Read the following extract from the short story 'Janey Mary' by James Plunkett and think about how it might be transformed into a short film.

Janey Mary

When Janey Mary turned the corner into Nicholas Street that morning, she leaned wearily against a shopfront to rest. Her small head was bowed and the hair which was so nondescript and unclean covered her face. Her small hands gripped one another for warmth across the faded bodice of her frock. Around the corner lay Canning Cottages with their tiny, frost gleaming gardens, and gates that were noisy and freezing to touch. She had tried each of them in turn. Her timid knock was well known to the people who lived in Canning Cottages. That morning some of them said, 'It's that little 'Carthy one, never mind opening. Twice in the last week she's been around – it's too much of a good thing.' Those who did answer her had been dour. They poked cross and harassed faces around half-open doors. Tell her mammie, they said, it's at school she should have her, and not out worrying poor people the likes of them. They had the mouths of their own to feed and the bellies of their own to fill, and God knows that took doing.

The school was in Nicholas Street and children with satchels were already passing. Occasionally Janey Mary could see a few paper books peeping from an open flap, and beside them a child's lunch and a bottle of milk. In the schoolroom was a scrawled and incomprehensible blackboard, and rows of staring faces which sniggered when Janey Mary was stupid in her answers.

Sometimes Father Benedict would visit the school. He asked questions in Catechism and gave the children sweets. He was a huge man who had more intuition than intellect, more genuine affection for children than for learning. One day he found Janey Mary sitting by herself in the back desk. She felt him, giant-like above her, bending over her. Some wrapped sweets were put on her desk.

'And what's your name, little girl?'

'Janey Mary 'Carthy, Father.'

'I'm Father Benedict of the Augustinians. Where do you live?' Father Benedict had pushed his way and shoved his way until he was sitting in the desk beside her. Quite suddenly Janey Mary had felt safe and warm. She said easily, 'I lives in Canning Cottages.'

He talked to her while the teacher continued self-consciously with her lesson.

'So, your daddy works in the meat factory?'

'No, Father, my daddy's dead.'

Father Benedict nodded and patted her shoulder. 'You and I must be better friends, Janey,' he said. 'We must tell your mammie to send you to school more often.'

'Yes, Father.'

'Because we must see more of one another, mustn't we?'

'Yes, Father.'

'Would you always come?'

'I'd like to come, Father.'

 Understand

1. What do you learn about Janey Mary in the first few lines of the story?
2. What kind of narrative is the above extract, first-person or third-person?
3. Give three details that you have learned about Janey Mary's appearance from the short story.
4. Was this the first time Janey Mary had visited the neighbours' houses?

Now watch the short film, based on the full story. Your teacher might pause it after the first few minutes for you to compare the openings.

 vimeo.com/129351941

 Create

 1. **(a)** Compare the opening of the short story to the opening of the film, using the table on page 47 of your Portfolio.

 (b) Choose one of the following headings and describe how you would have filmed the story differently, in the space provided on page 48 of your Portfolio.

  ◄ Costumes
  ◄ Props
  ◄ Movement
  ◄ Sound effects

 (c) Which did you prefer, reading the story or watching the film? Explain your answer in the space provided on page 48 of your Portfolio.

Focus on ... storyboarding

Storyboarding is a way of preparing a story for the screen. It is when you break down all aspects of the story and record them in images. These images are then arranged in order to create the full story.

Notes and details can be added to each board, so that when it comes to filming you do not forget anything.

You can divide each scene into shots. Draw a picture of exactly how you want each shot to look and include any other relevant details, like sound, dialogue, lighting or other effects.

Storyboarding checklist

Ask yourself the following 10 questions:

- Where is the scene set?
- How many actors are in the scene?
- How are they dressed?
- From what angle will the camera capture each shot? (From above, below, etc.)
- Do you need any important props in the scene?
- What type of shot (close-up, wide, establishing) do you need?
- Is there any movement?
- Is there any dialogue?
- Is there any special lighting?
- Are there any other special effects?

Take a look at the sample storyboard on the next page.

this is tea is so skinny!

Skinnies gm xoxoxoxoxoxo

Establishing shot. Sounds of the street, other cars and passers-by.

Dialogue between the two men. One holds a gun, the other has empty bags.

Sounds of panic and an alarm. Shouting from the robbers.

The sound of his breathing and his heart beating quickly, other noises have become muffled and distant.

Dialogue between robber and worker. Worker struggles to get money into the bag, hands shaking. Noises continue as in third shot.

Noise begins to flow in from the street, distant sirens can be heard. Panic and chaos still heard inside the bank, along with the alarm.

 Discuss

Think of a particular scene that you enjoyed from a story or play you have read together as a class. How would you shoot it for the screen?

 Create

 Create your own storyboard in the space provided on pages 49–50 of your Portfolio.

This short piece is an extract from the film *The Lady in the Van*, based on the book of the same name by Alan Bennett. Miss Shepherd is an elderly, strange lady who has been living in her van, parked outside Mr Bennett's house. She has just had a visit from social services and is complaining to Mr Bennett as they walk through a busy London market.

Alan Bennett is telling the story and often comments on the scene in voice-over (V.O.). Voice-over is a narrative voice in a story told on screen.

The Lady in the Van

MISS SHEPHERD watches TV through Curry's window: Edward Heath arriving in Downing Street, 1970.

A.B. arrives with her shopping.

A.B.　　　　　　　I've got everything – sherbet lemons, Cup-a-Soup, the miniature whisky.

MISS SHEPHERD　　That's medicinal.

They walk together up the High Street, MISS SHEPHERD pushing her child's pushchair.

A.B.　　　　　　　She seemed very understanding, the social worker.

MISS SHEPHERD　　Not understanding enough. I ask for a wheelchair and what does she get me? A walking stick.

(And she looks at him meaningfully.)

　　　　　　　　　　And she says I don't get an allowance unless I get an address.

A.B.　　　　　　　'The Van, Gloucester Crescent' – isn't that an address?

MISS SHEPHERD　　No, it needs to be a house. A residence. Still, I may be going away soon, possibly.

A.B.　　　　　　　How long for?

MISS SHEPHERD　　Broadstairs, possibly.

A.B.　　　　　　　Why Broadstairs? Have you family there?

MISS SHEPHERD　　No. NO.

A.B.　　　　　　　Have you got any family?

MISS SHEPHERD　　I just need the air.

Cut to:

EXT. INVERNESS STREET MARKET. DAY

MISS SHEPHERD　　I saw a snake this afternoon. It was coming up Parkway. It was a long grey snake. It was a boa constrictor, possibly.

A.B.　　　　　　　No …

MISS SHEPHERD　　It looked poisonous. It was keeping close to the wall. I have a feeling it may have been heading for the van.

A.B.　　　　　　　No, Miss Shepherd …

MISS SHEPHERD　　I thought I'd better warn you just to be on the safe side. I've had some close shaves with snakes.

A.B.　　　　　　　Listen to me, Miss Shepherd. There are no boa constrictors in Camden Town.

MISS SHEPHERD　　Are you calling me a liar? I know a boa constrictor when I see one.

Pitying smile from A.B. A street trader calls over.

STREET TRADER   All right, my love? You're looking especially lovely today, sweetheart.

MISS SHEPHERD   Don't sweetheart me. I'm a sick woman. Dying possibly.

STREET TRADER   Well, chin up, love, we all got to go some time. Smells like you already have.

ALAN BENNETT (voice-over) I do not believe in the snake, still less that it was en route for the van.

Cut to:

EXT. 42 GLOUCESTER CRESCENT. DAY

The PERRY CHILDREN playing in their garden. Piercing scream. Fiona comes up.

CHILD (SAM)   Mummy! Mummy! There's a snake!

ALAN BENNETT (voice-over) Only next day I find there has been a break-in at the local pet shop, so there may have been a snake on the run …

A boa constrictor slithers through the flower bed.

   So of course I feel guilty.

The CHILDREN and FIONA run into the house shouting 'A snake! A snake!'

Understand

1. Name something that Alan Bennett buys for the lady.
2. What does Alan Bennett do for a living?
3. Where is Miss Shepherd currently living?
4. Why does the social worker refuse to give Miss Shepherd an allowance?
5. Why is Miss Shepherd thinking of going away to Broadstairs?

Explore

 1. Do you think Miss Shepherd is an easy woman to get along with?

2. Why does Alan Bennett struggle to believe her claim about the snake?

 3. Choose one of the following words to describe Miss Shepherd and explain your choice.

- Stubborn
- Pessimistic
- Quick-tempered
- Interesting

4. Miss Shepherd is a very independent woman. Do you think she should be allowed to continue to live in her van?
5. If you could ask Miss Shepherd three questions, what would they be and why?
6. Why do you think Alan Bennett continues to help Miss Shepherd and does not ask her to move along?

Investigate

 Work in groups to research one of the voluntary organisations listed below.

- Age Action Ireland
- ALONE
- Friends of the Elderly Ireland

Find out who they are and what they do, then share your findings with the class.

Create

1. Imagine what Miss Shepherd looks like. Write a paragraph describing her appearance and how she would walk and talk. Use the following types of words:

- adjectives
- adverbs
- verbs.

2. Write a formal letter from the local council of Camden, ordering Miss Shepherd to move along, as it is forbidden to park on streets with double yellow lines and reside in a vehicle. (For information on formal letters see pages 35–36)

The White Dress

Watch Vanessa Gildea's short film *The White Dress*, available in the Shorts section on the Irish Film Board website. www.irishfilmboard.ie/directory/view/7711/the-white-dress

On your first viewing of the film, keep your eyes closed. What sounds do you hear? Write down all the places you hear the action taking place.

Now, open your eyes and watch *The White Dress* again to see if you were right.

Understand

1. Describe the first setting in the film.
2. What is missing from this short film that you have seen in other plays and films so far in this unit?

Explore

1. If this were a short story and you were describing the settings in the film, how would you appeal to the other senses in your description?
2. What words would you use to describe the young girl?
3. Earlier in the unit, we looked at the importance of costume. Why is it important in this film?

Revising stage and screen

Reflect and review

1. Look back at the images on page 175.
   (a) Which image best represents the unit, in your opinion?
   (b) Which image least represents the unit, in your opinion?
   (c) Think of some alternative images that could be used to represent this unit.
2. Fill in the unit review on page 51 of your Portfolio.

Language skills

1. Change these adjectives into adverbs.
   - Quick
   - Calm
   - Hungry
   - Terrifying
2. Write out the following paragraph, adding adverbs to make it more descriptive.

   > She looked into the cold, dark corridor. It seemed empty. She placed her hand on the door handle and turned it. The door opened and she was hit by a shower of dust. The damp air was overpowering.

Oral assessment

1. Work in small groups to create a short script and perform it for the class. Include a short introduction which includes details of costumes, props, lighting, sound, etc.
2. Choose your favourite actor/actress/director/writer and prepare a three-minute presentation about them. You can use visual aids, slide shows or background music to make your presentation more engaging.

Written assessment

1. (a) Write a review of a film that you have seen recently in the space provided on page 52 of your Portfolio.

   (b) Redraft your review in the space provided on pages 90–91 of your Portfolio.

2. Read the extract from *Same Old Moon* on page 53 of your Portfolio, then add stage directions where you think they are necessary.

3. Read the extract from *Make Me A Vampire* on page 54 of your Portfolio, then create a storyboard for a screenplay inspired by the extract in the space provided on pages 54–55 of your Portfolio.

Unit 5

Media and Advertising

1. What do you associate with each of the images above?
2. Is there another aspect of media that you would expect to see represented?
3. How often do you **(a)** watch television, **(b)** listen to the radio and **(c)** go online?
4. **(a)** Examine the list below and number each item in order of importance to you. Which is of least importance to you? Which could you not live without?

   ◖ Television 3   5 ◖ Websites
   ◖ Film 4   6 ◖ Radio
   ◖ Newspapers 8   2 ◖ Music
   ◖ Magazines 7   1 ◖ Social media

   (b) Compare and contrast two forms of media in the list above. Consider the advantages and disadvantages of each.

 Create

Write your own definition of media in the space provided on page 63 of your Portfolio, by completing the sentence 'Media is…'. We will return to this definition later on.

Media

Media refers to the various means of communication that can reach a mass audience. It plays an important role in sharing news and ideas as well as shaping public opinion. There are many different forms of media. The word originally referred to print media, such as newspapers and magazines, but television and the internet have also become important forms of mass communication in the past century.

The internet and social media

The internet is one of the most popular forms of media. People rely on the internet to find information, stay in touch and shop for their favourite products.

Social media enables people to connect with others through apps or websites. These can be accessed on phones and other mobile devices, so it is easy to stay connected.

Features of social media include the following:

- personal account
- profile page
- friends, followers or subscribers
- hashtags, likes and comments
- photographs and videos.

Discuss

1. Imagine life before the internet. Share ideas about what life would have been like. What would you miss the most?

2. **(a)** Can you name these social networks or websites?

   (b) What do you know about them?

3. How many social media accounts do you have?

Explore

1. Explain how social media makes it easier to stay in contact with friends and family.
2. What do you like about social media?
3. Examine the following images.

(a) Describe what is happening in these images.
(b) List three advantages and three disadvantages of social media.
(c) Do you think people rely too much on social media?
(d) What are the dangers of social media?

Investigate

1. As a class, organise a survey to find out how First Year students use social media.
   - Make a list of questions to include in your survey.
   - Break into groups to conduct the survey. Each group should ask a different question from the list.
   - When each group has completed their part of the survey, work together to gather and review the results as a class.

Create

Organise a class debate on the following motion: *This house believes that you should be eighteen years or older in order to use social media.* (For information on debates see pages 47–48.)

Television

The way we watch television has changed throughout the years. Today, many people stream shows to watch on their mobile phones, tablets and laptops using software like Netflix. Smart televisions connect to mobile devices and the internet. Television remains a popular form of entertainment for most people.

The main broadcasters in Ireland are:

- RTÉ
- TG4
- TV3.

Other channels are provided by the likes of Sky and Virgin Media.

 Discuss

1. How do you watch your favourite television shows? Each person should share the statement that matches their viewing habits.

   (a) I watch my favourite show at the same time every week.

   (b) I record shows that I like and watch them later on.

   (c) I watch shows on Netflix, Showbox or similar.

   (d) I stream or download shows to watch on my device.

2. Name some of your favourite shows. What do you like about them?

The most popular genres of television programmes include:

- reality
- drama
- sports.

 Understand

1. Name one more genre of television programme to add to the list above.
2. Name one programme belonging to each genre listed above.
3. Name at least one television channel that shows one of the programmes named in your previous answer.

 Investigate

 Complete the survey task on pages 56–57 of your Portfolio.

Radio

Many years ago, the radio (or wireless) was the most thrilling advancement in technology. It meant that people were connected to the world in a new, exciting way. The radio has been a source of news and entertainment since the 1920s.

In Ireland, we have national stations including:

- RTÉ 2 FM
- RTÉ Radio 1
- RTÉ Raidió na Gaeltachta
- RTÉ Lyric FM.

Discuss

1. Do you or your family listen to the radio at home or in the car?
2. Compare the radio stations and shows that you know.

You may listen to radio breakfast shows as you get ready for school. These shows are very popular, especially with people commuting to and from work.

Today FM is broadcast nationally, but it is a commercial station that is funded through advertising. This station broadcasts the Ian Dempsey Breakfast Show live every morning. Like many other radio shows, it is led by a presenter and includes some of the following:

- music
- talk and interviews
- competitions
- comedy sketches
- news and sport
- advertising.

Those interested can stream or listen live through the Today FM website, or save the podcast and listen back later on.

Listen to the following clip from the Ian Dempsey Breakfast Show:

🔗 https://www.todayfm.com/13year-old-Conor-Byrne-Shaves-His-Head

Understand

1. How does Conor feel about being on national radio?
2. Conor is getting his hair shaved for charity. How much money has he raised?
3. What makes Conor and the others laugh?
4. What evidence is there to suggest that this event takes place on radio?

 Explore

1. How do you know that the presenter is a good communicator?
2. What, in your view, are the qualities of a successful radio presenter?

 Investigate

 The clip that you have just heard is from the Ian Dempsey Breakfast Show on Today FM. Work in pairs to find out about another radio show. Try to find the following information:

- name of the radio station
- name of the show
- name of the presenter(s)
- style – talk or music?
- is there a podcast to download or can listeners listen through live streaming?

 Create

 1. **(a)** Use Glogster to make a digital poster advertising the radio show that you have researched. Work with your partner to make your poster stand out.

 (b) When you have finished, present your poster to your classmates. Share the information you have gathered about your radio station.

Magazines

A magazine is a publication on glossy paper, usually containing images, articles and interviews. Magazines are usually published periodically, either weekly or monthly.

Magazines provide entertainment, but they can also be informative. They can be divided into two categories, depending on their content and readership:

- magazines that appeal to a **general, mainstream audience** (for example, the *RTÉ Guide* magazine includes television listings, entertainment and lifestyle features)
- magazines that appeal to a **specialised, niche market** (for example, *The Irish Garden* magazine appeals to readers interested in gardening and *Empire* magazine appeals to readers interested in film).

 Discuss

1. Name at least one magazine you are familiar with.
2. Do you think the magazine that you have named appeals to a mainstream audience or a specialised, niche market?

 Understand

1. For each magazine cover, decide whether it would appeal to a mainstream audience or a niche market.
2. Which of these magazines would you be most interested in and why?
3. Identify the target markets by deciding what group of people might like to buy each magazine pictured above.

 Create

 Create a magazine cover in the space provided on page 58 of your Portfolio. You should decide:

- target market (specialised/ mainstream)
- name of the magazine
- design of the front cover
- feature articles
- image to attract readers.

Newspapers

Before social media, people relied on newspapers to find out what had already happened nationally and internationally. Nowadays, many people get news updates on their devices and some read newspaper publications online.

Newspaper articles report events or offer opinions. The main purpose of an article is to inform readers about a particular topic or issue. When you write a newspaper article, it is important that it is structured or laid out correctly.

Features

- **Masthead**: the name of the newspaper – you can invent the name or use one you already know.
- **Headline**: tells you what the article is about. Your headline should capture the reader's attention.
- **Strapline**: straplines come after the headline. They are short statements that give a little more information about the headline.
- **Sub-headings**: you will often see sub-headings which are used to tell you what the next section of the article is about. You can use sub-headings if you want to break your article up and make it more accessible for your readers.
- **Name of reporter**
- **Date**
- **Accompanying image(s)**

tea!

 Discuss

Can you name any newspapers sold today?

 Investigate

Bring a clipping of a newspaper article into school. If you do not have newspapers at home, find one online.

(a) Does the article include any of the features outlined above?

 (b) Work with a partner to compare the features of both of your newspaper articles. Discuss which article is more effective.

There are two main types of newspapers.

◀ **Broadsheets** directly report the news without emotion or commentary.

◀ **Tabloids** report the news along with the writer's own viewpoint. These commentaries are intended to entertain the readers.

Broadsheets

◀ Usually A2 – large in size

◀ More text than images

◀ Headlines are serious and reflect the tone of the news

◀ Mastheads are printed in black with a white background

◀ Factual, serious language

◀ Focus is on current affairs, politics and business

◀ Examples include *The Irish Times*, *The Irish Independent* and *The Financial Times*.

Tabloids

◀ A3 – smaller in size

◀ Large pictures or images

◀ Large headlines

◀ Mastheads are printed in white with a red background

◀ Sensational, emotive language

◀ Use of slang and puns

◀ Focus is on human interest, gossip, entertainment and celebrities

◀ Large sports section

◀ Examples include *The Irish Sun*, *The Sunday World* and *Irish Daily Star*.

 Investigate

 Work in groups to research one of the following newspapers:

◀ *The Irish Times*   ◀ *The Irish Independent*   ◀ *The Financial Times*

◀ *The Irish Sun*   ◀ *The Sunday World*   ◀ *Irish Daily Star*

Try to find the following information:

◀ Is it a broadsheet or a tabloid newspaper?

◀ On average, how many copies are sold each day/week?

◀ What is the latest front page headline in your chosen newspaper?

◀ What is the focus of your newspaper, to entertain or to inform?

Present your findings to the class.

Homophones and puns

Homophones are words that sound the same but have different spellings and meanings.

Leak   Leek   Pause   Paws

Understand

Make a list of five homophones, but write only one of the words.
For example, your list might look like this:

◄ Leek   ◄ Paws   ◄ Wear   ◄ New   ◄ Aunt

Swap your list with a partner and examine the words you have been given.
Complete each pair of homophones by finding the other word with the same sound but a different meaning and spelling.

A pun is a play on words that uses homophones or words with multiple meanings for a humorous effect.

Puns are often used in tabloid newspapers, particularly in the catchy headlines.

Understand

1. Find the homophone used in each of the puns below.

RIP
Boiled Water
You will be mist.

Finally achieved world peas

2. In pairs, use your lists of homophones from the task above to create puns. You should write three sentences, playing around with the words you have chosen. Try to make your puns amusing.

Grammar Primer: pages 35–38

Examine the front pages of newspapers A and B and answer the accompanying questions.

THE IRISH Sun

Wednesday, January 11, 2017

€1 (50p NI)

ONLY €1

SUPER STAYS

www.thesun.ie

New World Order

FIFA'S 48-TEAM CUP

SEE PAGE 5 AND SUNSPORT

Reform . . . Creighton

'Health leaders lacking'

LUCINDA Creighton has launched a searing attack on "cowardly" politicians who will do nothing to end our hospitals crisis.

In her Irish Sun column, she writes: "Reform requires bold leadership which is clearly lacking."

The ex-Fine Gael TD cites Mary Harney as the only recent Health Minister to make a difference.

Read her Column — Page 11

BARGAIN BREAKS

TOKEN 5 — SEE PAGE 20

THE IRISH Sun CAMPAIGN VICTORY GIVE US A BRAKE

BRAKE THROUGH

Series of proposals to end car insurance rip-off

By NEIL COTTER

THE Government yesterday paved the way for cheaper motor insurance costs — following an Irish Sun drive to lower premiums.

We had demanded proposals to tackle fraudulent claims, personal injury compensation and uninsured driving during our Give Us A Brake campaign.

A source said: "This issue cannot be fixed in the morning but work is well under way, every tree has been shaken."

Full Story — Page Four

METRO EDITION

Irish Independent

IRELAND'S BEST-SELLING DAILY NEWSPAPER · www.independent.ie · **Monday 28 October 2013** · €1.90 (£1.25 in Northern Ireland) · R

New era for schools in radical overhaul of exams

Major reforms will spell end of rote learning for students

Katherine Donnelly
Education Editor

STUDENTS will get marks for sporting performance, writing computer code or devising mental health campaigns under major changes to the Junior Cert syllabus.

Radical reform of the Junior Cert will provide teenagers with unprecedented opportunities to earn grades for showing what they can do outside the exam hall.

Change is aimed at encouraging students to think and to get away from a system dominated by a single, terminal exam that has spawned a reliance on "teaching to the test" and rote learning.

Eight new optional "short courses" will be rolled out in the coming years, offering 15- and 16-year-olds a suite of options for study – and massive changes in how they are assessed.

Now details of four of the short courses have been revealed by the National Council for Curriculum and Assessment (NCCA), the Government education advisory body which is developing the courses.

Draft proposals have now been outlined for four of the subjects that will be on offer – physical education; computer coding; social, personal and health education; and civic, social and personal education. The NCCA is inviting feedback on the new courses until Christmas.

To date it has produced proposals for:

● A new short course in programming and coding where pupils will learn how to design, write and test computer code.

● A physical education (PE) course where students gain half their marks from their sporting performances.

● An end to the written exam in civic, social and personal education (CSPE), with marks based on work carried out in school instead.

● An option to be assessed in projects as part of social personal and health education (SPHE).

Continued on Page 8

COMMENT
KATHERINE DONNELLY
Page 8

Rock icon Lou Reed dies

LOU REED, the American musician and frontman of seminal rock band The Velvet Underground, has died. The 71-year-old, responsible for songs such as 'Walk on the Wild Side' and 'Perfect Day', had undergone treatment for a liver transplant earlier this year. He died of a liver-related ailment, it was confirmed last night.

FULL REPORT: PAGES 2 & 3, OBITUARY: PAGE 32

Hospital boss says patients at risk of TB

Eilish O'Regan
Health Correspondent

PATIENTS in the overcrowded emergency department of a major hospital are being put at risk of a range of infectious diseases including TB, MRSA and flu on a daily basis.

The stark admission is made in an unpublished letter by Liam Duffy, chief executive of Beaumont Hospital in Dublin. The hospital was recently castigated in a report by inspectors for poor standards of hygiene.

Mr Duffy outlined the potential dangers to patients in a letter to the Health Information and Quality Authority (HIQA) months before it sent in its inspectors and produced the damning findings.

He said the emergency department was struggling to cope with a huge volume of patients, that space was limited and that toilet facilities were inadequate.

Continued on Page 5

Tributes paid after deaths of two former TDs

FIANNA Fail has suffered the loss of two former TDs who had a combined Dail service of 50 years.

Noel Davern (67) served as education minister under Charlie Haughey, as junior agriculture minister under Bertie Ahern and was a TD for 32 years in total for the Tipperary South constituency.

Denis Foley (79) represented the Kerry North constituency for 18 years, but controversially resigned from Fianna Fail and as chairman of the Public Accounts Committee following revelations that he held an offshore Ansbacher account.

Fianna Fail leader Micheal Martin paid tribute to both men and extended his sympathies to their families.

Continued on Page 19

Recommended retail price of the Irish Independent compact edition in ROI is €1.90
Vol. 122 No. 258 Irish Independent

Understand

1. Name the two newspapers.
2. Identify which newspaper is a tabloid and which is a broadsheet. Explain your choice.
3. What is the main headline of each newspaper?
4. Is newspaper A's front cover eye-catching? Give reasons for your answer.
5. Is there evidence to suggest the reporting in newspaper B is factual?

 Explore

1. Would you buy newspaper A? Give at least two reasons for your answer.
2. Why might some people prefer less text in a newspaper?
 3. What differences can you find between newspaper A and newspaper B?
 4. Both newspapers feature a sports story. Which headline makes you want to read the full story the most? Explain your choice.

 Create

 1. **(a)** Complete the headline task on page 59 of your Portfolio.

   (b) Write an article using one of the headlines from the previous task, in the space provided on page 60 of your Portfolio.

Read the following two articles on the same topic. As you read, see if you can guess which article is from a broadsheet newspaper and which is from a tabloid newspaper.

Article 1

PUPPY DOG CRIES

A number of puppies and dogs were seized at Dublin Port last night and will be available for adoption within the next week

The puppies were being exported without a pet passport and are now in the care of the Dublin Society for Prevention of Cruelty to Animals

By Jack Cahill   2nd April 2017

A number of puppies and dogs were seized at Dublin Port last night as they were being exported out of the country.

The majority of puppies are just ten weeks old and will now be in need of a new home.

The good news is the cute pooches can be adopted from the DSPCA within the next week.

This is the fourth seizure of its kind this year and according to the DSPCA, it brings the total number of puppies seized to over 500 in the last 18 months.

The comments on the puppy pics show how desperate people are to see those responsible for this kind of thing prosecuted.

One said: 'Makes me livid that people know the scum who do this! And they condone it by doing nothing! When will people wake up and grow a conscience!?'

With any luck the puppies will be re-homed quickly.

Article 2

Five puppies among 10 dogs seized at Dublin Port by customs officers

Two men travelling on ferry from Holyhead did not have pet passports for animals

Fiachradh McDermott   **July 4th 2017**

Customs officers seized five puppies and five adult dogs at Dublin Port when they stopped two men disembarking a ferry from Holyhead on Tuesday morning.

The men, both Irish nationals in their 50s, were driving a van pulling a horsebox. A random check showed the men did not have pet passports for the animals.

The Pomeranian and Spaniel-type dogs and puppies are in the care of the DSPCA, who work in co-operation with other animal welfare organisations and Revenue to confront the illegal puppy trade.

Brian Gillen of the DSPCA said that while one of the animals is micro-chipped, it is not properly registered so he had 'no clue' where the dogs came from. Since four of the dogs were adult females, he suspected they were for breeding.

He said it was 'most unusual' to seize inbound dogs or puppies, since the majority of seizures are of animals leaving the country.

A follow-up investigation is now in progress.

Understand

1. How many dogs were seized at Dublin Port?
2. Article 2 quotes a representative from the DSPCA. What do they say?
3. Is the language in article 1 formal or informal? Give an example to back up your answer.
4. Choose one of the newspaper articles and find the following:
   (a) headline   **(b)** name of the reporter   **(c)** strapline.

Explore

1. Article 1 has an accompanying image. Do you think this makes the article more or less effective than article 2? Explain your answer.

2. In your opinion, which newspaper article is most trustworthy?

3. Which of these articles is from a tabloid newspaper, in your view?

Create

Write a newspaper article for either a broadsheet or a tabloid newspaper. Base your article on one of the following topics:

- The cost of starting secondary school
- Patients on hospital trolleys
- *tabloid!!!* Café shut down due to poor hygiene
- We need change!

Remember to include the features outlined on page 224 and to write in an appropriate style.

Advertising

Companies use advertising to promote their product or service. If an advertisement is successful, consumers will feel the need to buy the product or service being advertised.

Advertisements are also used to raise awareness of serious issues in society. People may be moved to support a cause following a successful advertising campaign.

Advertising is everywhere. It is impossible to go about your daily life without encountering an advertisement in some form. Advertisers target us when we:

- go online or use social media
- watch television
- listen to the radio
- use public transport
- read newspapers or magazines
- receive leaflets or take-away menus through our letter boxes.

Here are just some of the places where we might see adverts. Can you think of some more?

Digital advertising

One of the most effective ways for advertisers to reach people is by advertising online. It is easy to make a product, service or issue visible online.

Banner advertisements

Advertisements often appear on websites as banners made up of text and/or images.

Pop-up advertisements

Internet users will also be familiar with pop-up advertisements, which appear at the front of the screen.

Video advertisements

Video advertisements are used to target consumers on sites such as YouTube.

Social media advertisements

Products and services are often advertised through social media platforms, such as Facebook and Snapchat. These adverts may appear in your feed or as a sidebar.

Social media accounts

Many companies advertise their brand through social media simply by creating an account. Look at how Specsavers opticians reached people on Twitter by posting this humorous tweet after the wrong film was named Best Picture at the 2017 Oscars:

 Understand

1. Name four kinds of advertisements used to promote products, services or issues online.
2. Advertisements appear at the beginning of YouTube videos. Name one other website where companies can advertise.
3. List the benefits of advertising online.

 Explore

1. In your experience, are online advertisements effective? Include a personal anecdote in your answer.
2. Do you think that internet users are against or in favour of online advertising? Give two reasons for your answer.

Television advertising

Television remains an extremely popular medium through which advertisers reach a large variety of audiences. You will notice that television advertisements vary depending on the time of day, the time of year and the programme being shown.

What makes a good television advertisement?

- Use of humour
- Catchy song or jingle
- Effective language
- Visually interesting

- Causes a reaction: the advertisement should make you feel something – joy, sorrow, even guilt
- Memorable: annoying advertisements do their job as they are difficult to forget.

Watch the following television advertisement for Specsavers:

(link) youtu.be/g0xG0c6jT0c

 Understand

 Work with a partner to answer the following questions.

1. What is being advertised?
2. Who might be interested in this brand?
3. What information is given in this advertisement.
4. What makes this advertisement memorable?

Take a look at another television advertisement, this time for Aer Lingus.

(link) https://youtu.be/1XWfRWNj9ms

 Discuss

1. How did this advertisement make you feel?
2. Do you think it is effective? Use the list above to help you.
3. Share some of your favourite television advertisements. How have the advertisers made them memorable?

what did I even do!

Radio advertising

Radio advertising is extremely popular in Ireland. Radio and television advertisements differ in that radio advertisers cannot use any visual tools.

Listen to the following advertisement for Brennans Bread:

http://greatirishradioads.com/brennans-evoke-nostalgia/

 Discuss

1. According to the advertisement, what three things will Brennans Bread always be about? *freshness, quality or taste*
2. Find evidence from the advertisement to show that Brennans Bread is an Irish product.
3. To what is Brennans dedicated?
4. Do you like the advertisement? Why or why not?

Listen to the next clip and answer the questions that follow.

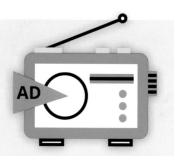

http://greatirishradioads.com/its-ok-to-break-the-rules/

AD

 Understand

1. Name two places mentioned in this advertisement.
2. Where do 'they' live?
3. Who are 'they'?
4. What website is mentioned at the end?
5. What can you be in with a chance of winning?

 Explore

1. What did you learn about radio advertising from this clip?
 2. In your opinion, is this a memorable radio advertisement?
3. Which do you prefer, television or radio advertisements? Give reasons for your choice.

Print advertising

Print advertising is advertising that appears in or on:

- newspapers
- magazines
- posters
- leaflets
- bus stops
- buses
- billboards.

Print advertisements make use of text and visuals rather than voices or sounds.

Can you think of any effective print advertisements? Maybe a film poster such as this one encouraged you to go to the cinema!

Understand

1. Name the film advertised above.

2. **(a)** Select one of the following words to describe this poster and explain your selection.

   - Amusing
   - Unexpected
   - Fun
   - Cute

   (b) Choose one other word to describe the poster. Give reasons for your choice.

Investigate

1. **(a)** Find the trailer for the film advertised above. Watch it carefully. Which do you think advertises the film best, the poster or the trailer?

   (b) Compare your preference with a partner and discuss the reasons for your choices.

Features of advertisements

Advertisers use a number of devices to produce an advertisement that will appeal to their target audience. Look closely at the advertisements that you see as you go about your day. Most of them will include at least some of the features of advertising.

Refer to the following advertisement as you are introduced to each of the features of advertising on pages 239–240.

When examining advertisements, ask yourself the following questions.

Is there a brand name?

Brand names are carefully chosen to appeal to a particular group of people who may be interested in the product, service or issue that is being advertised. In some cases, the company or organisation is the brand.

Do you recognise the logo?

A **logo** is a design, symbol or image that is unique to a particular brand. Companies use logos to make their product more identifiable.

What does the copy say?

In advertising, the words used are known as **copy**. The copy in advertisements often includes:

- **buzzwords**: words that trigger a response from the consumer, such as **free**, **best** and **powerful**
- **emotive language**: words and phrases that appeal to our emotions, such as **traditional**, **home** and **love**.

Can you find a caption?

A **caption** is a heading sometimes included in advertisements to introduce the product, service or issue. Captions are mainly used in print advertisements.

Is there a slogan?

A **slogan** is a catchphrase associated with a particular brand. Slogans differ from captions as they may appear in several advertisements for the same product or service. Techniques used in slogans include:

- **alliteration**: the words are catchy because they begin with the same sound
- **humour**: silly or funny slogans stand out
- **puns**: a play on words can catch our attention
- **repetition**: slogans may repeat a word, phrase or message.

What images and colours do you see?

Most advertisements will include an **image** that is designed to get your attention. Advertisements aim to persuade you to buy a product, pay for a service or support a cause. It is very important that all images associated with the product are enticing and draw consumers in.

Colours can be linked to particular products. For example, bright colours like yellow and blue are often used to advertise cleaning products. These colours are associated with freshness and sunlight.

Is someone famous endorsing the product?

Celebrities are often paid to **endorse** (say that they use) a particular product, making it more desirable to the consumer. For example, the singer Ellie Goulding endorses Pantene, as seen on page 242.

Who is the target audience?

Particular products are aimed at different groups of people. Generally, an advertisement will try to reach its **target audience** – the group of people most likely to buy the product or use the service. The target market or audience is determined by age, gender and interests.

 Understand

1. Identify the following in the advertisement on page 238.
   - Brand
   - Logo
   - Buzzwords
   - Emotive language
   - Caption
   - Slogan

 2. Work in pairs to come up with at least three well-known brand names for each of the following items:
   - cereal
   - a soft drink
   - sportswear
   - a car.

3. Look at the logos below and see if you can name the brands they are associated with.

4. Suggest one example of a buzzword.
5. Suggest one example of a word or phrase that appeals to the emotions.
6. List five slogans that you know and choose your favourite.
7. List the images or colours associated with the following brands:
   - Coca-Cola
   - Pepsi
   - Fanta
   - Ballygowan

8. Describe the images and colours in the advertisement on page 238.
9. **(a)** Can you think of three famous figures who promote a well-known brand?
   (b) Why might someone buy a product that is endorsed by a celebrity?
10. Identify the target audience for the advertisement on page 238. Give reasons for your answer.

Exclamation marks

To exclaim is to cry out or express a strong feeling.

Gosh, that hurt!

An exclamation mark is used at the end of a sentence to show when something is surprising, exciting or even annoying.

Exclamation marks are used when writing dialogue. Notice how the examples below capture ordinary speech.

- ❮ *'The rain is so heavy the river has burst its banks!'*
- ❮ *'The view from our hotel is spectacular!'*
- ❮ *'Somebody, please help me!'*
- ❮ *'Don't panic, Alice!'*

 Grammar
Primer: page 39

ℹ️ Try not to use exclamation marks too often or they will lack impact. You should never use more than one exclamation mark to end your sentence or use one with another punctuation mark.

👍 Understand

1. The end of every sentence in this passage lacks punctuation. Write out the passage, adding a full stop or exclamation mark to the end of each sentence.

> It's so unfair She always gets her own way Every time she asks for something, you give in When I ask for something, you always say no It's so obvious that she is your favourite I hate having a sister When she does something wrong, you blame me Sometimes I wish I could swap families I'm fed up with all of you I'm going to my room, don't disturb me

2. Correctly punctuate the dialogue below.

> Quick the dog has escaped

> Are you sure I think I saw him in the garden Look There he is

Look closely at the following advertisement and answer the questions that follow.

Understand

1. What is being advertised – a product, service or social issue?
2. Identify the following in this advertisement:
   - ◖ brand
   - ◖ buzzwords
   - ◖ caption.
3. In your opinion, who would be interested in buying the item advertised?

 Explore

As seen in this advertisement, Ellie Goulding endorses Pantene. Suggest one other celebrity to endorse this product. Give reasons for your choice.

 Create

Imagine you work for Pantene. Write an email to the celebrity of your choice, asking them to endorse your product.

- ◖ Structure your email correctly (for information on emails see pages 39–40).
- ◖ Share information about the brand.
- ◖ Explain to the celebrity why they should endorse the brand.

In pairs, examine the advertisement below. Try to identify the target audience for the product advertised.

Fitness is now in fashion

One tracker. Every occasion.

The **Fitbit Alta**™ features interchangeable bands so you can switch your tracker to fit your style. With auto-exercise recognition, all-day activity tracking, call and text alerts and reminders to move, finding your fit has never looked better.

 fitbit alta

| ALL DAY ACTIVITY | AUTO SLEEP TRACKING & ALARMS | CALL, TEXT & CALENDAR ALERTS | REMINDERS TO MOVE | ACCESSORY BANDS | AUTO EXERCISE RECOGNITION |

Understand

1. Name the brand.
2. Find the slogan.
3. What is the dominant image in this advertisement?

 Explore

1. Is the vocabulary used in this advertisement effective? Explain your answer.
2. In your opinion, who is the target audience? How do you know?
3. Do you think the advertisers stereotype or make assumptions about their target audience? Explain your answer.

 Create

1. **(a)** Design a print advertisement for one of the products listed below in the space provided on page 61 of your Portfolio.

   ◖ The latest iPhone
   ◖ Your favourite snack food
   ◖ A car that is new to the market
   ◖ A holiday destination
   ◖ This year's must-see film

   Before you begin, you should identify your target audience. Try to appeal to this group of consumers in your advertisement. Use the list of key advertising techniques on pages 239–240 to help you.

 (b) When you have finished, swap advertisements with another student. Assess one another's work, using the questions on page 62 of your Portfolio.

 (c) Imagine your classmates represent the company whose advertisement you have made. Present your advertisement, explaining how your concept will promote their brand.

Here are two film posters advertising *Beauty and the Beast*. Poster A is advertising the 1991 animated film, while poster B is advertising the 2017 live-action version. Examine both carefully before completing the tasks on page 247.

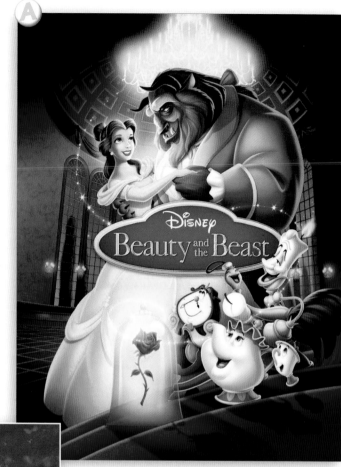

Understand

1. Describe both advertisements under the headings below.
   ◖ Colour
   ◖ Images
2. Based on the two posters, what is the most obvious difference between both films?

Explore

1. In your opinion is the target audience for both films the same? Identify the target audience for each and explain your answer.
2. Which poster do you find more appealing? Give reasons for your answer.
3. **(a)** List three advertising techniques that could be used to make **one** of these advertisements more appealing.
   (b) Explain how each of the techniques you have listed would help to improve your chosen advertisement.

Investigate

Find out which film was more popular by researching the total box office earnings of both movies. Were you surprised by the result? Think of three reasons to explain why one film attracted more viewers than the other.

Create

Create a poster advertising a film of your choice. Make use of at least three of the following advertising techniques:
◖ images
◖ colour
◖ copy (name of film, director, actors, release date, quotes from reviewers, etc.)
◖ humour
◖ star rating.

Advertisers may also bring a particular issue or campaign to our attention. The aim is not to sell a product or service, but to raise awareness of an issue in society. Often, the organisations behind these advertisements work to persuade people to donate to a cause.

Understand

1. Identify the issue this poster aims to address.
2. Suggest one means of support available for people affected by this issue.
3. According to the advertisement, 'Lending an ear is lending a hand'. What does this mean?

Explore

1. What group of people might find the image in this advertisement appealing? Explain your answer.
 2. In your view, is this an effective advertisement? Refer to the features of advertising in your answer.
3. Explain why it is important for people to look after their mental health.
4. Write about a time when you shared a problem or worry with another person. How did it help?

Investigate

Use your research skills to learn more about the #littlethings campaign. Use the questions below to guide your research.

- What is mental health?
- How can people feel happy and well?
- What other posters were used to advertise this campaign?
- How can people connect with or share the campaign?
- What other images and advertisements promote positive mental health?

When you have finished, bring all the information you have gathered into school to share in groups.

Create

Use the information you have gathered for the Investigate task to create a poster in support of the #littlethings campaign to promote positive mental health in your school.

Revising media and advertising

Reflect and review

1. Look back at the images on page 217.

   (a) Which image best represents the unit, in your opinion?

   (b) Which image least represents the unit, in your opinion?

   (c) Think of some alternative images that could be used to represent this unit now that you have completed it.

 2. Fill in the unit review on pages 63–64 of your Portfolio.

3. **(a)** Your teacher will say the following terms out loud. As you hear each term, make a list of associated words.

   ◁ Media   ◁ Newspapers

   ◁ Television   ◁ Magazines

   ◁ Communication   ◁ Advertising

   (b) Compare your responses with a partner. Were some of your responses similar? Why might this be?

Language skills

1. Put these homophones into sentences:

   ◁ Buy   Bye   ◁ Which   Witch   ◁ Wood   Would   ◁ Seen   Scene

2. Name the homophone of the images shown:

3. Revise what you learned about puns by writing a tabloid headline including a play on words. This headline about a lightning storm might help you: Lightning strikes in shocking storm!

4. Rewrite the following passage, adding in the end marks (full stop, question mark or exclamation mark).

   > What time does the match begin I'm so excited to play I really hope we win Do you think we have a good chance If we play the way we did in training I think victory will be ours

Oral assessment

 Prepare a presentation on the role of media or advertising in our lives.

- Research your topic.
- Prepare your presentation – use an image, slideshow or prop.
- Practise your presentation, focusing on the delivery of your message.
- Deliver a two-minute presentation in front of your classmates.

Written assessment

 1. (a) Write the text of a radio advertisement in the space provided on page 65 of your Portfolio for one of the following:

- an upcoming concert of a band or singer of your choice
- an appeal for donations to a charity of your choice.

 (b) Redraft your advertisement in the space provided on page 92 of your Portfolio.

 2. (a) Think of a significant event in one of the novels that you have studied in First Year. Write a newspaper article reporting on the events as they happened in the space provided on page 66 of your Portfolio. You may like to include quotations from those involved.

 (b) Redraft your article in the space provided on page 93 of your Portfolio.

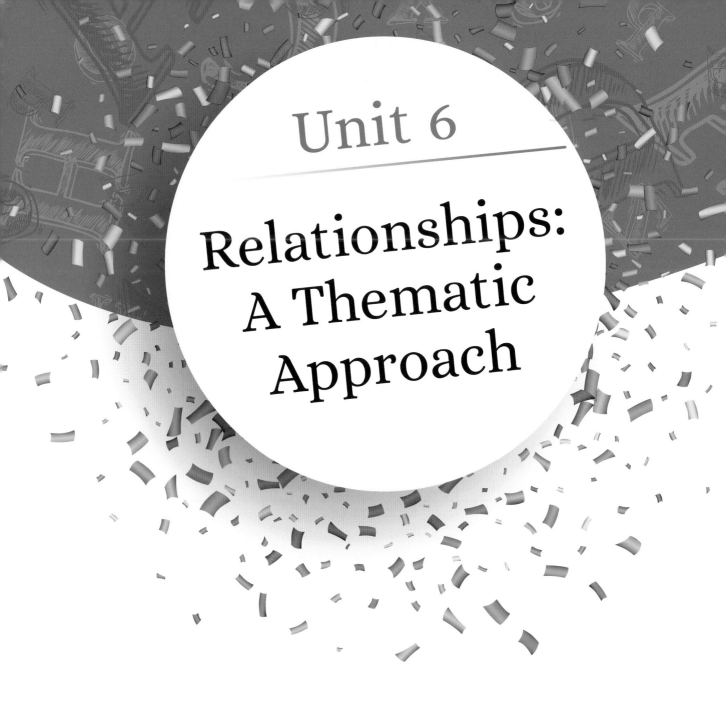

Unit 6

Relationships: A Thematic Approach

Why study a theme?

A theme is a central idea or message that runs through a piece of literature. This unit is a thematic approach to English. All areas of English that you have encountered in this book will now come together under a specific theme. The theme for this unit is relationships.

Why study this theme?

A relationship is the way in which two or more people, things or ideas are connected. Characters in literature can be connected in any number of ways. A few examples are love, family, friendship and work. Relationships are an integral part of our development. This unit aims to strengthen your understanding of relationships by looking at the benefits and challenges they can present.

Learning intentions

◖ Develop a deeper insight into and understanding of the theme of relationships.

Writing With Purpose

◖ Read and write articles, reviews and personal essays with the theme of relationships.

Poetry and Song

◖ Study a selection of poems that deal with different types of relationships.

Fiction

◖ Analyse the development of relationships that are both positive and negative.

Stage and Screen

◖ Encounter special relationships portrayed in drama.

Media and Advertising

◖ Enhance your understanding of how powerful a relationship can be.

Language Skills

◖ Learn about prepositions.
◖ Understand the correct use of 'there', 'they're' and 'their'.

Discuss

1. What do these images have in common?
2. Which image do you feel best represents relationships?
3. Why did you choose this image?
4. What are the different types of relationships people can have?

Create

Write your own definition of relationships in the space provided on page 72 of your Portfolio, by completing the sentence 'Relationships are …'. You will return to this definition later on.

Interactions in relationships

The way characters act towards one another is a key feature of relationships within a text. Dialogue, body language and tone of voice can tell the reader a lot about a relationship. The interaction between two characters is an interesting area to focus on when studying the theme of relationships.

In Sarah Crossan's novel *One*, Tippi and Grace are conjoined twin sisters who share everything, from clothes to friends to their body. In the excerpt below, the twins are about to start their first day at a new school. Pay attention to their interactions with each another.

One

Truth Is What Happens

Tippi,
half dipped in sleep,
drains her coffee mug and
stares into her scrambled eggs
as though she can read her future in the
yellow and white
        swirls.

I never
usually
rush her,
but we can't be late,
not on our first day of school,
so I quietly clear my throat
      —ahem, ahem—
hoping it will stir her from daydreaming long enough
to get going on the marbled eggs.

Instead it is like pouring
icy water into a
pan of hot fat.

Tippi pushes away her plate.
'You know I'm owed a
goddamn gold medal
for all the times you've kept *me* waiting
over the years.'

So I whisper,

'I'm sorry, Tippi,'

because I can't lie and pretend the

throat clearing

meant nothing.

Not with her.

Truth:

It's what happens

when you're bound like we are

by a body too stubborn

to peel itself apart at conception.

Uniform

Unlike Dragon's school

where they can wear what they like,

Hornbeacon expects all students to wear

uniforms—

bright white shirts, stripy green ties,

a plaid skirt

      with pleats down the front.

The idea

is to make everyone look the same.

I know that.

But it doesn't matter how we dress.

We will always

      stand out,

and trying to look like everyone else is stupid.

'It isn't too late to back out,' Tippi says.

'But we agreed to go,' I reply,

and Tippi clicks her tongue.

'I was forced into saying yes.

You think I want *this*?' she asks.

She tugs at the tie knotted around her neck,

pulling it up

and into a noose.

I reach for the skirt and step in.
Tippi doesn't resist
but pulls it into place.

'I feel so ugly,' Tippi says.

She laces her fingers through my hair and
　　　separates it into three thick strands
　　　which she plaits and unplaits.

'You're not ugly.
You look like me,' I say, smirking,
and squeeze her hand
tight.

What is Ugly?

I've been in enough hospital wards to have seen horrors:
a kid with his face melted down one side,
a woman with her nose ripped off and ears hanging loose
　　　like strips of bacon.

That's what people call ugly.

Not that I would.

I've learned to be less cruel than that.

But I know what Tippi means.

People find us grotesque,
especially from a distance,
when they see us as a whole,
the way our bodies are distinctly two
　　　then merge,
　　　suddenly,
　　　at the waist.

But if you took a photograph of us, head and shoulders only,
then showed it to everyone you met,
the only thing people would notice is that we are
twins,
　　　my hair to the shoulders,
Tippi's a little shorter,
both of us with pixie noses

and perfectly peaked eyebrows.

It's true to say we're different.

But ugly?

Come on.

Give us a break.

 Discuss

1. What difficulties do you imagine conjoined twins would have in their daily lives?
2. The novel is written in an unusual format. Why do you think the author chose to use this format?

 Understand

1. Why does Grace say they cannot be late?
2. How does Tippi react when Grace tries to hurry her?
3. Describe the uniform that students at Hornbeacon are expected to wear.
4. What are the 'horrors' that Grace has seen in hospital wards?
5. How does Grace reassure Tippi when she says that she feels ugly?

 Explore

 1. Why is Grace unable to lie to Tippi, in your opinion?

 2. In what ways do you think the personalities of the two sisters differ? Give reasons for your answer.

 3. Would you say the sisters have a good relationship with one another based on the extract? Support your answer with reference to the text.

 Create

 Write a diary entry Grace might have written after her first day at Hornbeacon in the space provided on page 67 of your Portfolio. (For information on diaries see page 5.)

Read Nicholas Tucker's review of Sarah Crossan's novel *One*.

One by Sarah Crossan, book review: An admirable and affecting tale of conjoined twins

Now is a golden time for minorities in children's fiction, with Sarah Crossan's *One* currently exploring the relatively unchartered fictional waters surrounding the topic of conjoined twins. Her main characters, 16-year-old Grace and Tippi, talk, joke and feel very much like other US teenagers. Yet they still attract ignorant or unkind comments, finding a note stuck to their school locker reading, 'Why don't you go back to the zoo?' This is in addition to being openly filmed by others when on public transport and having to field frequently agonising personal questions.

Grace and Tippi have two heads, four arms but are joined at the hip. Home-schooled and under constant medical and psychological care, this support is threatened when their mother loses her job and already unemployed Dad can't stay off the booze. The only way open to the family is for the twins to sell their story, something they are loath to do. Luckily for them they find an unusually compassionate British television producer.

At their new school, meanwhile, they quickly make two firm friends: Yasmeen, who is HIV positive, and Jon, who lives in squalor after his mother had left him. This little gang of outsiders go on forbidden smoking and drinking sprees and Grace soon falls heavily for Jon. Her feelings are reciprocated while Tippi, literally, looks the other way. But an attack of flu leaves the twins in failing health, with separation – however dangerous – the only alternative to certain death for both.

Sarah Crossan tells this affecting story through the voice of Grace, employing a loose but readable form of blank verse that often takes up only a few lines on the page. She narrates directly and honestly until towards the end when emotions finally burst their banks, drowning further plot developments in torrents of raw feeling. Grace also creates one of those 'bucket lists' of things to do in case she dies, one of which includes climbing a tree. Making and then fulfilling an uncomfortable and unrealistic final choice of this sort has become a cliché in fictional accounts of young people coping with possibly terminal illness. This example rings as hollow as most of the others.

But Crossan has researched her subject thoroughly, referring to past examples of conjoined twins including Chang and Eng, who managed to dodge King Rama of Siam's death sentence as babies and went on to have two wives and 21 children. The medical procedures involved in the twins' separation are clearly described, but with details of the actual operation left to the imagination. Only overtly sentimental in the last few pages, this is still a story to savour and admire.

Understand

1. Why do Grace and Tippi have to sell their story?
2. What does Grace have on her bucket list?
3. What do Grace and Tippi like to do with their new friends?
4. According to the reviewer, what did the author research before writing this novel?
5. What typical features of a review can you identify in this piece?

 ## Explore

 1. Would you consider this to be a positive or a negative review? Give a reason for your answer.

2. Would this review encourage you to read the novel? Give two reasons for your answer.

 ## Create

 1. In pairs, come up with an alternative heading for this review.
2. Write a review of a novel or short story that you have read. (For information on reviews see pages 53–54.)

Prepositions

Prepositions are words that show the relationship between nouns or pronouns.

For example:

*   *The bag is **beside** the door.*
*   *The shoes are **under** the table.*
*   *The cat is **near** the bowl.*

Grammar Primer: pages 40–42

In each case the preposition shows the relationship between a noun (bag, shoes, cat) and another noun (door, table, bowl).

The following are examples of the most commonly used prepositions.

about	because	by	into	outside	toward
above	before	down	near	over	under
across	behind	during	like	past	until
against	below	except	next	round	upon
along	beneath	for	of	since	up
among	beside	from	on	through	with
around	between	in	onto	till	within
as	beyond	inside	out	to	without

 Understand

1. Find the prepositions in the following sentences.
   (a) Nicola is about to go to school.
   (b) Geoff was born before Ciara.
   (c) The book is under the bed.
   (d) The bird sat on the bench.
   (e) James held the sign above his head.
   (f) Ethan ran to the finish line.

2. Write out the following sentences and select a suitable preposition to fill the blanks.
   (a) Valerie walked home _____ the meeting.
   (b) A rabbit lives _____ that bush.
   (c) Grainne climbed _____ the boat.
   (d) Sarah hid _____ the bed.
   (e) The shop is located _____ the stop sign.
   (f) _____ midnight we were all exhausted.
   (g) Put your pencils _____ the desk.
   (h) Sean arrived _____ Eithne.

3. How many prepositions can you count in the review of *One* on page 258?

Changing relationships

As characters develop, their thoughts and feelings can change. This can have an impact on their relationships with other characters. The development of a relationship can make the characters more believable and relatable to the reader.

In the novel *Goodnight Mister Tom* by Michelle Magorian, young Willie Beech is evacuated from London to the countryside on the eve of the Second World War. In the countryside he develops and flourishes under the guidance of Tom Oakley. He eventually receives a letter from his mother telling him to return home to London. At the beginning of this extract he has just stepped off the train and sees his mother waiting on the platform. After such a long absence, the relationship between these two characters has changed.

Goodnight Mister Tom

Willie ran over to her.

'Mum!' he cried. 'Mum!'

'Go away,' she said sternly. 'You won't get no money from me.'

'Mum,' he repeated, 'it's me.'

She glanced down and was about to tell him to clear off when she recognised him. Yes. It was Willie but he had altered so much. She had been looking for a thin little boy dressed in grey. Here stood an upright, well-fleshed boy in sturdy ankle boots, thick woollen socks, a green rolled-top jersey, and a navy blue coat and balaclava. His hair stuck out in a shiny mass above his forehead and his cheeks were round and pink. It was a great shock to her.

'I'm awfully pleased to see you, Mum. I've such a lot to tell you and there's me pictures, like.'

She was startled at his peculiar mixture of accents. She had expected him to be more subservient but even his voice sounded louder.

'I'm sorry,' she said. 'I'm not very well, you see, and I'm a bit tired. I wasn't expectin' such a change in you.'

Willie was puzzled.

He thought that it was his mother that had changed. He had learnt new things, that was true, but he was still him.

He studied her face. She was very pale, almost yellow in colour and her lips were so blue that it seemed as if every ounce of blood had been drained from them. The lines by her thin mouth curved downwards. He glanced at her body. She was wearing a long black coat, fawn stockings and smart lace-up heeled shoes. A small shopping bag was now leaning against her leg.

He touched her arm gently.

'I'll carry that for you, Mum,' he said, picking it up. She spun round and gave his hand a sharp slap.

'I'll tell you what I wants when I wants and you know I don't approve of touching.'

'Sorry,' he muttered.

They stood silently and awkwardly as the large noisy train station roared around them. Willie felt his heart sinking and the spark of hope that he had held was fast dissolving, but then he remembered. Mister Tom had said that they would feel awkward at first and that it would take time to get used to each other.

Mrs Beech, meanwhile, surveyed her small son, her mind racing. She'd be lenient with him for the moment. After all it was his first evening back and he had a lot to learn before accepting his manly responsibilities.

'Let's go for a cup of tea,' she said at last. 'You can take my bag.'

'Thanks, Mum,' and he smiled.

She stepped sharply backwards, horrified. She couldn't remember ever having seen him smile before. She had hoped that he had remained a serious child. The smile frightened her. It threatened her authority. She swallowed her feelings and stepped forward again, handing him her bag. Everything was going to be fine, thought Willie.

 Discuss

Have you ever met up with a friend or a family member after being apart for a long time? Did this relationship feel different when you met up?

 Understand

1. How does Mrs Beech react when Willie first approaches her?
2. Mrs Beech notices that Willie has changed. What changes does she notice?
3. What advice did Mister Tom give to Willie?
4. What do Willie and his mother decide to do?

 Explore

 1. What impression do you get of Willie's mother? Explain your answer.

 2. Think about how Willie's mother responds to him carrying her bags. What does this tell us about their relationship?

 3. Do you agree with Willie that 'Everything is going to be fine'? Give reasons for your answer.

 Create

 1. Work in pairs to rewrite the dialogue between Willie and his mother to portray a more loving and supportive relationship. When you have finished, act out your dialogue.

2. Write the letter Willie would have sent to Mister Tom telling him about the reunion with his mother in the space provided on page 68 of your Portfolio.

There, they're and their

'There', 'they're' and 'their' are homophones. They may all sound the same but they have entirely different meanings.

'There' means in or at that place.

*You left your coat over **there**.*

'There' is also used as a pronoun to introduce a sentence.

***There** is a chill in the air tonight.*

'They're' is a contraction of 'they are'.

***They're** going to the cinema.*

> Grammar Primer:
> pages 43–44

'Their' is the possessive case of the pronoun 'they'.

*They are riding **their** bicycles.*

 Understand

Write out the following sentences and insert 'there', 'their' or 'they're' in the blanks.

1. The exit is over _____.
2. Iveagh and Ibar are always late; _____ friends never expect them to be on time.
3. Deirdre has two dogs and _____ very loud.
4. Jessica and Alex cling tightly to the envelopes containing _____ exam results. _____ both hoping that they passed.
5. _____ are seven types of trees in this park. If you look over _____ you will see one of them.
6. Mark and Jennifer both hoped _____ would be enough time to see _____ grandad.
7. If they want to get _____ phones back they need to attend detention. In this school _____ are rules.
8. Where are _____ bags? I thought they left them over _____.
9. _____ going over _____ to get _____ exam results.

Friendships

A friendship is a relationship between two people born out of similarities, kindness and mutual appreciation. Friendships are an important part of our development as people.

Facebook created the following advertisement to celebrate World Friendship Day.

 https://youtu.be/iUdQflaG8ro

 Understand

1. What event does this advertisement promote?
2. List two adjectives that are used to describe friends.
3. According to the speakers in the advertisement, why can it be difficult to maintain friendships?

 Explore

 1. Do you think this is an effective advertisement? Give reasons for your answer.

2. Come up with some ideas that could improve this advertisement.

3. Why do you think one of the speakers says that it is unlikely grown men would say 'I love you'? Do you agree with him?

 Create

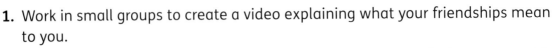 1. Work in small groups to create a video explaining what your friendships mean to you.

 2. (a) Work in small groups to come up with some suggestions for how you could celebrate World Friendship Day in your school.

(b) When you have agreed on an idea, write the email you would send to your principal explaining why it is important to celebrate friendship, and asking for permission to organise whatever type of celebration your group decided on.

Friendships do not only exist between one person and another. Many people have strong friendships with their pets and some view their pets as family.

The following article explores the relationship between humans and dogs.

A dog is a human's best friend

A dog is not just a human's best friend; a dog can be anyone's best friend.

When coming home feels like your very own surprise birthday party, you know you have something good in your life. Rover almost gives himself a heart attack when he even hears my car pull into the drive. I sometimes wonder if he spends his time alone with his supersonic hearing tuned in, waiting for any familiar sounds so that he can react with an explosion of excitement.

Humankind and dogs have had a loving relationship for many years, with domestic dog remains being found beside human remains dating back 14,000 years.

So, why do we love our pet pooches so much? Well, it is simple really. They love us unconditionally. Dogs have developed through the years and have an acute understanding of humans. They can sense our mood, pick up on our emotional state and sympathise with our sorrow.

Not only are they our loyal companions, but research has shown that dogs can save our lives. Dogs can recognise cancerous smells from metabolic waste products in our bodies. The difference in smell is so significant that dogs can identify cancer in the early stages. A black Labrador named Marnie was able to detect with 97% accuracy colon cancer in 200 humans.

Dogs have graduated beyond being pets and have become fully-fledged members of our family. They give us the best of themselves, and in return it is our responsibility to give them the best care we can. Dogs are not entertained by television or social media, so after a long day when your dog nudges you for a walk or a play, remember that being best friends is a two-way street, and be sure to reward your dog for their love, loyalty and compassion.

 Understand

1. Why does the writer say that a dog is not just a human's best friend?
2. What does Rover do when the writer comes through the door?
3. What can the black Labrador Marnie detect?

Investigate

1. (a) Many animals are abandoned in Ireland each year. Work in groups to research one of the following animal charities.

   ◖ Dogs Trust
   ◖ Dogs Aid Animal Sanctuary
   ◖ Paws Animal Rescue
   ◖ Dogs in Distress
   ◖ ISPCA
   ◖ MADRA
   ◖ DSPCA
   ◖ Ash Animal Rescue

   Try to find out the following information about your chosen charity:
   ◖ where they are based
   ◖ how many animals they take in each year
   ◖ how many animals they successfully rehome
   ◖ what the public can do to help to rehome these animals or decrease the number of abandoned pets each year.

   (b) When you have finished researching your chosen charity, work as a group to create a presentation, then present your findings to the class.

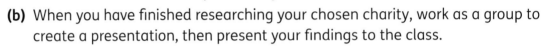

Create

Write a debate speech proposing or opposing the following motion: *This house believes that dogs make better friends than humans.* When you have prepared your speech, carry out a class debate. (For information on debates see pages 47–48.)

Family relationships

Family relationships are very important. We all have different relationships within our own family structures. Our relationships with our family members can have a huge impact on our lives.

Everyone's family home experience is unique. In the following podcast, Cathy Moorehead reveals her experience of growing up as a child of deaf parents.

www.rte.ie/radio1/doconone/2016/0527/791374-the-loudest-house-on-the-street/

Discuss

1. Imagine that you have not completed your homework because you watched a series on Netflix instead. Deliver this information as you would to your friend. Afterwards, deliver this information as you would to your teacher. What do you notice about the difference in your tone of voice and the language you use?

2. Why do you think tone is an important tool in oral communication?

Understand

1. Fill out the worksheet on page 69 of your Portfolio.

2. Write a personal profile for Cathy by answering the following questions.

   (a) What was Cathy's family life like?

   (b) How many people were in Cathy's family?

   (c) Where was Cathy raised?

   (d) What did Cathy like to do?

   (e) What are Cathy's regrets?

   (f) How was Cathy's house different to other people's houses?

   (g) How did Cathy's parents meet?

   (h) What does Cathy do now?

Create

Work in groups to create a two-minute podcast on one of the topics below. Remember to include appropriate sound effects where possible. You can use sound.org to source sound effects.

◖ School life

◖ A visit to the park

◖ The school run

◖ A visit to the zoo

Our families often protect and care for us. The following poem deals with the desire most parents have to protect their children from negative experiences.

Nettles
By Vernon Scannell

My son aged three fell in the nettle bed.

'Bed' seemed a curious name for those green spears,

That regiment of spite behind the shed:

It was no place for rest. With sobs and tears

The boy came seeking comfort and I saw

White blisters beaded on his tender skin.

We soothed him till his pain was not so raw.

At last he offered us a watery grin,

And then I took my hook and honed the blade

And went outside and slashed in fury with it

Till not a nettle in that fierce parade

Stood upright any more. Next task: I lit

A funeral pyre to burn the fallen dead.

But in two weeks the busy sun and rain

Had called up tall recruits behind the shed:

My son would often feel sharp wounds again.

regiment:
a unit in the army

hook:
traditional cutting tool

honed:
sharpened

pyre:
wood on which a corpse is burned

Discuss

1. Did you ever injure yourself when you were younger?
2. Who did you go to for comfort?
3. What did this person do to comfort you?
4. Have you ever been stung by a nettle? Describe how it felt.

Understand

1. What happened to the poet's son when he was three?
2. Why does the poet think 'bed' is a curious name for the nettles?
3. What did the poet do after his son offered him a watery grin?
4. What happened two weeks later?

5. Work with a partner to list all of the military imagery that you can find in this poem.

Explore

1. Do you think 'Nettles' is an appropriate title for this poem? Give a reason for your answer.

2. What do you think the poet means by the line 'My son would often feel sharp wounds again'?
3. Choose a poem that you have studied that deals with a brave or heroic moment. Name the poet and give the title of the poem. How did the poet convey this moment of heroic bravery to the readers?

Create

1. **(a)** Write a speech about the importance of friends and family in the space provided on pages 70–71 of your Portfolio. (For information on speeches see pages 42–43.)

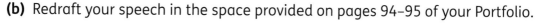
   (b) Redraft your speech in the space provided on pages 94–95 of your Portfolio.

   (c) Read your speech to the class.

Family traditions are an important part of life. They can help us to emulate the people we are closest to and shape the way of life for future generations. However, family traditions can sometimes cause issues if an individual wants to find their own path in life. In the following poem, Seamus Heaney explores the concept of family traditions and of making your own mark in the world.

emulate:
copy the actions of

Digging
By Seamus Heaney

Between my finger and my thumb
The squat pen rests; snug as a gun.

Under my window, a clean rasping sound
When the spade sinks into gravelly ground:
My father, digging. I look down

Till his straining rump among the flowerbeds
Bends low, comes up twenty years away
Stooping in rhythm through potato drills
Where he was digging.

The coarse boot nestled on the lug, the shaft
Against the inside knee was levered firmly.
He rooted out tall tops, buried the bright edge deep
To scatter new potatoes that we picked,
Loving their cool hardness in our hands.

By God, the old man could handle a spade.
Just like his old man.

My grandfather cut more turf in a day
Than any other man on Toner's bog.
Once I carried him milk in a bottle
Corked sloppily with paper. He straightened up
To drink it, then fell to right away
Nicking and slicing neatly, heaving sods
Over his shoulder, going down and down
For the good turf. Digging.

The cold smell of potato mould, the squelch and slap
Of soggy peat, the curt cuts of an edge
Through living roots awaken in my head.
But I've no spade to follow men like them.

Between my finger and my thumb
The squat pen rests.
I'll dig with it.

Understand

1. **(a)** How does the pen rest between Heaney's finger and thumb in the second line?

   (b) What poetic device is Heaney using in this line?

2. What is Heaney's father digging at the beginning of the poem?

3. Heaney reflects on the image of his father and grandfather digging. What sounds does he recall?

4. What does Heaney remember bringing to his grandfather?

 Explore

 1. How are Heaney's father and grandfather portrayed?

2. In what way is Heaney different to these two men?

3. What image stands out most to you in the poem? Explain your choice.

 4. Aside from relationships, what other themes do you think this poem deals with?

5. What does the closing line 'I'll dig with it' suggest?

6. The poem suggests that digging can be similar to writing. With that concept in mind, what do you think Heaney meant by the line 'going down and down / For the good turf'?

 Create

Write a paragraph about a memory you have of a parent or grandparent carrying out an activity, hobby or job.

Sometimes, generational differences can mean that family members do not always understand one another.

In the short film *My Strange Grandfather* by Dina Velikovskaya, a young granddaughter is dismissive and even ashamed of her grandfather's strange behaviour, but she learns that his peculiar actions allow him to create a real miracle.

 https://youtu.be/wYBpxPRn_nw

 Understand

1. What music do you hear in this film?
2. What sound effects are included in this film?

 Explore

1. Do you think the grandfather and granddaughter in this film have a good relationship? Give two reasons for your answer.
2. There is no dialogue between the grandfather and his granddaughter. In your opinion, does this add to or take from the film? Explain your answer.
3. Are there any similarities between the Aer Lingus advertisement on page 235 and the short film *My Strange Grandfather*? Write a paragraph exploring the similarities between the family relationships shown in each.

 Create

 Choose one scene in which the grandfather and granddaughter are together. Work in pairs to write a short piece of dialogue between the two characters. When you have finished, act out your dialogue for the class.

Think about some common phrases that a parent might use.

- *Because I said so.*
- *If you keep staring at that screen, your eyes will go square.*
- *If I've told you once, I've told you a thousand times.*

 Work with a partner to list 10 sayings you might expect to hear a parent say to a teenager.

Watch the following video about Irish mammies:

https://youtu.be/m-kvto8XYNU

 Discuss

1. Were any of these sayings on your list?
2. Would you consider this video to be humorous?

 Understand

1. What problem is the mammy having in the first scene?
2. What does the mammy take out of the drawer?
3. What does the mammy tell us the weather was like an hour ago?
4. What does the mammy shout up the stairs?
5. What county name is printed on the cup that the mammy is holding?

 Create

 1. (a) Amy has asked her mother countless times if she can go to the local disco. Her mother refuses to allow her to go, as she thinks that Amy is too young. This is the last disco of the year and Amy really wants to go. Work with a partner to write the dialogue that you think would take place in this scenario.

 (b) Read over your dialogue and add stage directions. List some props you could include and the lighting, sound effects and costumes you could use to bring your scene to life.

 (c) Act out your scene for the class.

Sometimes we can have a family-like relationship with people who are not our relatives.

In the following extract from *The Member of the Wedding* by Carson McCullers, Frankie's brother is getting married and Frankie feels as though she is being left out. She has a conversation with the family cook, Berenice, who is like a mother to Frankie. As you read this extract, pay attention to the interactions between Frankie and Berenice.

The Member of the Wedding

[Frankie sits miserably, her shoulders hunched. Then with a sudden gesture she bangs her forehead on the table. Her fists are clenched and she is sobbing.]

Berenice: Come on. Don't act like that

Frankie *[her voice muffled]***:** They were so pretty. They must have such a good time. And they went away and left me.

Berenice: Sit up. Behave yourself.

Frankie: They came and went away, and left me with this feeling.

Berenice: Hosee! I bet I know something. *[She begins tapping with her heel: one, two, three – bang! After a pause, in which the rhythm is established, she begins singing.]* Frankie's got a crush! Frankie's got a crush! Frankie's got a crush on the *wedding*!

Frankie: Quit!

Berenice: Frankie's got a crush! Frankie's got a crush!

Frankie: You better quit! *[She rises suddenly and snatches up the carving knife.]*

Berenice: You lay down that knife.

Frankie: Make me. *[She bends the blade slowly.]*

Berenice: Lay it down, *Devil*. *[There is a silence.]* Just throw it! You just!

[After a pause Frankie aims the knife carefully at the closed door leading to the bedroom and throws it. The knife does not stick in the wall.]

Frankie: I used to be the best knife thrower in this town.

Berenice: Frances Addams, you goin' to try that stunt once too often.

Frankie: I warned you quit pickin' with me.

Berenice: You are not fit to live in this house.

Frankie: I won't be living in this one much longer; I'm going to run away from home.

Berenice: And a good riddance to a big old bag of rubbage.

Frankie: You wait and see. I'm leaving town.

Berenice: And where do you think you are going?

Frankie *[gazing around the walls]***:** I don't know.

Berenice: You're going crazy. That's where you going.

Frankie: No. *[Solemnly]* This coming Sunday after the wedding, I'm leaving town. And I swear to Jesus by my two eyes I'm never coming back here any more.

Berenice *[going to Frankie and pushing her damp bangs back from her forehead]*: Sugar? You serious?

Frankie *[exasperated]*: Of course! Do you think I would stand here and say that swear and tell a story? Sometimes, Berenice, I think it takes you longer to realize a fact than it does anybody who ever lived.

Berenice: But you say you don't know where you going. You going, but you don't know where. That don't make no sense to me.

Frankie *[after a long pause in which she again gazes around the walls of the room]*: I feel just exactly like somebody has peeled all the skin off me. I wish I had some good cold peach ice cream.

 ## Discuss

1. Do you have a relationship with someone who is not related to you, but who you consider to be family?
2. Can you think of a time when you felt left out of a family event? What happened? How did it make you feel?

 ## Understand

1. What does Berenice say to Frankie to make her feel so angry?
2. What does Frankie do with the knife?
3. What is Frankie planning on doing after the wedding?
4. Why does Berenice think that Frankie is not serious about running away?

 ## Explore

 1. In your opinion, do Frankie and Berenice have a good relationship?

 2. What evidence is there to suggest that Frankie and Berenice have a parent-child relationship?

3. How do you think the audience would feel when Frankie picks up the knife?
4. Do the stage directions help you to visualise the play? Without the stage directions would the play still make sense?
5. Imagine you are staging this scene. What props, set, costumes and lighting would you use to bring the play to life on stage? Explain your choices.

 ## Create

Imagine you are the casting director for *The Member of the Wedding*. Decide on the characteristics you would like the actors playing Frankie and Bernice to have and create an advertisement for each of the roles.

Romantic relationships

Romantic relationships are deep emotional connections between two people. Over time, romantic relationships can develop into love.

Romantic relationships can be expressed powerfully through poetry. When we love someone we want to be able to give them everything to show them how much they mean to us.

In the following poem, W. B. Yeats uses metaphor to express these feelings.

He wishes for the Cloths of Heaven

By W. B. Yeats

Had I the heavens' embroidered cloths,
Enwrought with golden and silver light,
The blue and the dim and the dark cloths
Of night and light and the half-light,
I would spread the cloths under your feet:
But I, being poor, have only my dreams;
I have spread my dreams under your feet;
Tread softly because you tread on my dreams.

 Understand

1. What does the speaker want to give to his beloved?
2. Why is he unable to give this to her?
3. What does he give her instead?

 Explore

 1. Do you agree that this poem conveys a powerful message about love? Give two reasons for your answer.

 2. In your opinion, why does the poet not include the word 'love' in this poem? Give one reason for your answer.

 Create

 Work in groups to create a video to go with this poem. Think of suitable music, backdrop and imagery to represent the poem. iMovie is a useful app that could help you to create this video.

Not all romantic relationships are happy. In the following poem there seems to be some distance between the couple. As you are reading, pay particular attention to the poem's form.

40 — Love

By Roger McGough

middle	aged
couple	playing
ten	nis
when	the
game	ends
and	they
go	home
the	net
will	still
be	be
tween	them

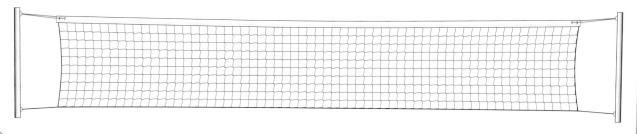

 **Discuss**

1. Do you think '40 — Love' is an appropriate title for this poem?
2. At what age would you consider people to be middle-aged?
3. Considering the relationship between this couple, why do you think they play tennis together?

 Explore

1. Think about the form of this poem. What does it suggest? Why do you think the poet wrote the poem this way?
2. What does the poet mean when he says 'the net will still be between them'?

 Create

Write a poem about a relationship between two people.

Revising relationships: a thematic approach

Reflect and review

1. Look back at the images on page 253. Now that you have studied relationships, would you change any of those images? Think of some alternative images that could be used to illustrate relationships.

2. Fill in the unit review on pages 72–73 of your Portfolio.

Language skills

1. Write out the following sentences, adding 'there', 'their' or 'they're' as needed.
   (a) Carl has a great relationship with his grandad, _____ the best of friends.
   (b) Martha's neighbours are a nightmare, she only gets peace and quiet when _____ not _____.
   (c) David and Shauna love _____ dog Coco.
   (d) _____ is a strong wind this evening.
   (e) I think _____ going to the park later.
   (f) If I see _____ bags I'll tell them.
   (g) _____ are 12 months in a year.

2. Find the prepositions in each of the sentences below.
   (a) Brian drove around the roundabout.
   (b) The dog fell asleep underneath a warm blanket.
   (c) George sat on his new bed.
   (d) I ran through the park.
   (e) The cat crawled towards us.
   (f) Class begins at 8.45 a.m.
   (g) We got there by plane.

3. Write out the following sentences, inserting an appropriate preposition in the blank space.
   (a) Daisy walked her dog _____ the street.
   (b) I walked _____ the pet shop.
   (c) My classroom is _____ the lockers.
   (d) He worked _____ his father.
   (e) Caleb and Harrison placed their trophies _____ the cabinet.
   (f) Sarah was going on her holidays _____ August.
   (g) I received a letter _____ Jane.

Oral assessment

Choose a film, novel, short story or play you have studied that deals with an interesting relationship between two characters. Prepare and deliver a presentation on this relationship to your classmates, using the prompts below as a guide.

- ◖ Background information on the characters.
- ◖ How their relationship started.
- ◖ How their relationship developed.
- ◖ What you found interesting about this relationship.

Written assessment

1. **(a)** Choose one style of writing from the list below:
   - ◖ personal essay
   - ◖ diary entry
   - ◖ short story
   - ◖ poem
   - ◖ article
   - ◖ blog post.

   In your chosen style of writing, create a piece entitled 'The Importance of Relationships in our Lives' in the space provided on pages 74–75 of your Portfolio. Be sure to include the features from the particular style you have chosen.

   (b) Redraft your piece in the space provided on pages 96–97 of your Portfolio.

   (c) After you have written your second draft, write a paragraph explaining your choice of writing style, in the space provided on page 97 of your Portfolio.

Exam skills

1. Choose two characters from a novel you have studied that have a relationship.
   (a) Name the novel, the author and the two characters involved in the relationship.
   (b) Describe the relationship between these characters.
   (c) In your opinion, is the relationship between these characters positive or negative? Use a key event from the novel to support your answer.

   Write your answer in the space provided on pages 98–99 of your Portfolio.

Acknowledgements:

'BLACKBERRY-PICKING', 'DIGGING', and 'MID-TERM BREAK', Copyright the Estate of Seamus Heaney, first appeared in Death of a Naturalist. Reproduced by permission of Faber & Faber Ltd.; 'Don't Be Scared' from The Oldest Girl in the World by Carol Ann Duffy. Published by Faber, 2000. Copyright © Carol Ann Duffy. Reproduced by permission of the author c/o Rogers, Coleridge & White Ltd., 20 Powis Mews, London W11 1JN; 'MIDSUMMER, TOBAGO', Copyright Derek Walcott, first appeared in Sea Grapes. Reproduced by permission of Faber & Faber Ltd.; 'Stopping by Woods on a Snowy Evening' by Robert Frost (ebook) from THE POETRY OF ROBERT FROST edited by Edward Connery Lathem. Copyright © 1916, 1939, 1969 by Henry Holt and Company. Copyright © 1944, 1958 by Robert Frost. Copyright © 1967 by Lesley Frost Ballantine. Used by permission of Henry Holt and Company. All rights reserved. (print) from Collected Poems by Robert Frost. Published by Vintage. Reprinted by permission of The Random House Group Limited. © 1930; 'THE GIRL WITH MANY EYES', Copyright Tim Burton, first appeared in The Melancholy Death of Oyster Boy & Other Stories. Reproduced by kind permission of Faber & Faber Ltd.; "40—Love" by Roger McGough from "After the Merrymaking" (© Roger McGough, 1971) is printed by permission of United Agents (www.unitedagents.co.uk) on behalf of Roger McGough; Back in the Playground Blues by Adrian Mitchell by kind permission of the Estate of Adrian Mitchell, c/o United Agents; Base Details by Siegfried Sassoon Copyright Siegfried Sassoon by kind permission of the Estate of George Sassoon; Dream Variations and I, Too by Langston Hughes by kind permission of Alfred A. Knopf Inc. c/o David Higham Associates; Extract from A Shop Selling Speech by Sabrina Mahfouz by kind permission of Bloomsbury; Extract from Antarctica by Claire Keegan, by kind permission of the author c/o Curtis Brown; Extract from Goodnight Mister Tom by Michelle Magorian by kind permission of Penguin Random House UK; Extract from The Hitchhiker's Guide to the Galaxy by Douglas Adams reproduced with permission of Pan Macmillan through PLSclear; also by kind permission of Curtis Brown; Extract from Janey Mary by James Plunkett reprinted by permission of Peters Fraser & Dunlop (www.petersfraserdunlop.com) on behalf of the estate of James Plunkett; Extract from Jessica Ennis Unbelievable - From My Childhood Dreams to Winning Olympic Gold by Jessica Ennis by kind permission of Hodder & Stoughton; Extract from Noughts and Crosses by Dominic Cooke by kind permission of Oxford University Press; Extract from One by Sarah Crossan by kind permission of Bloomsbury; Extract from Pygmalion by kind permission of the estate of George Bernard Shaw, c/o The Society of Authors; Extract from The Martian Chronicles by Ray Bradbury by kind permission of the estate of Ray Bradbury c/o Don Congdon Associates; Extract from The Member of the Wedding by Carson McCullers by kind permission of the estate of Carson McCullers c/o Andrew Nurnberg Associates; Extract from Yellow Cake by Margo Lanagan, by kind permission of the author; Extract taken from 'THE LADY IN THE VAN', Copyright Alan Bennett and Reproduced by permission of Faber & Faber Ltd.; Feeling Good by Anthony Newley and Leslie Bricusse by kind permission of The Richmond Association; Five puppies among 10 dogs seized at Dublin Port by customs officers by Fiachradh McDermott by kind permission of the author; Homework! Oh, Homework! by Jack Prelutsky by kind permission of HarperCollins; 'I Found A Reason' Words and Music by Lou Reed © 1970, Reproduced by permission of Oakfield Avenue Music Ltd/ EMI Music Publishing Ltd, London W1F 9LD; Learning Lettering by Nathalie Marquez Courtney by kind permission of the author; Mel Churcher on the differences between stage and screen acting by kind permission of Mel Churcher (author of A Screen Acting Workshop + DVD published by Nick Hern Books); Nettles by Vernon Scannell by kind permission of the estate of Vernon Scannell; Powder from The Night in Question by Tobias Wolff, copyright © 1996 by Tobias Wolff. Used by kind permission of Bloomsbury; Property For Sale by Rachel Rooney by kind permission of David Higham Associates; PUPPY DOG CRIES by Jack Cahill by kind permission of the Irish Sun; Review of One by Sarah Crossan by Nicholas Tucker by kind permission of independent.co.uk; Rosa Parks by Jan Dean by kind permission of the author; Saoirse Ronan on how Brooklyn is her own Irish-American journey by Sheryl Garratt by kind permission of Telegraphmediagroup; The ABC by Spike Milligan by kind permission of Spike Milligan Productions; The Capitol – Washington DC by Alex Stringer by kind permission of Kate, Matt and Alex Stringer; The Fault in our Stars by John Green – review by awkwardunicorn Copyright Guardian News & Media Ltd 2017; The Pig by Roald Dahl by kind permission of Jonathan Cape Ltd. & Penguin Books Ltd.; The Q&A Louis Walsh: 'Which book changed my life? My chequebook' by Rosanna Greenstreet by kind permission of Rosanna Greenstreet; Tula by Margarita Engle by kind permission of Houghton Mifflin Harcourt; 'When I'm 64' Words and Music by John Lennon and Paul McCartney © 1967, Reproduced by permission of Sony/ATV Tunes LLC, London W1F 9LD; Xbox, Xbox - A Love Poem by Kenn Nesbitt by kind permission of the author; You Can't Judge A Book By The Cover Words and Music by Willie Dixon Copyright © 1962 Hoochie Coochie Music. Copyright Renewed. All Rights Administered by BMG Rights Management (US) LLC. All Rights Reserved. Used by Permission. Reprinted by Permission of Hal Leonard LLC.

Photo acknowledgements:

ACORN 1 / Alamy Stock Photo; Action Plus Sports Images / Alamy Stock Photo; Adam Welz / Alamy Stock Photo; AF archive / Alamy Stock Photo; Alan Wilson / Alamy Stock Photo; Art Directors & TRIP / Alamy Stock Photo; Ben Molyneux / Alamy Stock Photo; Catharine Collingridge (The Bright Agency); CBW / Alamy Stock Photo; Clynt Garnham Publishing / Alamy Stock Photo; Collection Christophel / Alamy Stock Photo; Cover of I Am Malala by Christina Lamb and Malala Yousafzai by kind permission of The Orion Publishing Group; Cover of Looking for Alaska by John Green by kind permission of Penguin Random House; Cover of Roll of Thunder, Hear My Cry by Mildred D. Taylor by kind permission of Penguin Random House; Cover of The Test by Brian O'Driscoll Copyright © Inpho/Billy Strickland and Penguin Books Ltd, 2015; Cristina Fumi / Alamy Stock Photo; David Kilpatrick / Alamy Stock Photo; dpa picture alliance / Alamy Stock Photo; Ed Endicott / Alamy Stock Photo; Entertainment Pictures / Alamy Stock Photo; Extract from Coraline by Neil Gaiman, P. Craig Russell by kind permission of HarperCollins; Five puppies among 10 dogs seized at Dublin Port by customs officers – image by kind permission of the Office of the Revenue Commissioners; Geraint Lewis / Alamy Stock Photo; Granger Historical Picture Archive / Alamy Stock Photo; INTERFOTO / Alamy Stock Photo; Irish Independent front page 28.10.13 by kind permission of Independent News & Media; Irish Times website front page 24.10.17 by kind permission of the Irish Times; Isabelle Plasschaert / Alamy Stock Photo; ITAR-TASS Photo Agency / Alamy Stock Photo; J.F.T.L IMAGES / Alamy Stock Photo; Janine Wiedel Photolibrary / Alamy Stock Photo; Janne Tervonen / Alamy Stock Photo; Jeff Morgan 03 / Alamy Stock Photo; Jim Newberry / Alamy Stock Photo; Jocelyn Kao (The Bright Agency); koerie / Stockimo / Alamy Stock Photo; Learning Lettering image Copyright © Nathalie Marquez Courtney by kind permission of Nathalie Marquez Courtney; M. Stan Reaves / Alamy Stock Photo; Michael Rooney / Alamy Stock Photo; Moviestore collection Ltd / Alamy Stock Photo; OMG! I just got born! by Mick Stevens by kind permission of Condé Nast; Over, damn you, over! by Zachary Kanin by kind permission of Condé Nast; Pako Mera / Alamy Stock Photo; Paul Hennessy / Alamy Stock Photo; Pictorial Press Ltd / Alamy Stock Photo; PUPPY DOG CRIES – images by kind permission of the DSPCA; Radharc Images / Alamy Stock Photo; Roger Sedres / Alamy Stock Photo; Shutterstock; Specsavers sponsored tweet by kind permission of Specsavers Optical Group; Sport In Pictures / Alamy Stock Photo; Steven May / Alamy Stock Photo; Sydney Alford / Alamy Stock Photo; The Advertising Archives / Alamy Stock Photo; The Irish Sun front page 11.01.17 by kind permission of The Irish Sun; TheCoverVersion / Alamy Stock Photo; urbanbuzz / Alamy Stock Photo; WENN Ltd / Alamy Stock Photo; Wikimedia Commons; World History Archive / Alamy Stock Photo; ZUMA Press, Inc. / Alamy Stock Photo.

Special thanks to EmojiOne.com for emoji icons © 2018, EmojiOne, Inc.

The author and publisher have made every effort to trace all copyright owners, but if any material has inadvertently been reproduced without permission, they would be happy to make the necessary arrangement at the earliest opportunity and encourage owners of copyright material not acknowledged to make contact.